Mesoamerican History

A Captivating Guide to Four Ancient Civilizations that Existed in Mexico – The Olmec, Zapotec, Maya and Aztec Civilization

© **Copyright 2018**

All Rights Reserved. No part of this book may be reproduced in any form without permission in writing from the author. Reviewers may quote brief passages in reviews.

Disclaimer: No part of this publication may be reproduced or transmitted in any form or by any means, mechanical or electronic, including photocopying or recording, or by any information storage and retrieval system, or transmitted by email without permission in writing from the publisher.

While all attempts have been made to verify the information provided in this publication, neither the author nor the publisher assumes any responsibility for errors, omissions or contrary interpretations of the subject matter herein.

This book is for entertainment purposes only. The views expressed are those of the author alone, and should not be taken as expert instruction or commands. The reader is responsible for his or her own actions.

Adherence to all applicable laws and regulations, including international, federal, state and local laws governing professional licensing, business practices, advertising and all other aspects of doing business in the US, Canada, UK or any other jurisdiction is the sole responsibility of the purchaser or reader.

Neither the author nor the publisher assumes any responsibility or liability whatsoever on the behalf of the purchaser or reader of these materials. Any perceived slight of any individual or organization is purely unintentional.

Free Bonus from Captivating History (Available for a Limited time)

Hi History Lovers!

Now you have a chance to join our exclusive history list so you can get your first history ebook for free as well as discounts and a potential to get more history books for free! Simply visit the link below to join.

Captivatinghistory.com/ebook

Also, make sure to follow us on:

Twitter: @Captivhistory

Facebook: Captivating History:@captivatinghistory

Contents

FREE BONUS FROM CAPTIVATING HISTORY (AVAILABLE FOR A LIMITED TIME) 5

PART 1: OLMECS 10

A CAPTIVATING GUIDE TO THE EARLIEST KNOWN MAJOR ANCIENT CIVILIZATION IN MEXICO 10

INTRODUCTION 1

CHAPTER 1 – WHO WERE THE OLMECS? 2

CHAPTER 2 – EMERGING FROM THE JUNGLE 5

CHAPTER 3 – FADING INTO OBSCURITY 8

CHAPTER 4 – OLMEC ART 11

CHAPTER 5 – THE OLMEC TRADERS 16

CHAPTER 6 – THE OLMECS AND THEIR NEIGHBORS 20

CHAPTER 7 – OLMEC MILITARY 23

CHAPTER 8 – THE OLMECS AT HOME 28

CHAPTER 9 – RELIGION AND BELIEFS OF THE OLMECS 33

CHAPTER 10 – CULTURAL INNOVATION OF THE OLMECS 37

CHAPTER 11 – THE OLMECS, A MOTHER CULTURE OF MESOAMERICA? 44

CONCLUSION 46

PART 2: ZAPOTEC CIVILIZATION 48

A CAPTIVATING GUIDE TO THE PRE-COLUMBIAN CLOUD PEOPLE WHO DOMINATED THE VALLEY OF OAXACA IN MESOAMERICA 48

INTRODUCTION 49

CHAPTER 1 – LOOKING BACK OVER HUNDREDS OF YEARS 51
- THE CLOUD PEOPLE 51
- THE OAXACA VALLEY 53
- THE DOMAIN OF THE CLOUD PEOPLE 54

CHAPTER 2 – UNDERSTANDING THE ZAPOTECS IN PHASES 57
- THE FOUNDING OF THE MONTE ALBÁN 57
- MONTE ALBÁN PHASE 1 58
- MONTE ALBÁN PHASE 2 58
- MONTE ALBÁN PHASE 3 59
- MONTE ALBÁN PHASE 4 60
- MONTE ALBÁN PHASE 5 60
- THE PROMISE OF TOMORROW 61

CHAPTER 3 – EARLY AGRARIAN ROOTS AND THE BUILDING OF A CIVILIZATION 62
- FROM NOMAD TO VILLAGERS 62
- THE EARLY STRUCTURING OF SOCIETY 63
- A MOVE TO HIERARCHIES AND AWAY FROM AUTONOMY 64
- THE RISE OF ALLIANCES AND COMPETITION 65
- WAR AND THE BEGINNINGS OF WRITING 66

CHAPTER 4 – RELIGION, MYTHS, AND POWER 68
- THE ZAPOTEC PANTHEON 68
- RITUALS, SACRIFICES, AND MYTHS 69
- DISTRIBUTION OF POWER 70
- DETERMINING THE NEXT LEADER 71
- THE DEAD 72

CHAPTER 5 – A FAMILIAR, TIERED SOCIETY 73
- THE ROYAL FAMILY AND CLASS 73
- THE COMMONER CLASS AND ITS LAYERS 75
- THE RELIGIOUS ORDER 76

CHAPTER 6 – A DAY IN THE LIFE OF THE ZAPOTECS 78
- WIDE VARIETY OF LIVING STANDARDS 78
- AT HOME 79
- EARLY ASTRONOMERS AND THE PASSAGE OF TIME 79
- BUMPER CROP 80

    OTHER CROPS AND FOOD 81
    THE ROLE OF TRIBUTES 82

CHAPTER 7 – THE ARTS, ATHLETICS, AND TECHNOLOGY 83

    A HIGHLY DEVELOPED LANGUAGE 83
    THE INTRICACIES OF THE WRITTEN WORD 84
    INTRICATE ARTIFACTS 85
    A HEALTHY SENSE OF COMPETITION 85
    A LOOK INTO TECHNOLOGY'S ROOTS 86

CHAPTER 8 – TWO WORLDS COLLIDE 88

    THE END OF A WAR 88
    THE CONQUISTADORS' ARRIVAL 89
    A TENTATIVE PEACE 90
    THE FALL OF AN EMPIRE 91

CONCLUSION 93

PART 3: MAYA HISTORY 95

A CAPTIVATING GUIDE TO THE MAYA CIVILIZATION, CULTURE, MYTHOLOGY, AND THE MAYA PEOPLES' IMPACT ON MESOAMERICAN HISTORY 95

INTRODUCTION 96

CHAPTER 1 – MEET THE MAYA 98

CHAPTER 2 – FROM TRIBAL VILLAGES TO EARLY STATES 104

CHAPTER 3 – THE GOLDEN AGE 112

CHAPTER 4 – FROM THE GOLDEN AGE TO THE AGE OF DISASTER 121

CHAPTER 5 – THE MAYA GOVERNMENT AND SOCIETY 129

CHAPTER 6 – THE MAYA WARFARE 138

CHAPTER 7 – ECONOMY OF THE MAYA CIVILIZATION 146

CHAPTER 8 – THE MAYA ACHIEVEMENTS IN ARTS AND CULTURE 154

CHAPTER 9 – RELIGION AND RITUALS IN THE MAYA SOCIETY 163

CHAPTER 10 – MYTHS, LEGENDS AND THE GODS OF THE MAYA 171

CHAPTER 11 – THE MAYA EVERYDAY LIFE 177

CHAPTER 12 – FROM COLONIAL TIMES TO TODAY, THE MAYA PERSIST 182

CONCLUSION 189

PART 4: AZTEC HISTORY ... 191

A CAPTIVATING GUIDE TO THE AZTEC EMPIRE, MYTHOLOGY, AND CIVILIZATION ... 191

INTRODUCTION ... 192

CHAPTER 1 – WHERE DID THE AZTECS LIVE? ... 194

CHAPTER 2 – WHO WERE THE AZTECS? ... 196

CHAPTER 3 – GOVERNMENT, CITY-STATES, AND EXPANSION ... 199

CHAPTER 4 – THE ARRIVAL OF THE SPANISH AND THE DECLINE OF THE EMPIRE ... 204

CHAPTER 5 – A DAY IN THE LIFE OF AN AZTEC CITIZEN ... 207
THE SOVEREIGN, THE DIGNITARIES, AND THE NOBLES ... 207
THE SOVEREIGN ... 208
THE DIGNITARIES ... 210
NOBLES ... 210
COMMONERS ... 212
LANDLESS PEASANTS ... 215
SLAVES ... 216

CHAPTER 6 – AGRICULTURE AND DIET ... 219

CHAPTER 7 – RELIGION ... 222
CREATION, LIFE, DEATH, AND THE FOUR SUNS ... 222
HUMAN SACRIFICE ... 224
THE GODS ... 226
QUETZALCÓATL ... 226
HUITZILOPOCHTLI ... 227
TLALOC ... 228
CHALCHIHUTLICUE ... 229
COATLICUE ... 229
THE CALENDAR ... 230

CHAPTER 8 – SPORTS ... 233

CONCLUSION ... 235

READ MORE CAPTIVATING HISTORY BOOKS ABOUT ANCIENT HISTORY ... 236

BIBLIOGRAPHY ... 243

Part 1: Olmecs

A Captivating Guide to the Earliest Known Major Ancient Civilization in Mexico

Introduction

When most people think about pre-Columbian Mesoamerica, they often jump straight to Aztecs and Mayans, arguably the most famous and well-known native civilizations of this region. Of course, they are not to blame as historians themselves give those cultures most of their attention. This often leads to misconceptions about how civilized life actually began in the Americas. Some people think that civilization didn't exist in North America until the Europeans arrived; others think it all began with the Mayans.

In reality, the first people that managed to elevate themselves to civilized life were the Olmecs. They remain relatively unknown, hidden in the long and dark corridors of forgotten history. Most of their culture remains wrapped in mystery, which may explain why so few historians are ready to tackle the task of uncovering the true story of the Olmecs. It is a difficult job, and even after many decades devoted to researching Olmecs, answers may not show up. And usually, with every answer, a new question arises. In a way, it's a Sisyphean task. Because there aren't written sources and histories of the Olmecs, their exact story remains unknown. And most of our knowledge about them are just theories based on archeological findings.

So, anyone brave enough to take on the task of learning about the Olmecs should be prepared for a lot of ifs, maybes, probabilities, and likelihoods, not to mention the conflicted opinions of various historians. With all that in mind, one could get discouraged from even trying. But, as the earliest known civilization in America, they deserve some of our attention. Their tale deserves to be told.

Chapter 1 – Who Were the Olmecs?

The most honest answer you'll get for this question is "We are not exactly sure." These people, known as the Olmecs, occupied southcentral parts of present-day Mexico, in what are today states of Veracruz and Tabasco, on the shores of the Gulf of Mexico. They emerged in these tropical lowlands somewhere around 1400 BCE and created what is considered one of the first civilizations in Mesoamerica. For roughly one thousand years, they were the most developed and most powerful nation in this area. During that time they dominated the region through trade and military might, spreading their more sophisticated culture and civilization to neighboring tribes. And then around 400 BCE, just as suddenly as they arrived, they had disappeared into the thick Mexican jungles.

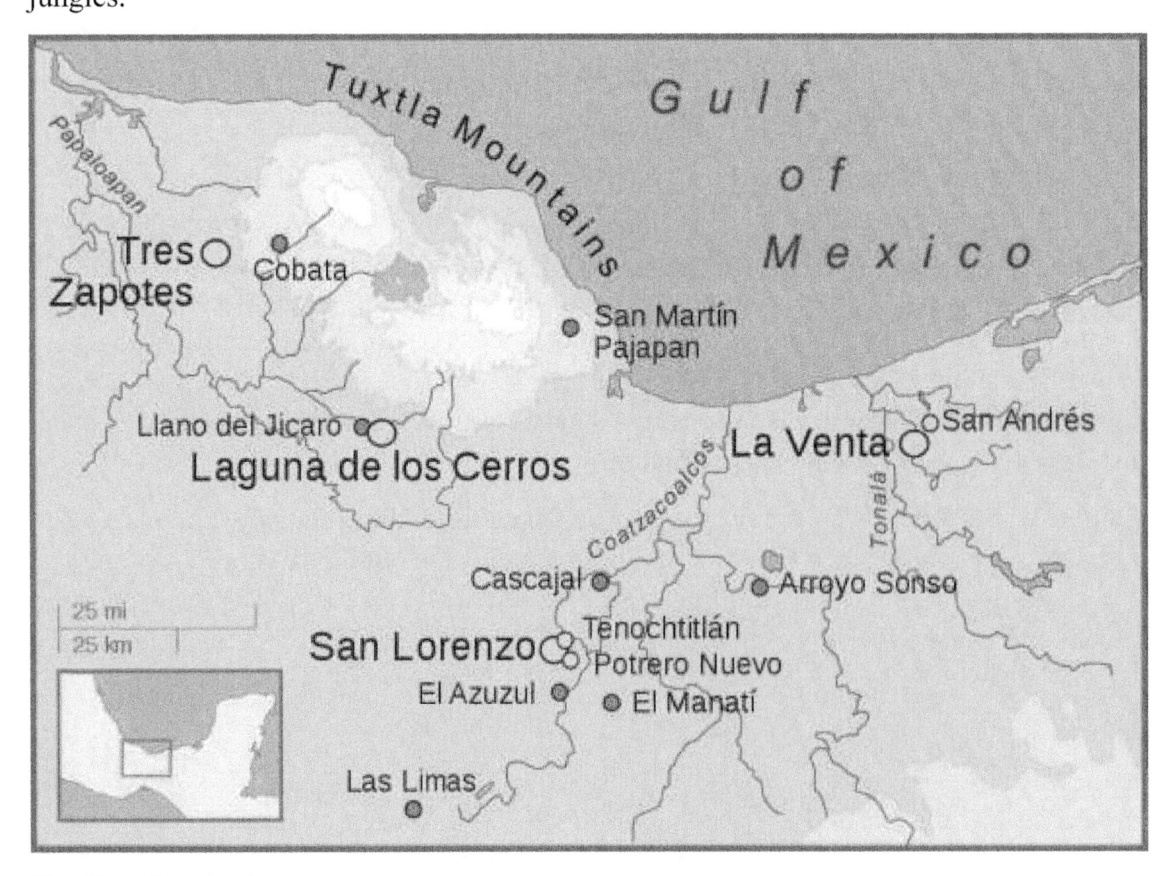

The Olmec heartland.

For almost two thousand years they were forgotten, but during the 19th century, as archeology began to expand and evolve into a serious science, historians started to notice a specific type of jade sculpture with jaguar-like features. It was a unique and powerful style that caught their attention. After some research, they found out that they came from the region we now know as the Olmec heartland, located along the Gulf coast. Early modern archeologists weren't sure how to name this new civilization, but one of them remembered that Aztecs from the 16th century CE told Spaniards about the people living in that area, who they called Olmeca (Ōlmēcah). In Aztecan Nahuatl language that means "rubber people". The name came from the widespread usage of rubber among the population of that region. Even though there is no real connection between the civilizations that in different times occupied the same territory, the name stuck. But we are almost certain that they didn't call themselves Olmeca.

It is worth mentioning that a poem in Nahuatl, recorded long after Europeans came to the Americas, tells a tale of a legendary land on the banks of "the eastern sea." In the poem, this mythical land, Tamoanchan, was settled long before the Aztecs founded their cities, in an era no one can remember. And its rule existed for a long time. What is even more intriguing about this poem is that the name Tamoanchan wasn't of Aztecan origins, but rather Mayan, the word Tamoanchan meaning "In the land of rain or mist." Some historians believe that the Olmecs heartland was described in the poem and that they actually spoke a variation of the Mayan language. But others disagree, claiming that the tongue of original Olmecs was actually an archaic form of Mixe–Zoquean language, which is still spoken in the area. Although the latter theory is now widely accepted, the truth is that due to the lack of archeological findings, we're still not certain about what exact language the Olmecs spoke.

After archeologist started to explore the Olmec sites more thoroughly during the early 20th century, they discovered many sites that could be linked with the so-called rubber people. But two of them stood out as the biggest and most important cities of the Olmecs. The first one was San Lorenzo, situated in the Coatzacoalcos River Basin. The first signs of human communities on that location are sometimes even dated way back to 1800 BCE. But those earliest settlements are usually considered to be pre-civilized societies. The actual rise of this city coincides with the rise of Olmec civilization itself, around 1400 BCE. But by 900 BCE, this site was mostly abandoned. The center of Olmec power and culture had moved by that time.

The second important Olmec archeological site is La Venta, located to the northeast of San Lorenzo in the swampy basin of the Tonalá river. It started to emerge around 1200 BCE, but after the fall of San Lorenzo, it took over as the center of the Olmec civilization. It stood as a bastion of the Olmecs, being home to some of their most important architectural creations. This city was abandoned around 400 BCE, which also marked the end of the Olmecs (at least in the way we think of them now). Of course, these weren't the only cities. There were many others, like Tres Zapotes, Laguna de Los Cerros, and El Manatí, but those never managed to match the wealth and power of San Lorenzo or La Venta. To avoid any misconceptions, it is important to note that these names aren't Olmecan names, but were given to the sites by the archeologists working on them in the unhospitable Mesoamerican jungles.

At first glance, even to the trained eye of an historian, the location of the Olmec heartland might seem a bit unwelcome for the start of a young civilization since it is located among the dense jungles and swamps with a humid climate. But when one takes into account that all major cities were located near rivers, which provided both fertile soil and easier travel, things start to make much more sense. And stepping back to see a wider geographical picture, we can notice that the Olmecs were located on an important trading route that connected regions which later spawned the Aztecs and Mayans. The location of the Olmecan civilization could be compared to other major civilizations, like the Sumerians in Mesopotamia, the Egyptians on the banks of the Nile, or the self-explanatory Indus Valley civilization. Combining those two essential elements explains why the earliest Mesoamerican civilization started right on that spot.

These few broad and vague details about the Olmecs given in this chapter only serve as an introduction to this civilization. Now it's time to dive deeper into the Olmec story, and like archeologists and historians, get a more explicit answer to the question posed in this chapter. And hopefully, by the end of this book, you'll have your own impression of who they were.

Chapter 2 – Emerging from the Jungle

Although it is not certain where the Olmecs actually came from, one shouldn't think that people just magically appeared in the Americas or that they evolved separately from humans on other continents. The currently accepted theory is that during the last Ice Age, somewhere between 30,000 and 10,000 years ago, the first humans came to North America. They crossed over a land bridge named Beringia that connected Alaska to the far eastern shores of present-day Russia. Another theory that is less accepted maintains that early settlers actually traveled by boats along the Pacific Coast. No matter which theory is closer to the truth, one thing is for certain—people slowly migrated south towards warmer climates and more fertile lands.

Around 8,000 BCE, due to the changes in temperature and sea level which came with the end of the Ice Age, early settlers in present-day Mexico started to change their lifestyle. They started to rely more on domesticated plants as their main source of food. Yet, their tribal organization remained on a rather basic level, more similar to how we see prehistorical humans. The next important step in the development of more complex lifestyle happened roughly around 2000 BCE. That is when an early village life started. It was a more organized way of living than before, a vital step in the development of civilized life in the Mesoamerican region since it brought growth in population and food surpluses, a necessity for the rise of more complex social and cultural life. Those crucial changes in society and way of life led to developments in the arts, as well as political and class stratification of most Mesoamerican societies.

At the same time, in similar circumstances like all others around them, the Olmecs started to build their civilization. In the beginning, around 1800-1700 BCE, they probably weren't much different than other tribes around them, having something similar to chiefdoms which had both limited power and cultural development. But by the 1300s, the Olmecs in their San Lorenzo settlement came to entirely new heights of cultural complexity. Looking at how sophisticated their art became, how majestic their huge statues were, and how big the city grew, archeologists concluded that San Lorenzo was unequaled by any other settlement in Mesoamerica at that time.

Besides being breathtakingly beautiful and intriguing for archeologists, these magnificent building projects of the Olmecs at San Lorenzo show that they had, at the very least, basic social and political stratification, with one small group of ruling elites and a large group of common people. Because without at least some social organization, such endeavors are practically impossible. Of course, since we don't have any written evidence, we can't be sure that they didn't manage to develop more finely diversified classes and to what extent their society was stratified. But looking at those impressive creations, it is evident that the Olmec rulers and elite were capable of mobilizing their population and force them to work in constructing architectural wonders. This meant Olmecan leaders held more power than their peers from other tribes around them. In fact, it could be argued that the power the ruling class held over their people is actually the most critical thing that differentiated Olmecs from other Mesoamerican people at the time.

The Olmec colossal head statue found at San Lorenzo.

That authority of the Olmec elite, which proved to be vital for their development as a civilization, was most likely based on the ruling classes controlling the fertile lands near the river, similarly to the elite in Ancient Egypt and Mesopotamia. And, unlike neighboring chiefdoms, the Olmec elite also managed to take control of trading with their neighbors. That allowed the Olmec ruling elite to become the elite, and gain command over the lower classes and force them to work on public projects, like building temples and statues. Of course, it should be kept in mind that this gathering of political authority and control of the Olmec elite didn't happen overnight, but was a slow process that lasted for a really long time.

Thanks to these factors, the Olmec settlement at San Lorenzo managed to keep its dominance for about three centuries, with its "Golden Age" lasting from about 1200 to 900 BCE. By the end of that era, it started to decline, losing its power and inhabitants. It became an empty shell of its previous glory. Historians aren't entirely sure what caused this downfall. Some think it could be due to natural problems like diseases or bad harvest years. Others believe it could be a result of an internal struggle for power or some kind of civil war. There were suggestions that an external military threat, either from neighboring Olmecs or some other tribes, managed to bring the San Lorenzo settlement to its knees. The one thing that archeologists are certain about is that by 800 BCE this city was pretty much abandoned. But that didn't mark the end of all Olmecs. As San Lorenzo started to fade, La Venta began to rise. And around 900 BCE it became the new center of power for the Olmecs and all of Mesoamerica.

Chapter 3 – Fading into Obscurity

As it usually happens in history, when one city or state falls, another rises to take its place. In the case of the Olmecs, La Venta took the place of San Lorenzo as the most important Olmec city during the 10th century BCE. As noted in the previous chapter, it likely wasn't a sudden change, but gradually happened. And under La Venta supremacy, Olmec civilization reached its peak. But unlike San Lorenzo, the natural swampy surroundings of La Venta wasn't quite suitable for farming, which raises the question of what gave that settlement the edge it needed to become the new center of Olmec power. Again, here is where historians disagree. One theory suggests that the Tonalá River had a different path at the time, so the swamps weren't as pervasive in that area. The other theory is that the La Venta Olmecs used nearby fertile lands as a source of food and labor by some way of occupation and exploitation. But considering that archeological surveys showed that the area of La Venta was settled as far back as 1750 BCE, the first option seems more likely, as it is more analogous to the San Lorenzo settlement.

Because of that, it's not unsurprising that La Venta based its own supremacy on a similar basis as San Lorenzo where the Olmec elite had the control of agricultural production and trading. But there was also one more crucial difference. Looking at the archeological evidence, historians concluded that this settlement also served as a religious and ceremonial center. This meant that the rulers of La Venta had even more power than their predecessors which probably spanned over a greater area, since this meant that all surrounding Olmecs came to La Venta, bringing offerings to their gods as well as the rulers of the city. With even more monumental buildings and statues that displayed their wealth and power than San Lorenzo, it is clear that the La Venta settlement reached greater heights than any city in Mesoamerica at the time, and it seems it had a lot to do with the religious aspect of the settlement.

But one should dismiss this site as a purely religious city. There is archeological evidence that it was a thriving town, with people living both in it and in the smaller settlements around it. And within that large number of residents, there were more specialists than in the older Olmec societies. Besides the priests and artisans that created the marvelous pieces of art the Olmecs are best known for today, there were traders, builders, and even indications of military-oriented professionals. We can only guess how many more professions and skilled laborers there were in La Venta. It is important to note that the Olmecs most likely weren't limited to just the ruling elite and working commoners at this time. Their society probably became more diverse based on their classes. With social complexity, Olmec culture also became more sophisticated.

Statue of an Olmec chief at La Venta.

Thanks to that complexity and sophistication of the Olmec society, for about five centuries, La Venta managed to maintain its dominance in both the Olmec civilization and the entire Mesoamerican region. But its power eventually started to decline. By 400 BCE, the La Venta settlement began to fade into obscurity. In the next century, the city was pretty much abandoned. Unlike San Lorenzo, archeologists are sure that the downfall of La Venta was a violent one, as they have found traces of a deliberate destruction of monuments and buildings. Although they aren't quite sure if the attack came from outside forces or if it was some kind of uprising, most believe it was a foreign power that invaded La Venta, since it is highly unlikely that the domestic population destroyed their own monuments. And although the Olmecs abandoned La Venta, the city didn't seem to lose its significance as a cultural center. Archeologists found buried offerings that are dated to the early Colonial Era that contain products like Spanish olives. This means that for more than a millennia people came back to this site to practice their religious rituals even though they forgot who built it and for what exact purpose. This is perhaps the best proof of how important and powerful the Olmecs and La Venta were.

However, this does not change the fact that at some point this settlement was abandoned. Whatever may be the exact cause, with the fall of this Olmec center, Olmec civilization also came to an end. And just like how we don't know exactly where they came from, we're not sure where they went, or to be more precise what happened to them. It is likely that most simply relocated or were assimilated into other cultures or some mixture of both. And assimilation with different cultures, which were so influenced by the Olmec civilization by this time, wasn't too much of a transition for most of the people. Ultimately, we can only be sure they didn't magically vanish or were all killed, as there is still some native population in the Olmec heartland that speaks a language that is descended from one we assume the Olmecs spoke.

Chapter 4 – Olmec Art

The first thing archeologists discovered about the Olmecs was their art, so it seems to be a fitting place to begin our journey to better understand their civilization. There wasn't some groundbreaking discovery of Olmecan sculptures or other art forms that brought them to light. For a long time, a lot of smaller statues and carvings from the Olmecs were circulating around the archeological artifact and ancient art markets. But most experts thought they were part of either Mayan or Aztec civilization or at least some derivation of those. So, they didn't attract much attention on their own. However, all of that changed in the second half of the 19th century when José Melgar y Serrano, one of the Mexican explorers, found the now famous Olmec colossal heads. After that discovery, the Olmecs were finally recognized as a separate and unique culture. At first many thought this strange new civilization flourished in about the same period as the Mayans and that they took over some aspects of Mayan culture which would explain the similarities between them. But opposed to them stood Matthew Sterling, archeologist of the Smithsonian Institute, who argued that the Olmecs predated others, such as the Mayans and Aztecs. The struggle between the two historical schools of Mesoamerican history was finally settled in the 1940s when Mexican archeologist Alfonso Caso managed to sway most of the scientific community to Sterling's side. Further carbon-dating tests, to the dismay of many Mayanists, people who were specialized in Mayan history, gave more conclusive support to the theory of Olmecs being one of the earliest known Mesoamerican civilizations.

The colossal heads that brought the Olmecs back into the limelight of history rightfully became the best-known symbol of their civilization and their art. Although all of them are rather big, they vary in sizes, weighing between 6 and 50 tons and ranging in height from 1.6 to 3.5 meters (5.2 to 11.4 ft). All of them were made from basalt mined in the Sierra de los Tuxtlas Mountains of Veracruz on the northern edge of what is now considered the Olmec heartland. These statues depict mature men with flat-faced and thick-lipped features, fleshy cheeks, and wearing various types of headgear that resemble today's rugby helmets. Because of those helmets, some researchers at first thought they represented winners and champions of some Mesoamerican ballgame, but that theory is now largely abandoned. They most likely represent rulers, considering they were the ones who had enough power to make that type of monument which researchers think took at least 50 years to carve out and move. Besides, the headgear is now usually associated with military or ceremonial symbolism.

One of the most prominent characteristics of these huge heads is naturalism, which is one of the staples of Olmec art in general. Naturalism means the art usually depicted real objects with natural, although typically stylized, features. The men depicted on those statues don't seem to be represented in an idealized image, but rather as the artists saw them. Some of them have a more serious look while others look like they are relaxed or even smiling. Since some traces of paint were found on them, there is a real possibility that they were brightly colored at the time of their construction. Of course, as time passed, the characteristics of the art style started to change a bit as well. So even though they are quite similar in style, there are slight differences between the earlier heads from San Lorenzo and the later ones from La Venta. The San Lorenzo ones seem to be more skillfully executed and more clearly realistic, while the La Venta ones show more of a tendency towards a more stylized art form.

While on the subject of the Olmec colossal heads, there is a myth about them that has to be debunked. Some researchers, after looking at the fat lips and other features of these monuments, claimed that they looked more like Africans than Mesoamericans and came to the conclusion that the Olmecs were of African origins. But various historians have since proven this wrong. By comparing these statues with the present-day native population living in the area, they showed that the features of the Colossal heads' faces were and still are common among Mesoamerican Indians. Also, other types of Olmec art don't depict those features as clearly or as much. Archeologists explain this fact by stating that basalt is different to work with compared to other materials that the Olmecs used. It is a harder substance that only allows shallow carvings on it, forcing the artists to make certain features on the faces that may not have been common among the Olmec population. With that being said, most of the scientific community disagree with this theory of Olmec African descent, putting it in more of a pseudohistory category.

Looking past the iconic colossal heads, the Olmecs also created other examples of monumental arts, such as altars and stelae. Made out of stone, they were decorated with beautiful carvings which showed off the Olmecs skill in both high and low reliefs. The most common depiction on these monuments was of an older person holding a child in his lap. Here it is seen that the Olmecs differ from most of the other cultures around the world since this iconography is usually connected with a mother-child motif. But in the Olmec reliefs, the older person is always shown as having masculine traits, which makes deciphering the meaning of these carvings rather tricky. Some scholars think they represent a connection with religion, displaying representations of deities. Others lean towards more of a dynastical meaning, like the passing of power from father to son. Of course, there were other motifs carved as well, like a clearer representation of rulers and priests, as well as warriors and animals, like snakes and jaguars. Almost all of them are created with the naturalistic style that was so common in the Olmec art. But the most stunning feature of their art is the capability of the Olmec artist to capture movement in their reliefs. Carving various scenes in which the subjects are caught in middle of an action, made their art feel more energetic.

Olmecs, of course, didn't only produce monumental art pieces. They are also quite well known for statues, small figurines, celts (ax-like tools), and pendants, all made from various materials with the most beautiful and finely-detailed ones made out of jade and serpentine. Since these were rare and precious stones, it is clear that those statues were made for the richest people in Olmec society, probably the royal family. They also made effigies and small ritual axes which held more of a ceremonial than practical purpose since they were never sharpened enough to be used. All of these art forms kept the distinctive Olmec style and were rooted in naturalism and realism. This style wasn't only bound to Olmec sculptures of various sizes, but was also represented in bowls and vessels made out of clay. They had intricate reliefs that showed stylized representations of animals and plants. In some cases, the bowls were even zoomorphic, shaped like animals.

One step further away from naturalistic characteristics and more towards the stylized type of Olmec art is the small baby-faced figurines. The name is quite self-explanatory, as the main features of these small statues are plump bodies, infantile puffy cheeks, swollen crying eyes, and pouty frowns. These babies are usually posed in a sitting or lying position, mimicking how little kids crawl and play on the ground. And although they are always depicted naked, there are no signs of gender on them. Another interesting characteristic of these figurines is that most of them have helmets on their heads, similar, if not identical, to those that crowned the Colossal heads. With that in mind, there is a possibility that the baby-faced sculptures are a representation of rulers' children, but their true purpose and iconographical meaning is yet to be determined.

But the most prominent exception to the typical naturalism of Olmec art are the motifs of were-jaguars, in which human form is mixed with the characteristics of a jaguar. And those motifs were surprisingly quite common for something that we mark as an exception. These are usually seen on sculptures, where ware-jaguars are often represented as infantile. They have chubby bodies and puffy-faced features, but also snarling mouths, toothless gums, or long fangs. In some cases, they also have claws. And like the previously mentioned baby-faced figurines, they were also sexless. One of the most common compositions that included were-jaguar babies is that of a larger adult figure holding the infant on outstretched arms like it's being presented. Looking at some of the finer details, like their usually cleft heads and decorations on their clothes, archeologists saw similarities with how later Mesoamerican civilizations represented their gods, which led them to believe that were-jaguars are a representation of a certain divine being, probably a rain deity. But like all other Mesoamerican cultures, the Olmecs also believed in a number of gods, so the question remains why the were-jaguars were so frequent and representations of other gods were not.

A classical were-jaguar sculpture from San Lorenzo.

Another interesting type of artifact made in the distinctive Olmec style are jade face masks. They have asymmetrical open, downturned mouths, wide nostrils, and half-squinting eyes, which suggests they are part of the Olmec tradition. However, archeologists have never found this kind of mask on any Olmec site to this day, even though most of them were created during the Olmec era. This has led some researchers to hypothesize that those masks were not made by Olmecs and were only influenced by their style. Others point out that wooden masks, made at the very beginning of the Olmec civilization, clearly show they had a long tradition of making masks. And they think it's only a matter of time until archeologists will find the jade masks at an Olmec site. Another interesting detail surrounding these masks is that one of them was recently found in an Aztecan tomb, even though carbon dating puts its creation date at around 500 BCE. This suggests that these masks were highly regarded throughout Mesoamerican history and it is highly possible that they were raided from Olmec sites by their successors.

Of course, the Olmecs made a lot of other artifacts and artwork. These were just some examples of the most well-known and noteworthy representations of their style. Although most of the Olmec art we talked about in this chapter was made from some kind of stone, precious minerals, or clay, Olmecs also used materials like cloth and wood to make their art. But since those other materials were less durable, almost no traces of those type of artifacts are left. And even though there are many questions and controversies surrounding Olmec art, like with their whole history, there is no denying its beauty, craftsmanship, and their influence on other Mesoamerican cultures that came after the Olmecs. Another testimony to the excellence of Olmec art is that centuries after they were gone, other civilizations saw their artifacts as priceless works of art. That is why those were praised and gathered, probably even traded by later civilizations. Also, some of the Olmec features and motifs were copied by artisans of other civilizations for thousands of years and have by now become the trademark of how we imagine Mesoamerican art. The influence of Olmec art on Mesoamerican society can be paralleled with the influence of ancient Roman and Greek art had on later European society.

Chapter 5 – The Olmec Traders

Even though the archeologists have given more attention to their art, trade was a much more important part of Olmec life and society and played a crucial role in their rise to power. It is significant to note that even though the Olmecs were the first to achieve a level of development that we associate with civilized life, they certainly weren't the only complex society in Mesoamerica, especially in the later periods of the Olmec era. Around them were many chiefdoms, which varied in cultural and social development as well as in wealth and power. And together with the Olmecs, they created a trade network which allowed not only transportation of materials and resources but also an exchange of ideas and culture. But the question arises of how the Olmecs differed from their neighbors; what allowed them to use trade for amassing riches better than others? How were they able to gather strength and influence through trading, and use it to develop their culture and flourish as a civilization?

Indeed, being situated in a vital trading hub that connected resource-rich areas of the present-day Yucatán peninsula and Central Mexico was undoubtedly helpful. But historians also think it was because the Olmecs were probably among the first to use long-distance trade rather than trading only with their nearest surrounding. With such a widespread trading network in place, the Olmecs were able to trade for the same types of resources with different tribes, while at the same time exporting their goods to numerous buyers. That diversity of trading partners is most likely what made their success in this field greater and easier, making their civilization richer than any other at the time. But archeologists think that the Olmecs didn't start trading to get wealthy. They believe it all started because their fertile and food-rich region lacked obsidian, a glass-like volcanic rock which was an essential resource for making farming and other work tools, weapons, decorative objects, and many other things. And even in the later stages of Olmec development, it seems that the core of their trade remained the basic need for that precious stone.

But obsidian wasn't the only resource that the Olmecs had to import. As the power and riches of their elite grew, so did their demand for materials needed for luxury items. That is why in later periods they started importing iron ore, serpentine, magnetite, and most importantly jade - which the Olmecs accessed by trading with Mayan predecessors in the Yucatán Peninsula and present-day Guatemala. Jade probably became the most widely used precious mineral in the Olmec society and was most commonly used to create masks and figurines. Using that as a connection, some historians who lean towards speculations and wild theories devised another theory about the origin of the Olmecs, connecting them with ancient China, specifically the Shang dynasty (1600-1000 BCE). According to that theory, Chinese refugees crossed the Pacific Ocean to form, or at least influence, the creation of the Olmec civilization. The major connections between the two civilizations was their usage and high regard of jade and the similarities between Olmec artwork and Chinese art that circulated in that period. Of course, these speculations are rejected by the majority of the Mesoamerican historians and archeologists as a wild tale.

Stepping away from the luxuries, it is interesting that there haven't been any traces of food being imported on a large scale by the Olmecs since their lands were fertile enough to sustain the population on their own. However, the Olmecs did trade for salt and cocoa. Although they had access to salt from the Gulf Coast, it seems it wasn't enough to satisfy their needs, considering they expanded their salt trade network in many directions—to the south towards present-day Guatemala, to the west to the Pacific Coast of Oaxaca, and to the north to the central plane of Mexico, which was later inhabited by the Aztecs. There is also a possibility that the Olmec traders weren't just bringing salt to use in their homeland, but were also reselling it to other tribes, acting as a middleman in the salt trade. That way salt became not only an important commodity needed to sustain life, but also a valued strategic resource needed for trading. Cocoa, on the other hand, was more of a luxury item which came to the Olmecs from the south, from what is today Honduras. There will be a more detailed explanation of the use and importance of cocoa in Olmec society in one of the following chapters.

Other goods they traded for were also animal pelts and feathers of exotic animals. The Olmec elite used these for both ceremonial purposes and as a sign of their status. In fact, when we combine all of the listed items the Olmec traders acquired, we can see that most of their import was focused on the need of the higher class. This could to a certain extent be explained by the fact that lower class could find most of the things they needed to survive in the Olmec heartland. And it also explains why the trade was mostly beneficial to the elite, while commoners saw little direct gain from it. Of course, we should keep in mind that the extra wealth that was brought into the Olmec society also benefited the whole population in the long run as it was one of the main driving forces of the development of their civilization. So it could be said that the non-elite parts of the society had at least some kind of indirect benefit from the development of trade, even though the goods imported to their lands were not meant for their use.

So far, we have seen what goods the Olmecs brought into their country. But they also had a lot to offer in return. As we already know, the Olmec region was quite fertile, boasting various types of food like squash, beans, manioc, sweet potato, and most importantly maize. Not only that, but they lived next to the ocean and big rivers where they had access to fish, another important food group. So, it is reasonable to assume that food was one of the first resources they offered to their trade partners as it was their first step towards establishing their trade network they are now famous for — in the earliest stages of their civilization and their trade. Clearly food was the foundation of the Olmec trade. It should be mentioned that in the early Olmec era the extent of their trade was still limited to the local vicinity, trading only with their immediate neighbors. It took a while for the Olmecs to develop this significant part of their economy, which allowed them to move up from basic food trade.

Even though food most likely remained an essential part of their trade even in the later periods, as the Olmec civilization developed so did the skills of their various artisans. And since they seemed to be the first ones to achieve a certain level of intricacy and finesse, they also realized that others might be interested in products their craftsmen had to offer. So, in later periods, the Olmec traders started exporting their artisanal and artistic creations. These varied from ritual figurines and masks, to various pottery which held both aesthetic and practical use, to clothing and everyday life tools. As the artisanal craftworks were not as common, especially during the San Lorenzo supremacy, they were more valuable, giving Olmec traders the upper hand in trading with others. Creating these goods from the raw materials they imported and exporting them for higher prices allowed the Olmecs to amass wealth quickly. In fact, we could draw a parallel between the ancient Olmecs and Industrial Age Britain. Both of those powers used their technical advances and knowhow to transform imported raw materials in finished products they would then trade for much higher prices, making a considerable profit. But the Olmecs also had something else to export besides the handcrafts and food.

Although the Olmecs lacked many natural resources other than food, their region was rich with trees used to produce primitive rubber. The Olmecs were, unsurprisingly, the first to start harvesting the natural sap of the Hevea tree to make the rubberlike material. It's not surprising that the Olmecan traders used it as an important part of their exports due both to the scarcity of the product and the numerous applications it could be used for. We can assume rubber was a valuable product at the time, and it is certain that it played an important role in prestige and prosperity of the Olmec traders. That prestige was also important for them to make the next step in utilizing their trade network – assuming the role of middleman traders. They were able to assume this role partly because of their geographical location, but also because they were seen as reliable traders thanks to their reputation. And this type of trade is probably the most profitable, as it requires no effort in creating a product, and it brings pure gain. Of course, the role of a trade intermediary wasn't something the Olmec traders could do from the beginning. Only after they established their extensive trade network, connections and reputation were they able to fulfill this very profitable part of the trade.

But there is one last piece of the puzzle left that gives one more reason why the Olmecs were such successful traders, and which gave them the edge over their competitors. That was the monopoly in trade. It is true that the initial spark that lit the raging fire of the Olmecan trade was their geographical position, which allowed them to trade with almost all of Mesoamerica. But more importantly, they had a monopoly over the items they traded. They had the best artisans whose skillfully crafted products were unmatched for a long time and the unique rubber that was distinctive to their region. It is true, however, that the Olmecs lacked obsidian, jade, salt, and other resources which should have put them on equal footing to other chiefdoms and tribes. But that wasn't the case because many different tribes had the same resources the Olmecs needed. That meant they could choose different trading partners according to their needs and current circumstances. On the other hand, those tribes had no other choice than to trade with them for the unique items the Olmecs had to offer. That is the crucial last component in the success of the Olmec traders.

Chapter 6 – The Olmecs and Their Neighbors

It should be clear by now that the Olmecs weren't alone in the jungles and plains of Mesoamerica. Even in the earliest parts of their civilization's formation and development, they were surrounded by many other settlements, tribes, and people. The Olmecs not only prospered thanks to their trade with these neighbors but also gathered the power that came with the wealth they amassed and influence which came from their prestige. Those factors became instrumental to the rise of their society from obscurity into the civilized world. But it would be unwise to think that trade, no matter how important it was to them, were the only relations they had with surrounding tribes. However, it is still unclear to this day what the exact nature of these interactions and connections was. Without any clear evidence, there is plenty of room for uncertain theories. But, like before, that fact shouldn't stop us in search of the Olmec story.

Archeologists started to question the relationships the Olmecs held with other tribes from the early days of their exploration of the Olmec civilization and history. Going from the fact that many Olmec-styled artifacts were found over a wide area of Mesoamerica, those early researchers of the Olmecs came to the natural conclusion that at least at some point there was a clear supremacy of that civilization over the whole region. Archeologists theorized that the number of their artifacts found in settlements far from the Olmec heartland meant they directly controlled those settlements. That led them to think that the Olmecs had sort of an empire, similar to the one the Romans had in the Mediterranean. But during the mid-20th century with further archeological digs and findings, this theory became less attractive to historians as evidence that corroborated this theory was almost nonexistent. With the lack of proof of any kind, it became clear that the Olmecs didn't manage to unify Mesoamerica into one large empire.

Yet, historians were unable to leave this idea completely. In their minds, signs of Olmec supremacy were still there since all their artifacts were scattered around the region. So, some of them thought that if the Olmecs didn't subdue Mesoamerica with their direct control, they must have made colonies out of their neighbors. Either the local elites stayed in power, paying their respect and tributes to their Olmec masters, similar to the medieval vassals. Or they were removed and substituted by the Olmec officials as the Europeans did with their colonies in the 19th century. This more indirect rule could also explain the wide area of their supremacy, as in both types of colonist rule the locals would have tried to replicate Olmec art and would have close trading ties with the Olmecs themselves. That would explain all the artifacts found. But as with the previous theory of a large Mesoamerican empire, this was also more or less rejected by the majority of historians in recent years. The reason is the same – there is no clear foundation for it in the archeological findings. The most widely supported idea currently is that Olmec supremacy was rooted in their culture and trade alone, without any forcible subjugation of their neighbors.

The explanation of all the archeological findings of Olmec and Olmec styled artifacts scattered around Mesoamerica, in non-Olmecan settlements, became less based on violence and force. For once, historians finally accepted the possibility that the Olmec trade network was so vast and well-connected that their handcrafts could have reached much further than they thought before. Also, with the acknowledgment of their trading success as well as the recognition of their artisanal quality, historians now believe that their products would have been sought among their neighbors as a sign of prestige, as luxury items. And the explanation for the artifacts that weren't Olmec made, but only Olmec styled can be quite simple. Local artisans tried to copy their work as Olmec art, and since crafts were a sign of high status, even "knockoffs" could be valuable, as not everyone could afford the original Olmec creation. Now there are even some theories that the Olmecs were in a way exporting their artisans as well, meaning that rulers and elites of other chiefdoms who had enough wealth and power could hire Olmec artisans to create art for them. By now it has become more apparent that the Olmec rule was more localized to the Olmec heartland.

But knowing that the Olmecs were only ruling over their own region is only a partial answer to the question relating to the nature of the relationship they had with their neighbors. From new evidence found at both Olmec and non-Olmec sites across Mesoamerica, historians now think that relations between the chiefdoms and tribes were more on the equal footing and interlinked than it was thought before. This was definitely true in the later era of the Olmec civilization when the surrounding cultures managed to catch up with them in their level of development. That allowed for more complicated diplomatic relations between the Olmecs and their neighbors. One example of this rise in sophistication of tribal diplomacy is found at the archeological site of Chalcatzingo in the Valley of Morelos, located in the southern portion of the Central Highlands of present-day Mexico. That location was settled by an unnamed tribe as early as 1500 BCE, but it remained at a rather low level of development until 900 BCE when they came in contact with the Olmecs and started to emulate their style. They reached the height of their power between 700 and 500 BCE, at the time of La Venta supremacy. With the high number of Olmec products found at Chalcatzingo, archeologists have concluded they had a close relationship between each other and also believed there was an alliance between them that was most likely strengthened with a marriage.

The connections and diplomacy between the Olmecs and their neighbors were also likely fostered by personal visits and connections between rulers and members of the elite. These actions certainly helped the Olmecs to forge good relations with surrounding tribes. This shouldn't come as a big surprise considering that the trade was controlled by the upper classes of most cultures and civilizations in the early era of Mesoamerican history. From that we can clearly see that the backbone of the diplomatic relations was indeed trade. And profit seems to be the most likely reason why all of the elites strived for rather peaceful and good neighboring policies, as war meant that the trade would stop and that would be bad for all sides involved. One could even claim that rulers of these chiefdoms, including the Olmecs, were thinking more like merchants than generals. Of course, even though the Olmecs seem to be an overall peace-loving society of traders doesn't necessarily mean they didn't resort to violence and aggression towards some smaller villages around them to impose a diplomatic or trade agreement upon them or offer them protection from other chiefdoms or even from the Olmecs themselves. After all, if there was no outside threat, why would any tribe or state create alliances with their neighbors? Also, some historians also speculate that the Olmecs used their military power and diplomatic influence to interfere in local politics of some smaller tribes and settlements. That way they could favor the local elite who would benefit them and their trade more. This one more testament to the complicated nature of the Olmec diplomacy, and their relations with other Mesoamerican tribes.

It should be emphasized that all of the possibilities mentioned in this chapter are at the present time speculations and theories based on scant evidence, so the true nature of Olmec intertribal relations and diplomacy remain shrouded in the veil of mystery. At least until some new evidence sheds more light on this. And even though some theories are more likely than others, the historic community isn't able to completely agree on them. Thus, this question of how exactly the Olmecs interact with their neighbors remains open for the time being, but nevertheless, it is an essential piece of the puzzle in the Olmec story.

Chapter 7 – Olmec Military

In the previous chapter, it was shown that the Olmecs weren't an expansionistic and bloodthirsty society, but rather wealth-searching and peace-loving traders who avoided going to war. But that shouldn't lead to the conclusion that they didn't have any soldiers or weapons. Even in non-violent civilizations, there had to be some sort of a military to protect them from foreign threats and invaders, especially if they were as rich as the Olmecs were. Some historians tried to link the lack of defensive fortifications and walls around the Olmec settlements as a sign that they weren't threatened in their heartland and from that drew conclusions that the Olmec army didn't actually exist. But after more research, archeologists found evidence that confirms that the Olmecs had some sort of military, though the exact details about it are still debated about.

Like in most of the ancient civilizations worldwide, the military in the Olmec society was linked to the elite and the ruling class. This is most obvious in their art, as rulers were often depicted wearing helmets and carrying various types of weapons. Opponents against the idea of the Olmec military's existence tried to explain this art by suggesting that those weapons and armor had a more ceremonial and religious purpose, rather than practical. And it is likely that military equipment had some ritual importance and was a sign of power and prestige. But other evidence suggests that the equipment was used for more than just its symbolism. For one, in some artistic depictions, Olmec rulers are accompanied by naked and bound men. These were most likely captives from some sort of military endeavor, as the burned bones were found in some burial pits. It has been suggested that those were remains of foreigners, since the Olmecs buried their dead. It is also probable that they believed, like most other Mesoamerican civilizations, that burning the body would damn the soul of the deceased. So, for some historians, the logical explanation of why a large group of adult males would be desecrated like this would be if they were prisoners of war, captured during a battle by the ruling elite.

These artistic portrayals clearly show that the Olmecs had an actual army and that it was in the hands of the higher class. However, lack of written evidence limits our insight into the details of how exactly their military worked. That is why maybe the best source for a deeper understanding of this topic comes from the Olmec weapons which were found at archeological sites. In the early San Lorenzo period, the most commonly used weapons were fire-hardened wooden spears, which were both primitive and inefficient. So, it is likely they were used primarily for hunting rather than for war. But as that settlement started its golden age and trade expansion around 1150 BCE, the Olmecs also adopted an important innovation in their military equipment. They started using obsidian tips for their spears, which made them sharper, with longer edges that could also be used for both slashing and stabbing. Judging by some sculptures of that period, Olmecs also adopted the use of clubs and maces, which are more primitive type of shock weapons. This is an important step, since for the first time, weapons were made with a solely martial application and were not mere adaptations of everyday utilitarian tools. And as with many other things, it could be argued that the Olmecs were the first to make that kind of leap, giving them an edge in the arms race of ancient Mesoamerica.

An Olmec king holding a mace-like weapon.

Beside those hand-to-hand weapons, there is evidence that the Olmecs also used throwing spears and atlatls, which is a spear-throwing tool common in the Mesoamerican region. But their use seems to be limited since they would be ineffective in fights against raiders and in smaller skirmishes, which were probably the most common type of battles the Olmecs faced. Besides, the supply of projectiles would quickly be exhausted rendering them quite useless, especially in conflicts that are further away from their heartland. But probably more interesting is the fact that the Olmecs didn't use any kind of armor. Their soldiers are usually depicted without any protective gear on their bodies, with the exception of helmets. And archeologists think that those helmets were probably more a symbol of status rather than functional protection for the head. Not only that, but the Olmec warriors were never depicted carrying a shield. Some historians believe the reason behind this is that they needed extra mobility in hand-to-hand combat, while others think they didn't have advanced enough technology yet to build armor which offered enough protection while at the same time not weigh too much. Some even argue that armor in general wouldn't be useful against opponents who used hit-and-run tactics, which were probably the most common type of adversaries the Olmecs met. The use of armor spread through Mesoamerica only when most armies became more conventional in nature, but by that time the Olmecs had already faded into obscurity.

But the Olmec had one more crucial military contribution to give before they disappeared. That was another new weapon, a slingshot, which appeared among the Olmecs during the La Venta dominance. Archeologists aren't sure if they originally created it or if they adopted it from some other tribe, but from the archeological evidence that is scattered across Mesoamerica, historians believe that the slingshot was spread throughout the region by the Olmecs. It was at the time the most superior long-range weapon of the region. Unlike throwing spears, its ammunition was less likely to run out, as small stone projectiles could be carried in larger quantities. And they could be replenished pretty much everywhere, even on an expedition long away from home. Slingshots also had a much higher rate of fire than throwing spears. The biggest advantage of a slingshot, however, was their range, which in a best-case scenario was up to 500 meters (about 550 yards). When we take into account that the Mesoamerican soldiers weren't equipped with any kind of armor, a hit from a single slingshot projectile could be quite damaging, if not deadly if it landed in the right spot. This new weapon gave an edge to the Olmec forces in both offensive and defensive actions, and historians think it was also rather useful against the hit-and-run raids on merchant caravans.

The implementation of the slingshot surely changed the military strategy that the Olmecs used. But we can only give educated guesses to the exact tactic that might have been used by the Olmec warriors because there's no evidence about it at all - not even on statues and carvings. The main question is if they used any kind of cohesive formation. From other examples around the world, it is known that armies which used shock weapons like the Olmecs did often had at least some kind of simple formation that allowed the soldier to focus on the enemy in front of him while his fellow warriors protected his sides and back. It is possible that the Olmecs used some simple tactical formation which would allow this, but most military historians think that it's not likely. For one, their opponents didn't have organized armies and most likely used guerilla strategies, so the Olmecs wouldn't be able to utilize the advantages of the tactical formation. Also, the fact that they already had technical superiority meant that the Olmecs didn't have to bother with learning new ways of warfare. Also, formations require at least some kind of military training. And there is no compelling evidence for that. Thus, it is far more likely that the battles were fought more on an individual scale. They would start as a mass confrontation between two armies, but due to the lack of organized tactics, the fight would break into duels between two soldiers. But with the implementation of slingshots, it is possible that a primitive type of tactic was developed, where first the projectiles were fired in volleys and then the hand-to-hand combat commenced.

Apart from the tactics used, the size of the Olmec army is also an important and interesting issue. As the total Olmec population wasn't really that high, reaching in the most optimistic estimates about three hundred thousand in the heartland, their armies wouldn't be that large. The second limiting factor was the handling of new types of weapons. It required some specialized training for a soldier to be proficient with it, and common folks couldn't just derive military skills from their utilitarian usage of tools. This means that war became the business of the elite, who could afford the time to gain military expertise. Common people played only a secondary role in the army. With that in mind, the largest possible army the Olmecs could create, at least in theory, was around five thousand strong. And that is if we consider the whole Olmec heartland as the source for raising the army, which was also highly unlikely as there is no evidence that the Olmecs were united into a single state. In reality, their armies were a lot smaller than that. One more reason for the limited number of the Olmec troops was the necessity of developed logistics needed to sustain an army of a larger size for a more extended period or on a long-distance campaign. That was one area in which no matter how advanced the Olmec society was, it wasn't efficient enough.

Taking all these facts into consideration leads us to a conclusion that the true nature of the Olmec military was mostly linked with armed trading caravans. For one, both merchants and warriors came from the elite class and likely performed both tasks at the same time. Secondly, these were rather small parties whose primary goal was to protect the goods. Thirdly, their equipment and tactics weren't designed for large-scale battles, but more for small skirmishes with bandits and raiders. Ultimately, the role of the Olmec military was protective, not expansionistic. But it remained powerful enough to influence their trading partners and neighbors with the idea of their strength and capabilities. With that influence, the Olmecs were able to expand and maintain their trading network, making local elites of other tribes more willing to cooperate with them, providing more secure trading than before. In the end, even the military revolved and evolved around trading, which seems to be the backbone of the whole Olmec civilization.

Chapter 8 – The Olmecs at Home

So far, we have focused more on how the Olmecs interacted with their neighbors and surrounding tribes. But now it's time to ask the question of how the Olmecs' life and society were structured. These questions are important in understanding the Olmecs and their story. Especially considering that the story of the common people is often unintentionally neglected in ancient history because they weren't the moving force behind substantial historical events which meant that they left less of a trail of evidence after them. This is why in this chapter, we shall try to uncover as many details about the Olmec commoners as the archeological findings allow us.

The first significant question about the common Olmecs is what they did for a living since we know that the elite was busy with trade and military. It shouldn't be a big surprise that, like most of the other commoners in the ancient world, the lower classes of the Olmec society were mainly farmers working on fields which were located outside of their villages. As we mentioned before, they grew maize, squash, beans, sweet potato, and manioc. Besides farmers, there were fishermen, either on the rivers or on the Golf Coast, who brought in fish, crabs, turtles, snakes, and shellfish. As the Mesoamericans didn't develop herding until the Europeans came, they still had hunters providing meat to supplement the vegetable and fruit diet. They caught rabbits, possums, raccoons, peccary (also known as skunk pig), and even deer. Also, they hunted for birds as well. It should be mentioned that those animals weren't used only for meat, but also for their hide and feathers which were used in various products and handicrafts made by artisans. These professions were the foundation of the Olmec society on which all others were built upon. But they were the least influential strata in it and were in a way exploited and controlled by the elite class which took the fruits of their labor for themselves and at the same time made them work on their grand project.

The common people, in most cases, didn't live in the central towns like San Lorenzo or La Venta. Instead, they lived in the villages that surrounded them. Common villages were rather small, with scattered wooden shacks and in some cases, if the village was large enough, even a small temple. They usually searched for higher ground to build up their villages and surrounding them were the fields most of them worked on. Of course, their wooden homes were rather modest and small. But they usually had a nearby garden which was used to grow medicinal and cooking herbs they needed for everyday life. Also, most of them had at least one storage pit dug nearby, which they used to preserve food, similar to the function of a root cellar. But their lives gravitated towards the center of town to which their village was associated, as they were the true social, political, economic, and religious centers of the Olmec society where the elite lived. The true nature of the elite-commoners relationship is unknown to us. We can't be sure if the villagers or the higher class owned the land, nor if or how exactly the commoners paid tributes. And if they did pay, how did the elite justify taxes? Were they paying for the land use or for protection, be it from outside attacks or from the elites themselves? Was the subordination of the commoners rooted in religion? All these and much more are still unknown to us, and at this stage, the only thing we could do is merely guess.

Another distinctive class, in a broad meaning of the word, were artisans, from those that created the wonderful pieces of the Olmec art, to those who created tools and weapons, to builders, etc. They probably resided in both villages and towns centers, but certainly more in the latter. On a social scale, they were probably a step above the farmers since their work involved skilled labor. And more importantly, their products and craftsmanship were sought by the elite, making them a bit more valuable, especially considering they were less numerous than the farmers. While some of them could have gained access to a cozy way of life if they were really good in their craft, they were by no means near the elite. We can't even compare them to the middle class of our time. Artisans were definitely still a lower class, nowhere near the elite, who most likely lumped them together with the farmers. That is why the elite had no problem to exploit their products for their own gain, like they did with the farmers. Although, as we've seen from the idea of export of artisans, if an artisan would show a high enough level of skill, he could gain a considerable level of respect from the higher class, which was clearly not possible for the farmers.

Other details about the everyday life of the lower class Olmecs are pretty much unknown. The things we can say with a degree of certainty is that there were no schools, as there is not even a hint for it among the archeological findings. Not even in the elite circles. Any education they got came from their families and neighbors. The cultural and religious life was centered in towns, as well as the trade. So, the commoners from surrounding villages had to commute to the towns if they wanted to participate in those spheres of life. Also, by looking at the scale of buildings and monuments in the town centers, we can assume that the elite had a way of mobilizing those villagers to participate in those great public projects. Some historians think it was done by use of religion, while others associate it with the use of force. Another possibility is that, like in some other ancient civilizations around the world, public work labor was one of the ways to pay taxes.

But not all is so gray for the Olmec commoners. As they lived in relative peace, they had calm although hardworking lives. When this is compared with some other examples in history, it wasn't all that bad.

Another part of the everyday life of the Olmecs — that is rather unimportant when compared with others we have talked about, yet quite interesting — are the clothes they wore. And unlike most of the other topics, thanks to the archeological evidence we can talk about this with more certainty. For men, the most common thing they wore was a simple loincloth, usually without any decoration on it. This isn't surprising considering the warm climate in which the Olmecs lived. In some cases though, they did wear tunics or mantles, most likely on some special occasions like ceremonies and religious rituals. Women also kept it rather simple, wearing only dresses and belts. As the evidence for this lays in the stone carvings and other forms of art, since no actual textile has been preserved, we can only give educated guesses on the exact material the Olmec clothes were made from. The most likely candidates are cotton and possibly in some cases leather. It also seems that these types of clothing were the same for both elite and commoners, with the difference being the quality of the textile and some minor decorations and color.

A carving of an Olmec woman.

Now, this doesn't mean that you wouldn't be able to differentiate a member of the elite from a commoner if you saw them next to the other. The biggest and most obvious distinction between these two classes would be the headdresses the elite wore. Unlike other types of clothing, these were complex and adorned with various decorations like beads, bird feathers, and tassels. The assumption is that the larger and more majestic examples shown in the Olmec art were reserved for ceremonies, while in everyday life they wore something that would be more similar to a simple turban. It is also rather interesting to note that there are representations of hats with brims, which are rather uncommon in the pre-Columbian Mesoamerica. The Olmec elite is also commonly seen in art having various adornments and jewelry on them. Those ranged from nose and ear plugs, through bracelets and anklets, to pendants and necklaces. These pieces of jewelry were usually made from jade and other precious stones, with the possibility that in some cases the less wealthy had them made from other perishable materials like wood.

Alas, it is time to turn our attention away from the fun and exciting story of fashion and trinkets, back to more serious topics. We have to examine the roles the Olmec elite played in everyday life. They were a clear minority in the Olmec society like elites usually are in all cultures around the world. They lived almost exclusively in the town centers, like Tres Zapotes or La Venta, where they enjoyed all the benefits of being the ruling class. Their homes were larger, built from more durable materials than wood, and decorated with various art pieces. And unlike the lower classes, they didn't have to work as hard, and it could be even hypothesized that they had servants of some sorts, though there is no clear indication of slavery. Taking into account that in the later Mesoamerican cultures slavery wasn't common nor had it played a substantial role, we can assume it also wasn't an important part of the Olmec society. Another perk of being a member of the elite was traveling. Thanks to trade, they were not only able to amass wealth, but also journey across the region, which wasn't something that the commoners did much. With more free time, members of the elite could focus more on religious ceremonies, feasts, and also on learning new important skills. Looking at all of that, their lives seemed to be quite carefree, with the only worry being how to better show off their power and riches and confirm their place at the top of the social hierarchy.

This is a good moment to repeat one more time that the rule of the elite over the commoners was rooted in their command over three things: religion, trade, and military. With the development of more sophisticated weapons, the military power of the elite grew substantially, because for one, only the elite knew how to use them proficiently. Also, those new types of weapons were something that a common farmer could not afford. As a result, the Olmec elite became distinctively stronger than the lower class. That made most of the rebellions of the commoners futile. And as the trade grew, it became harder for a commoner to get into the merchant circles, if not impossible. Also, wealth allowed the elite to amass more influence and power. For example, it made connecting with elites of other tribes possible, which amplified their political dominance. And as the rich had more time to practice their fighting skills, the elite also expanded its military domination.

The last segment, religion, is where things become a bit less clear. We cannot be sure how and when the elite grabbed this power. Some speculate that it began way before the Olmecs started developing their civilization. At the time, when the Olmecs' ancestors first switched to agriculture, a certain group of people or individuals may have gained a level of expertise in the calendar. With that skill, they could have helped with the harvesting of food, which would seem to others like they were talking to the gods through the skies. Or the first religious leaders came from the early military leaders who achieved victories which benefited the whole community and were seen as magical. Another possibility is that they gained their divine recognition when they were able to mobilize other common populations for building temples and shrines.

Whatever may be the root of it, it is certain that the Olmec elite had a dogmatic religious role in their society, which wasn't that uncommon. We can simply look at ancient Egypt as a comparison, where the pharaoh was a god on the earth. Some have theorized that the Olmec chiefs had the same divine justification for their rule, but this is uncertain. With these characteristics in mind, some historians have tried to label the rule of the Olmec elite as a form of military theocracy. With that came the debate if the Olmecs had developed a state or not. In this debate, there are two sides. One claims that the Olmec society wasn't diffused enough, with only two social classes, and that the rule of the elite wasn't sophisticated enough. With that, they meant that the elite didn't develop a mechanism of what we think as proper government. That part of the historian community is more willing to label the Olmec rule as a chiefdom, which is seen as a transitional type of rule that evolved from egalitarian tribes of the prehistoric times towards a fully developed state. The opposing side points to the major public projects as proof of the firm control the elite held over the masses. The sheer complexity of the Olmec culture is more than enough for historians to conclude that the Olmecs had a state. But no matter how historians label it, the rule of the elite was more or less absolute.

While on the subject of the Olmecs rule in their heartland, there is also an important question that has to be answered—were the Olmecs united in a single state/chiefdom? Some historians believe that they had to be in order to achieve such a success in both spreading their culture and trading. The lack of defensive fortifications and signs of serious battles in the Olmec heartland indicate that they lived in peace among each other (some form of military confrontation would also be expected if there was no political unity among them). But on the other side, there are no clear indications that the major town centers were in any way politically connected. The connection via culture is evident but looking at ancient Greece and the Mayans, one can see that sharing a culture does not necessarily mean a unified state. That is why some historians tend to believe the idea that the Olmecs were divided into several smaller city-states. Evidently close ties between those city-states could be identified as the alliance among the elites, possibly even with arranged marriages. And if those alliances were interconnected, there is also a chance that the Olmecs even had a sort of a league of city-states. Connection of that type would help them present a more unified front towards all of their neighbors, helping them with the trade. At the same time, the league would help to keep the peace between the city-states, explaining the lack of fortifications.

Chapter 9 – Religion and Beliefs of the Olmecs

As stated in previous chapters, religion played an essential role in the Olmec society. It was a source that legitimized the rule of the elites. And we have seen that the town centers were also used as ceremonial and religious centers. This status gave them enormous prestige and drew crowds from other settlements to come and pay their respects in both offering and prayer. But how was the Olmecs' religion structured? What did they believe in? Luckily for us, the Olmecs left us traces in their art, as well as in the religions of their successors, like the Mayans and the Aztec. Even though we don't have the exact knowledge of their rituals, we have a general idea of what they believed in.

It is generally accepted that the Olmec rulers played an important, if not central, part of religious practices. They may even have been seen as a representation of god(s) on earth. Beside them, there were also full-time priests, whose only concern was maintaining rituals, performing ceremonies, and appeasing the gods. They were almost certainly connected with the temples, like in other ancient civilizations. One of their jobs as priests was also to connect with the spiritual powers through various disciplines like meditating, fasting, and even ritualistic self-harming. Some scholars even go so far as to claim that the Olmecs also practiced human sacrifices, even though there is no hard evidence for that. It is possible that the ritual self-harming of the Olmecs was a stepping stone towards human sacrifice of the later Mesoamerican cultures. But it is evident that religion was mostly centralized and revolved around the temples in the major city centers.

There is one last possible religious figure in the Olmec society, and that is the shaman. They were likely remnants from the non-organized religion of their ancestors, linked more with the commoners. And unlike priests, it is likely that every village and community had one. Their exact practices are unknown, but after looking at other indigenous people of the Americas, scholars think that they were likely focused on altering the human state of mind with hallucinogens, trying to transcend human consciousness and connect with animals like the jaguar. That is why some archeologists think they wore masks that represented the were-jaguar, a mixture of human and jaguar, which as we already know was a common motif in the Olmec art. Some also link these shamans with astronomers and astrologists, or even possibly with the medicine-men. But it's clear that they were focused on helping their community in everyday life.

Based on available evidence, shamans were somewhat an opposite to the town priests. The priests were focused on the larger questions of religion, tasked with pleasing the gods, practicing ceremonies, and giving and taking the offerings. Their role was in the grander scheme of the universe. Shamans, on the other hand, weren't focused on praying to the gods as much as trying to understand and interpret their action. They were focused on smaller problems that on a large scale weren't as important to the whole Olmec society. But they played an important role in the local communities. We can assume that as the Olmec civilization grew stronger and more developed, the balance between shamans and priests shifted. In the beginning, they were equally important, at least to the common people. But in later periods, when priests got their large temples and gained more authority as well as a monopoly on the religious issues, significance and prestige of shamans dropped. It is something that is common for all early civilizations of the world during the process of moving towards what we today call organized religion.

Moving away from the subject of rituals and ceremony, it is time to see what and who the Olmecs believed in. We know that they were polytheists who believed in a number of gods, though we don't know their exact names. Their view of the universe was through energy and spiritualism linked closely with animals. That is evident from the fact that their gods were in shapes of different animals, sometimes even crossed with humans or with other animals. Their exact roles as gods are a matter of speculation, but they were certainly linked to various natural phenomena which were essential to preserving life such as the sun or rain. As previously mentioned, the were-jaguar was represented the most in Olmec art, which led many early archeologists to recognize it as the most important deity of the Olmecs. But recently, more scholars see it as one of the equals in the Olmec pantheon of the gods. The most widely accepted role of the were-jaguar is as the rain deity, but some also link it with military and/or sexual conquest. It is certain that the jaguar was an animal that played an important part in the lives of the Olmec. It was a fierce predator, hunting both day and night, which gave the feeling of raw power to it. It also seemed to represent the unification of three elements, water, air, and land. That symbolism comes from the fact that they lived in the jungle where they were comfortable walking on the ground, swimming in the rivers and climbing way up onto the trees. It is possible that the Olmecs wanted to emulate that energy and that is why they revered it so much.

Another important deity was the feathered or plumed serpent. This iconography may be recognizable to those who have heard about Quetzalcoatl of the Aztecs or Kukulkan of the

Mayans. Many speculate that these two cultures adopted this deity from the Olmec tradition. From these later societies, we know they respected the plumed serpent as the creator of humanity as well as a hero who played a messianic role, promising to lead the humans to some kind of a better future. Interestingly, it was able to shift its roles between a god, human hero, and an intangible myth. Even its mixture of a snake and a bird represented its important dualism and ability to change. A bird represented more divine attributes. Because it can fly, it can be close to the sky. And flight was a representation of its godly virtues. But a snake represented more down to earth attributes, since they were less virtuous and more human. The reason for that kind of symbolism was the fact that the snake crawled on the ground and dirt, far away from the divinity of the sky. That dualism represented the idea of transformation and inconsistency in life. But at the same time, being constantly around it represented some more permanent aspects of life, that can't be so easily transformed. Even though we clearly see that they revered this god, its importance to the Olmec culture is uncertain. As in some later Mesoamerican civilizations, the plumed serpent deity was the most significant in the pantheon, which was even divinely linked with rulers, so some thought it was important to the Olmecs as well. That is why in earlier periods of the Olmec research, some archeologists believed that the Olmec rulers were identified with this god in particular. But now, not everyone is so convinced, as this deity isn't as prevalent in the Olmec art, and there are no signs of its prestige among other gods.

The oldest representation of feathered serpent in Mesoamerica found at La Venta.

There were numerous other gods as well within the Olmec pantheon. There was a maize deity which is commonly represented with a cleft on its head with corn sprouting from it. In some cases, it also had a jaguar snarl on it, again showing the mysterious connection the Olmecs had with this animal. Usually on par with the maize god is the water god, which looks like a baby were-jaguar. The water god was connected to all water, including lakes and rivers. They seem to be paired together because maize and water were the sources of survival for the Olmecs. They also revered an anthropomorphic shark or fish creature. It is recognizable by its crescent eyes and a shark tooth. Some think it was the god of the underworld. Another important deity was the so-called Olmec dragon, which is a crocodile-looking god, with an occasional addition of human, jaguar or eagle features. It seems to have represented the Earth and fertility. As such, it was connected to agriculture, fertility, and fire. Of course, there are more that scholars haven't identified or singled out yet, but these examples seem to be the most important.

But the level of their importance to the Olmec society isn't entirely certain yet. Some earlier scholars were even doubtful if these were true representations of the gods the Olmecs believed in, although that is the currently accepted theory. The connections of deities and their roles are in some cases guesses based on connections with later cultures and their religions. Even their mutual ties are uncertain. Still, the biggest mystery of the Olmec beliefs remains the issue of the were-jaguar and its importance to the Olmecs. But no matter what the truth is behind these supernatural beings that were such an important motif of the Olmec art and focus of reverence, one thing is certain: their religious beliefs formed a complex and structuralized system. And from the ability to compare them with similar deities from other later Mesoamerican civilization, as well as the fact that some of their shrines were worshiped by people long after they were gone, scholars concluded that the Olmec beliefs became the foundation of others in the region. Though this shouldn't come as much of a surprise, in ancient times, gods were shared among civilizations like any other idea.

Chapter 10 – Cultural Innovation of the Olmecs

It has been mentioned in many places how the Olmecs were able to influence their successors in numerous ways, creating a foundation of the Mesoamerican culture as a whole, from trade networks and theocratic rule to religion and art. That was a remarkable feat on its own. But they also seem to be responsible for quite a few important cultural innovations which in later periods became the very things most people identify with pre-Columbian Mesoamerica. And some of these are still unmistakably a part of the present-day Mesoamerican culture. These cultural innovations are probably the very things that justify the idea of the Olmecs being the mother culture to all others in the Mesoamerican region which is another testament to their power and influence.

Architecturally speaking, probably the most iconic buildings seen in Mesoamerican cultures are the pyramids. Only slightly less famous than the pyramids found in Egypt, these Mesoamerican creations have been in the focus of both scholars and tourists for a long time. But most laymen associate them first with Mayans and Aztecs. They have indeed built some of the most breathtaking pieces, but as with many other things, they have only perfected something that the Olmecs have started. One of the earliest and biggest pyramids, at least at the time of building, is found at La Venta. It is actually seen as the center structure for the whole settlement. Today, after 2,500 years of erosion, the only thing left from it is a mound as it was built from clay that has a slightly conical shape At first, it made archeologists think it was purposely built that way to mimic the nearby mountains. But the recent studies have shown that they were similar to the pyramids of their successors. When it was still in its original form, it was a proper rectangular pyramid with stepped sides and inset corners. Being 34 meters (110 feet) high, it was the biggest building in that settlement, and maybe even of the whole Olmec world. That is why archeologists have aptly named it "The Great Pyramid."

The actual use of the pyramids in the Olmec civilization is still debated. At one side of the debate stand the scholars who think that these pyramids are temples, as were the Mayan and Aztecan pyramids. They think the Olmecs built them to be closer to the sky and the gods when performing religious rituals and ceremonies. On the other side of the debate, the less popular theory suggests that they were tombs, like those in ancient Egypt. Evidence that supports this is the fact that a magnetometer survey found an anomaly deep beneath an estimated 100,000 cubic meters (3.5 million cubic feet) of earth that fills The Great Pyramid. They speculate it could be a resting place of an important ruler. Another piece of supporting evidence to this theory is the fact that archeologists have found burial mounds with similar shapes which are seen as precursors to the pyramids. Though that may be true, the question remains—why would a tomb be the center focus of the whole city? Some researchers explain the anomaly as merely an unintentional byproduct of the building process or an offering built on the foundation of the temple to please the gods. Whatever may be the true function of the pyramids in Olmec society, the fact remains that they were among the first ones to build them, and through their influence, they were crucial in spreading them across the region.

What is left of the Great pyramid at La Venta.

The pyramids are now pretty much gone from the Mesoamerican cultures. But another Olmec innovation was so intertwined with everyday life that it's traces could be connected with the fact that one of the most popular sports in this region is football (soccer). That shouldn't be surprising considering that in the pre-Columbian era they played a Mesoamerican ballgame, which is quite similar to football, and whose earliest traces could be found on Olmec sites. The game was played in almost every civilization of Mesoamerica, but with the rules and exact details varying from culture to culture and from time period to time period. Even today, in certain areas of Mexico, people still play a game called Ulama, which came from the Aztec version of the game. The universal characteristic to all variations of the game was the rubber ball it was played with, though they varied in size. The oldest rubber balls came from El Manatí, a settlement close to San Lorenzo. These balls were dated to around 1600 BCE. Other evidence also corroborates this idea, like the number of ballplayer figurines found at San Lorenzo, from 1200 BCE. The fact that the balls were found in a sacrificial bog and that near it archeologists found a "yoke", which is a statue in the form of the upside-down letter U, made out of stone. That is usually connected to the Mesoamerican ballgame, led scholars to conclude that these balls weren't just a sacrificial offering. Rather, they think the game was played near the site in a form of a religious ritual of some sorts.

The evidence found in the cultures that came after the Olmecs confirm that the game was both religious in nature and recreational. It was an essential part of city life, usually played on special courts built only for the game. And while the significance of this game in the social life of the region is undoubtful, there is a major debate about another aspect of it. It is regarding the possibility of the human sacrifice being the part of the Mesoamerican ballgame. It is commonly considered that in the Mayan society the game ended with the losing side, or at least its captain, being ritually killed. Some theories even link this with the game being used to settle municipal grievances and inter-city conflicts. But so far, no such evidence has been found at the Olmec sites, leading scholars to believe that they played a more peaceful version of the game. Yet, its religious symbolism and importance in the Olmec society is certain. But how exactly it was connected to their beliefs is still under question. As it was played with two teams competing against each other, some see it as a ritual representation of the struggle of the day and night or life and underworld. Others concluded that the ball represent either the sun, which is more likely, or the moon. And the scoring hoops, through which the ball was supposed to be passed through for a point, was hypothesized to have represented equinoxes, sunrises, or sunsets. The last possible connection is fertility, as some of the ballplayer figurines of the period were found adorned with maize symbols. And some of those figurines seem to be representations of women. Both of these are often connected to fertility in the Olmec world, as well as other Mesoamerican cultures.

There is another cultural innovation that is surely connected with fertility, and that is the Mesoamerican Long Count calendar, popularly known as the Mayan calendar. The most striking characteristic of that calendar is that it revolves around the cycles. The shortest cycle is K'in, a single day, while most measures stop at the fifth cycle, B'ak'tun, which is approximately 394 years long. Interestingly, the longest cycle found is a ninth one, named Alautun, which is a bit longer than sixty-three thousand years. That cyclical nature of the Mesoamerican calendar made a lot of people believe that an end of a cycle meant the end of the world, which led to the 2012 media frenzy about the apocalypse. Of course, that faulty idea of the world ending came after an incorrect interpretation of an ancient Mayan text which mentioned that an old world ends and a new arises, meaning a new cycle starts after the end of the thirteenth B'ak'tun which ended on December 21st, 2012. On the other hand, the starting point of this calendar is 3114 BCE when translated to our calendar. Because of that it is considered that the Mesoamericans believed the world in which they lived was created at that date. But at this point, it should be noted that this calendar was not of Mayan creation; it was used across the whole region, and several archeological findings connected to the Mesoamerican Long Count calendar predates the Mayans by several centuries. And some of the earliest discoveries are connected with the Olmecs.

One of the oldest calendars was found at the Tres Zapotes site, which is located in the Olmec heartland and was at one point a part of the Olmec civilization. But it is also one of the few larger settlements that outlived the Olmec civilization as we see it today. The calendar found at that site is dated roughly to 32 BCE, which predates the rise of the Mayans by at least 300 years. But as it was found at the settlement which was at one point part of the Olmec culture, some see it as a direct connection with that civilization. Two other calendars of the same age have been found on the Guatemalan Pacific Coast and in the southern Mexican state of Chiapas. Both of them are similar in age to the one found at Tres Zapotes. Their link with the Olmecs is more indirect. These calendars were decorated in the Olmec style, not the Mayan, but were also in many other aspects far away from the Olmecs. The biggest problem with this theory of the Mesoamerican calendar being of Olmec origins is the fact that all these calendars were created about 300 years after the Olmec civilization had withered away, but that isn't the final nail in the coffin for it, as there could be some older calendars that still haven't been found. And their indirect ties to the Olmec are unquestionable. Looking at other important innovations and cultural advancements that came from this civilization, combined with this circumstantial evidence, it is not that unlikely that it was the Olmecs who first created the calendar, or at least created the foundation for it. But so far, most scholars tend to leave the question of the Mesoamerican calendar origin open until more concrete evidence is found.

The Mesoamerican calendar seems quite odd to most people nowadays because most people are used to the base 10 counting system, otherwise known as the decimal system, which is used in all measuring systems today. On the other hand, the Mesoamericans used base 20 in mathematics. The exception for that is the third cycle, which was 360 days long, and was based on the number 18, most likely so it would be roughly the length of a solar year. But one of the more interesting facts connected with the Long Count calendar is the usage of zero. That number is generally considered to be an essential step in cultural and scientific development as it is a sign of developed intellectual thought and also has a practical application in many fields of life. When the Mesoamericans needed to represent the absence of a number, they used a shell-like glyph, which in its essence was a symbol for nothing, mathematically speaking a zero. The Mesoamerican invention of zero happened at least few hundred years before the Arabs and Hindus. And if we connect the invention of the Long Count calendar with the Olmecs, then they could become the first to use a concept of zero. Of course, this claim is directly linked to the debate over if the Mesoamerican calendar was indeed an Olmec calendar.

Another heated debate over the contributions of the Olmecs is if they had developed writing, which is considered instrumental in forming a successful civilization. A stone tablet found near San Lorenzo, named the Cascajal Block, contains 62 glyphs. Some of these symbols resemble maize, pineapples, insects, and fish, while others seem to be more abstract, as they look like boxes and blobs. This, for some scholars, clearly represents a writing system, even if it was rudimentary. And as it was dated between 1100 and 900 BCE, it shows that the Olmecs had achieved basic literacy much earlier than others in Mesoamerica, with the oldest non-Olmec writing being dated to around 500 BCE. But as with all other aspects of the Olmec civilization, this is also a debated topic. For some archeologists, these symbols are too unorganized, without much similarities to other Mesoamerican writing systems. So rather than an example of writing, they suggest these glyphs may have individual meaning and are not mutually connected in a higher meaning. And if they are not connected, then they are just a compilation of symbols, not a written language. And some of them are similar to the symbols found on some pieces of Olmec art where they have been described as purely decorative. This could also indicate that the Cascajal Block could have some ornamental function rather than a practical use of relaying a message. But even if these glyphs are not a clearly developed writing system, it would at least indicate a formation of it.

Another piece of archeological evidence found at the San Andrés, a settlement near La Venta, is a much clearer sign that the Olmecs had their own writing system. Three artifacts, out of which a ceramic cylinder seal is the most important, were dated to 650 BCE, which is still about 150 years older than the oldest currently confirmed Mesoamerican writing. The seal contains three glyphs when combined in a way which the later Mesoamericans, most notably the Mayans, commonly used to represent a name of the ruler. Besides the seal, two small greenstone plaques have been found, both with only one (different) symbol each. But both of these symbols have been connected to well-documented glyphs in other Mesoamerican writing systems, again most notably the Mayan scripts. For the archeologists that agree with the theory of Olmec script existing, this is clear evidence of it, which when connected with the Cascajal Block, give a sense of continuity and development of the Olmec writing system. When compared with the traditions of the Mayan writing system, it indicates that the Olmec script no matter how rudimentary it may have been, has been the base on which all other Mesoamerican civilizations built their own writings. This would be another testament to the importance of the Olmecs in the development of the whole Mesoamerican region.

Presently, one of the most iconic foods linked with Mexico and the Mesoamerican region is tortillas, primarily the ones made out of maize. That type of food has been made in this area since before the Spaniards came, who actually gave it the name we call it now, since tortilla in Spanish means a small cake. In the Aztecan Nahuatl language, it is called tlaxcalli, which means something baked. We can't be sure what the Olmecs called it, but we know they made it. The evidence for this lies in archeological findings of comales, ceramic griddles on which tortillas were traditionally cooked. The interesting thing is that there weren't any comales found at the San Lorenzo site. But at La Venta, comales have been found, although they were not that common in the Olmec heartland. But like many other things, they were more commonly found at the Olmec-influenced sites. This means it was likely that both comales and tortillas had been developed in the later period of the Olmec civilization. Of course, this doesn't prove anything conclusively; they may have used those ceramic griddles for preparing other types of food and that those have been later adapted for making tortillas.

On the other hand, although traditionally tortillas have been made on comales, in some earlier forms they could have been made in some other way, which would suggest that tortillas could be older than the Olmecs. But even if they didn't invent the tortillas they could have perfected the way they were made. Clearly, tortillas played an important role in the development of Mesoamerica. At first glance, some people may see it as just food, without any further implications other than gastronomical culture. Tortillas have an advantage of staying fresh and edible for at least several days. Also, they were prepared and transported fairly easily. That would have improved the military and travel logistics of the Olmecs, making longer trips easier to organize and execute. In that way, tortillas may have been crucial for even the expansion of the Olmec trade network in the La Venta period, making it larger and more complex than before. And because the Olmec traders would almost certainly bring them on their travels, we can conclude they also spread it across Mesoamerica, making it a popular food in the region. So, even if they didn't invent or even improve tortillas, it is likely the Olmecs played a crucial role in spreading its use to other Mesoamerican civilizations.

While on the subject of culinary history, talking about Mesoamerica and not mentioning cacao and its usage would be a huge oversight. Cacao was an essential part of all Mesoamerican cultures, with a wide variety of application in everyday life. They made various types of beverages from it, used it in religious ceremonies, and at some points during the history of the region, it was used as currency as well. And the use of the cacao bean dates back all the way to the Olmec times. Evidence for that lies in the vessels found at various Olmec settlements, which after testing showed traces of cacao residue in them. This would confirm that the Olmecs drank one of the variations of the cacao beverages, which would put their civilization into the contest of being the first one to actually do so. The fact that the cacao tree grows naturally in the Olmec heartland also helps the case. It was only a matter of time before someone would think of some way to use its fruit.

From the vessels found, scholars are sure that at least one of the ways the Olmecs used cacao was to make drinks out of it. But some also think they used it in more spiritual and ceremonial ways, linking it from the very beginning of its usage to religion, as it was used in later Mesoamerican civilizations, but archeologists can't be sure about that. The third common usage of cacao as a currency seems rather unlikely for the Olmecs. Not only is there no evidence of cacao being used as one, but also, there is no evidence of a currency of any kind being used, although the Olmecs have traded with and for cacao, and its use as currency in later periods of Mesoamerican history rose from that trade. The biggest testimony to the crucial role the Olmecs played in making cacao a special part of Mesoamerican culture lies in the very word cacao. The word we use today is a Spanish transcription of Mayan word cacaw, which was their name for the cacao. But the Mayans got the word from the Olmec language, where this plant was called kakaw, according to the work of Mesoamerican linguists. That alone is enough to imply how important the Olmecs were to the spreading of cacao and its use over the region. But also looking at the bigger picture; it shows that this civilization didn't influence only the Mesoamerican civilizations, but that they with this word managed to influence the worldwide culture of the present era, as we even today love and use cacao, while still using the Olmec name for it. And other examples in this chapter also support the idea that the Olmec influence was much more widespread than they are usually credited for.

Chapter 11 – The Olmecs, A Mother Culture of Mesoamerica?

In this book, even from its title, the point has been in celebrating the Olmecs as one of the oldest, if not the oldest, civilization in Mesoamerica. And throughout the pages, the general tendency of the chapters has been to present all the ways in which the Olmecs have influenced both their contemporaries and their successors. Even when considering the theories that were against this notion, the idea that the Olmec civilization is a mother culture of all Mesoamerica should be obvious. And many scholars agree with this, though in various degrees. But there are also those who are completely against it. And this chapter is dedicated to the negative side of this important debate, as the positive side has been woven into all the previous chapters.

Looking at the Olmecs as a mother culture of the region, the religion seems to be the part where the Olmecs influence is the weakest. In previous chapters, it has been mentioned that their beliefs influenced others enough to pay respect to both Olmec holy sites and to at least some of their gods. Some scholars, however, believe it is also possible that these religious beliefs weren't solely Olmecan. It is possible that they actually predate the Olmecs. These beliefs could have come from the prehistoric Mesoamericans, who due to the fact that they lived in the same regions, started worshipping the same supernatural beings and animals, attributing to them similar connections to the natural phenomena in an attempt to explain them. With continued contact among the different tribes, their beliefs became more alike to the point when they became almost the same. In this sense, some scholars believe the religion and mythology of Mesoamerica didn't evolve from the Olmec beliefs and were instead merely one of many bricks in the wall.

And, as we have seen, a lot of their art stemmed from their religion. So, the issue regarding the cultural and artistic influence the Olmecs had on Mesoamerica through the times is also open for debate. As mentioned in previous chapters, the consensus among historians is that the Olmecs' style was copied by other chiefdoms and civilizations, spreading the characteristics of the Olmec culture across the region But contrary to that idea, some scholars think this explanation of mimicry is wrong. As with religion, they think that these similarities in art, which most have seen as copying of the Olmec style, are rooted in the cultural unity of the entire region, which predates the Olmecs. They think that nearly all of the people who lived in Mesoamerica had the similar aesthetics as well as beliefs, and without foreign influence made art with only minor, almost indistinguishable differences. That would mean that the Olmec style didn't exist. It was, in essence, a style of the entire Mesoamerica. If that's true, it would certainly make the Olmecs less special in the eyes of scholars, at least when talking about art.

Even when talking about the Olmecan cultural innovations mentioned in the previous chapter, theory is similar – they were created by the entire region, not only the Olmecs. There is no clear evidence that the Olmecs were first to make any cultural advancements. The oldest evidence for any of them have been dated to a similar age, and not all of them came directly from the Olmecs. This brings the question; did the Olmecs influence Mesoamerica? Or did Mesoamerica influence the Olmecs similar to the old conundrum of the chicken and the egg? While it is possible the Olmecs were actually the ones to make these innovations, it is also possible they copied them from their neighbors or trading partners. It is even possible that similar ideas on how to improve the quality of life were created in different tribes and chiefdoms without the Olmecs' influence. And with that mindset, they cannot be called the Mesoamerican mother civilization.

Some of the scholars even argue that the Olmecs weren't more advanced than any of their contemporaries and that they were more or less equal to other cultures of Mesoamerica at the time. They do not stand out in art, craftsmanship, or social complexity. The only thing that separates them from other tribes is their trade and their wealth. With all that being said, it could be concluded that the Olmecs were only a creation of modern times, a group of people that we linked into a civilization that wasn't as tangible as we would like it to be. And that in reality all the tribes and people of the region were actually unified in one widespread ancient Mesoamerican civilization. Of course, this is just another way of looking at the Olmecs and shouldn't necessarily be taken as the correct one. This debate is still not completely settled.

Conclusion

The Olmec story is filled with maybes, debates, theories, and ideas. With all these unanswered questions, the Olmecs are still largely a mystery to us. The Olmecs played an essential role in Mesoamerican history; from the beginning of their history, they started to stand out from their neighbors. They were able to create amazing temples, monuments, and other public projects. They had the finesse to create astonishing pieces of art of unparalleled quality for the time period. They were able to create a society which strived for more, which strived for greatness. And because of their excellence, the Olmecs served as a model to others around them at the time. That is why everyone tried to copy their ingenuity and why everyone wanted to be associated with them.

Of course, this doesn't mean that their society was perfect, nor their civilization a place where one would actually want to live. It should always be remembered that the majority of the Olmec people, the commoners, led hardworking lives, with very little leisure and luxury. The Olmecs shouldn't be viewed as some past utopia in any way. But even so, it was exactly these commoners who managed to achieve such proficiency in many diverse fields of work. They became the famous artisans whose products are still the focus of public attention. But with so many uncertainties and debates, some may ask if the Olmecs really deserve the hype that has been built up around them. Has the web of legend been spun around them only because they are one of the oldest civilizations of the Americas?

If nothing else, they deserve our attention because of the trade network they created, which in the end seems to be not only the core reason for their success, but also their greatest legacy. The Olmecs' influence and power stems from the fact that they had unprecedentedly capable merchants. With all the connections they had across the whole of Mesoamerica, they made the region feel much smaller, more linked, and more compact. This is possibly their greatest achievement. What didn't originate from them, they helped spread. So even if we can't or won't give the Olmecs the title of the Mesoamerican mother culture, we can't ignore the fact that they were important for the development of the region. They were the glue that stuck it all together in the first place.

For that reason, their story deserves to be told. That is why it is worth our time and patience to get to know the Olmecs. It is important to see them as artists and craftsmen, as warriors and rulers, as traders and priests, as shamans and inventors. Because even if their civilization is long gone and they have disappeared in dark corridors of the almost forgotten past, the Olmecs' have put their mark on history. Their impact can still be felt today, even if it is in a minor, almost unrecognizable way. And that fact should never be forgotten.

If you enjoyed this individual book on the Olmecs, can you please leave a review for it?

Thanks for your support!

Part 2: Zapotec Civilization

A Captivating Guide to the Pre-Columbian Cloud People Who Dominated the Valley of Oaxaca in Mesoamerica

Introduction

When people discuss the civilizations encountered by the Conquistadors as they traveled across South America and Mesoamerica, they will always bring up the Incans, Mayans, and Aztecs. These civilizations had large pyramids and structured societies that the Conquistadors studied, and history has assigned them a pivotal role in growth and development during the Pre-Columbian times. However, they were not the only civilizations.

Less well-known are the Zapotec. Even though they are obscure today, they lived and thrived, and became a civilization of interest to the Conquistadors. They did not leave behind the same kinds of massive structures and temples like other civilizations, so they have not left behind much for those people interested in learning about their culture. Historians have a wealth of details about these influential people through the writings of the Conquistadors. The journals and letters show how intensely interested the Europeans were in trying to understand the civilization and its complex system and relationships. While much of what is known today comes from these biased journals, archaeologists have spent decades trying to uncover the treasures and remains of this once great civilization.

Based on what is known, one of the greatest mysteries is why the Zapotec have not received the same attention and place in history as other well-known civilizations. As one of the largest Mesoamerican civilizations at the time, they helped to shape and form the world the Conquistadors encountered upon their arrival. Rivaling the size and complexity of their Mayan neighbors, the Zapotec were innovators and intellectuals who created a society that was markedly similar to the kingdoms and social structures.

One of the greatest mysteries about this sophisticated civilization is what happened to it. Roughly 2,500 years ago they were thriving. And then they were gone. After taming an area that was dry and difficult to navigate, they disappeared with almost no traces of what happened. These people who considered themselves to be children of the gods appeared to have returned to the clouds from whence they came, but not without leaving hints and pieces for archaeologists to find and interpret. Coupled with the writings of the Conquistadors, historians and archaeologists have been fleshing out every aspect of the Zapotec. From their early history where they tamed the Valley of Oaxaca to the society that met with the Conquistadors, there are many secrets of this once great civilization that have been uncovered.

The Zapotec were a fascinating people. They give a fresh look and understanding to civilizations that were just as complex, structured, and regal as any of their Mesoamerican, South American, or European counterparts.

Chapter 1 – Looking Back over Hundreds of Years

While the Zapotec civilization disappeared long ago, there are many remnants that show how influential and intelligent its people were at the height of its power. What is known about them today is based on a combination of the records left by the Conquistadors and educated guesses based on the remains of the civilization. Archeologists also have access to some descendants of the Zapotecs who still live in the Mesoamerica area. Although their knowledge of their past is limited, they have kept some myths and beliefs alive. There are still many unanswered questions, particularly about what led to the nearly complete disappearance of the entire civilization, but every day archeologists learn a little bit more about this fascinating civilization. .

While it is true that a wide gap will always remain in the understanding and truth about this ancient civilization, historians and archaeologists have worked with the knowledge that they have gained from the records left by the Conquistadors, the ruins and the descendants of the Zapotecs to build a comprehensive picture of the history, evolving social structures, politics, and daily lives of these people. Slowly, they have been constructing a timeline that extends over more than a millennium to capture the rise and decline of the Zapotec.

The Cloud People

To understand the Zapotec civilization, it is essential to have some basic knowledge of their religious beliefs (a fact that is true of every civilization, no matter how modern or ancient). Their civilization began to form roughly 2,500 years ago. Ancient Egypt had already seen the peak of its power and Rome was a republic, but not yet an Empire. The evolution of the Zapotec civilization was similar to the rise and evolution of the Roman Empire. The primary difference between the two was that the Zapotecs did not seek to take over the known world; they primarily sought to build and expand their culture over the surrounding area. Once they expanded their empire until it began to touch another empire, they frequently worked to build a relationship with that culture instead of trying to dominate it.

The Romans and the Zapotecs employed politics as a way of expanding their empires, and then resorted to war when they encountered resistance to their expansion. The Romans dealt with smaller bands of resistance compared to the world of Mesoamerica. Without any real power to counter their military in Europe, the Romans spread across Europe and northern Africa. In contrast, the Zapotecs were not the only significant power in the region. Shortly before the arrival of the Conquistadors, the Zapotecs had resolved yet another conflict with the Aztec civilization that lived to the north.

Like the Romans, the Zapotecs believed their existence was closely tied to their Pantheon. They also thought the upper echelons of their society derived from the gods. No living human, not even the high priest, was able to talk directly to the creator of the world, but that did not mean that the Zapotecs were ignored by the creator. Instead of having direct contact with humans, the creator and other gods showed their concern for the Zapotecs by the gift of almost everything that people encountered. All things that moved were considered to be significant, from the animals that they ate to the plants they harvested to the clouds in the sky where their ancestors lived. They believed everything that moved had a spirit that was given to it by the creator. From their place in the clouds, the ancestors of the upper class would offer the prayers of the people, both upper class and commoners, working to improve the lives of the entire civilization.

The Conquistadors spent several years studying the Zapotec civilization, learning about their culture and trying to correlate it to their own. Many aspects of Zapotec life were almost identical to European elements, but some were unfamiliar. This led to misleading information and representation about the Zapotecs that archaeologists have had to dispel over time. This has proven to be tricky since the civilization itself was gone by 1600 AD. However, there are still some descendants of the Zapotecs who have their own understanding of what the different rights and rituals meant, based on the myths and beliefs that have been passed down. This difference in interpretation in the Zapotecs' actions has given rise to a lot of skepticism among experts, and they have begun to construct their ideas and theories based on their findings in the ruins of the civilization.

One of the most notable discrepancies between what the Conquistadors noted and how archeologists interpret the religion is the number of gods worshipped. The Conquistadors based their information on questions and surveys with members of the Zapotec nobility. When they talked with the different leaders and kings of various areas, the Spanish found that each one tended to have their own pantheon beneath the main gods. Based on what the descendants of the Zapotecs say and the hieroglyphs, it is much more likely the "gods" that differed between the different cities and regions were not considered gods by the Zapotecs. It is probable that the reverence shown to these figures was similar to the reverence shown by the Catholic Church to saints at about the same time. The Zapotecs believed it was the ancestors of the nobles who could talk to the gods on behalf of the people, and so the ancestors were treated with respect after their death.

Part of the misunderstanding could have been that the Conquistadors considered their god to be above them, so when the Zapotecs indicated the clouds, the meaning was less clear. The Zapotecs had as much reverence for the clouds as any other moving part of the Earth, but it was easy for the Spanish to misunderstand it when it was juxtaposed with their own religion. While the Spanish believed humans came from the dirt, the Zapotecs thought they were from the clouds and that some of them would return to the clouds when they died.

The Oaxaca Valley

Referred to as the Valley of Oaxaca, the region where the Zapotec civilization thrived and worshipped was as much a testament to their intellect and abilities as it was a critical component in forming who they were. While civilizations in Europe and North Africa developed around fertile areas where water was plentiful, the Zapotecs opted for safety, setting into a region that was easier to fortify and defend. The rise of the Zapotec civilization at Monte Albán was the beginning of a shift from another minor civilization into something far more substantial and innovative.

The roots of what would become a dominant civilization in the region came from the area where the people decided to settle. Their first major city was San José Mogote, but it proved to be less than ideal because the Zapotecs were always at war with their neighbors in that area. With much of the best land already occupied, in about 500 BC the Zapotecs decided to move to a location that was at a higher elevation at the top of one of the mountains, which enabled them to keep an eye for any approaching travelers or hostile neighbors.. The new city was Monte Albán, and it was nestled in the Valley of Oaxaca.

There was a good reason why this region had not been populated before the Zapotecs arrived. One of the most prominent features of the Valley of Oaxaca is the mountains that surround it. Visiting the site of Monte Albán provides a sense of what it must have been like for the original settlers in the region. It is difficult not to feel isolated, and the remoteness made trade exceptionally difficult. For a people who had been in perpetual war though, isolation was welcome.

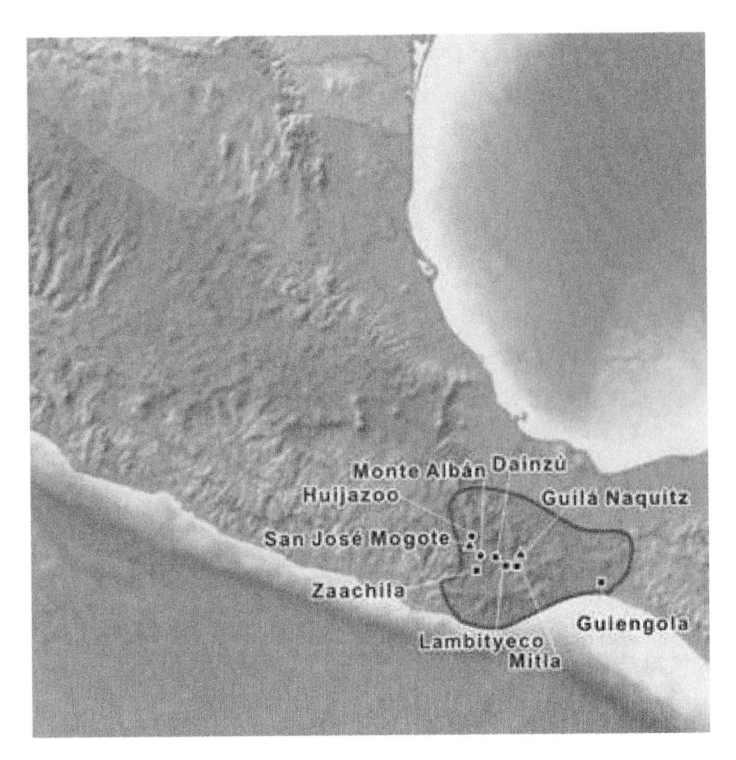

Source

Another major drawback to this region was how arid it was. Although the climate is temperate in the Valley of Oaxaca, there is only about 500 mm of rain a year – that is 2 inches a year. For a people who relied on agriculture for food, this was inadequate to sustain a large population. The minuscule amount of rain fell primarily between May and September. Today, scientists consider the area to be in "permanent drought.". Despite the lack of rain, agriculture has always been an essential part of the region, as much today as it was when the Zapotecs thrived in the area. The Zapotecs used the latest in technology and innovation to ensure crops could thrive. The need to be innovative to survive was probably one of the reasons the Zapotecs were more advanced than many of the other civilizations in the region. Archeologists have uncovered almost 3,000 sites that prove just how successful the Zapotecs were at ensuring their agrarian livelihood.

The Domain of the Cloud People

Like all civilizations, the boundaries and borders of the Zapotec civilization shifted and changed over time. In the beginning, the Zapotecs were divided into three groups based on where they resided. The Valley Zapotecs lived in the Valley of Oaxaca, which became the heart of the civilization. The second group is the Sierra Zapotecs, and they resided to the north of the valley. The third group was the Southern Zapotecs. Despite the name historians and archaeologists have given them, the Southern Zapotecs lived to the south and the east of the valley, and their area was around the Isthmus of Tehuantepec.

Many cities and towns were important to the culture. There were three capitals over the course of the Zapotec history: San José Mogote, Monte Albán, and Mitla. However, the cities of Dainzu, Lambityeco, Yagul, El Palmillo, and Zaachila played vital roles in the development and expansion of the Zapotec Empire.

After the Zapotecs had established the thriving city of Monte Albán, they began to conquer many of their neighbors by overpowering them with superior military power. Then, because they had a larger population, the Zapotecs were easily able to absorb the smaller, conquered villages into their culture. Often, they would focus on peaceful means of bringing villages and peoples into their civilization, such as arranged marriages and offering the use of their more advanced technologies to the less advanced neighbors around them. Whether out of fear or an interest in joining a larger defender, the smaller civilizations around Monte Albán were easily incorporated into the Zapotec Culture.

Over time, their influence stretched far beyond Monte Albán. It is difficult to know precisely how vast the empire was because the Zapotecs did not keep borders the same way that Europeans did. Civilizations blended, with people from different cultures living together on the boundaries. It was difficult to remain a small, independent state or city with so many competing civilizations trying to expand. However, the large civilizations worked together as much as they fought against one another. The relationship between the Zapotecs and Teotihuacans, a nearby civilization, was mostly positive. One of the exceptions was the Aztec civilization, a neighbor to the north of the Zapotecs that was more dominating than the other cultures in the area.

The Zapotecs also expanded through politics and marriage, similar to the traditions of European royalty, rather than always relying on military might. Despite this proclivity to more political conquest, they had a much larger and more advanced military structure than many of their neighbors. Having found their footing in Monte Albán, it was much easier for them to begin to pick up their smaller, less warlike neighbors. They were also talented political tacticians. During their war with the Aztecs, the Zapotecs made an agreement with the Mixtecs. The Mixtecs resided in an area of tropical lowlands near the Aztecs, and they were to attack the Aztecs while the Aztecs were passing through the Tehuantepec lowlands. In return, the Zapotecs would give the Mixtecs land. Since the area to be given was not specified before the assistance, the Zapotecs gave the Tehuantepec land unsuitable for habitation. Having lost the bloody seven months' struggle against the Aztecs, the Zapotecs negotiated a deal that did not remove too much of their influence from the region. One of the rulers of the Aztecs wed the ruler of the Zapotecs. The Aztecs were also given garrisons in the Valley of Oaxaca and would receive an annual tribute from the Zapotecs. The loss to the Aztecs was undoubtedly a blow to the Zapotecs, but it was not the catastrophe it could have been, especially when one considers how harshly the Aztecs had treated smaller cultures upon their defeat. Unlike the Zapotecs, the Aztec Empire began their wars with mercenaries and those who were accustomed to fighting. The Aztecs did not shy away from fighting, and they did not seek a new place to avoid fighting. When the Aztecs won a battle, their prisoners were almost always sacrificed, unlike the less wholesale practices of the Zapotecs. While the Zapotecs did sacrifice some of their prisoners, many became concubines or slaves, and one day they might be allowed to gain their freedom. The Zapotecs were good at turning losses, truces, and agreements in their favor through the use of skillful negotiation. Using Machiavellian tactics, they could build their empire and sustain it even in defeat.

Their ability to work situations to their advantage did not work against the Conquistadors, however. Nor could they counter the deadly diseases the Conquistadors brought that wiped out many of the natives in Mesoamerica.

Chapter 2 – Understanding the Zapotecs in Phases

Each empire and vast civilization reaches its peak in phases, and the Zapotecs are no different. The relics and ruins have provided a wealth of information about the growth of the Zapotec people, enough data to allow much of the extensive history of the Zapotecs to be divided into different eras or phases.

The identified phases of the Zapotecs revolves around their capital city. Even though the Zapotecs were a civilization before moving to Monte Albán, they did not have the prestige or security that helped them to thrive after the move.

The Founding of the Monte Albán

Archaeologists have found numerous implements and tools that suggest three civilizations were living in the Valley of Oaxaca, including the Zapotecs. The remains of weapons and other implements indicate the civilizations were at war with each other and the constant warring was probably the reason why the Zapotecs decided to relocate.

It was almost certainly a sense of danger that drove them from their homes. The number of security features that still surrounds their capital is an indication that protecting their people was a primary concern for the Zapotec civilization.

The Zapotecs' reach would eventually extend beyond Monte Albán, but the Zapotec people really began to thrive after its founding. Their superior fortifications gave them the security necessary to grow in other ways. Because of their extensive security around the exterior of the Monte Albán, they became one of the most advanced and innovative peoples in Mesoamerica and perhaps around the world. They would develop their own type of writing that is comparable to Egyptian

Hieroglyphics (the Zapotec writing are also called hieroglyphics). None of this would have been possible had they remained in the wetter, more populous regions where they had lived before moving to Monte Albán.

Monte Albán Phase 1

The first phase lasted for roughly 300 years, from 400 BC to 100 BC. During the early history of the city that would eventually become the capital of an entire civilization, life was a struggle. The rainfall was negligible, so they needed to ensure famine would not be a greater enemy than the two civilizations they had encountered before their move to the area. The former center of the civilization, San José Mogote, had proven to be difficult to defend and too close to neighbors with militaries as capable as the military of the Zapotecs. Monte Albán gave the Zapotecs a place where they could grow and develop with fewer outside threats. It also gave them time to build their military.

During this time, many other people outside of Monte Albán were tied to the Zapotec civilization. While they were not yet looking to expand their reach to the extent that they would in later phases, the Zapotecs did begin to pull people from the surrounding areas into their civilization. They were still in the early stages of their civilization, so their hierarchical structure was more fluid than it would be at the peak of the Zapotecs' power. The nation was beginning to be centralized around this one city that was secure from outside threats, but it was still in the early days and people were still determining their place in the culture and society. This was a time of growth and development, and many of the ideas and innovations that would help them thrive later began during this phase.

Many of the structures that can be seen today were built during this early stage. Once they were secure, the Zapotec began developing language, jewelry, and structures that were far more advanced than any they had previously produced. There are also many pots and ceramics from this time, showing how interested the people were in creating and defining themselves through art. One of the most interesting items from this period is called the whistling jar. By dividing a jar into two different sections, the Zapotecs were able to pour water and store it at the same time. As air pushed the water out of one chamber, the jar would whistle. The whistling jar would continue to be made over the course of the civilization's history. They also began to sculpt with jade and other precious materials. The delicate jewelry and pottery, as well as the easily identifiable style that marks their civilization, are still one of the most intricate and unique of its kind today. For those who would like to see examples of the buildings and artifacts, pictures are available on the internet or you can check for a museum near you to see them in person, if you can't visit the sites themselves.

Monte Albán Phase 2

Phase 2 was a shorter period of time, lasting from about 100 BC to 100 AD, but it was a time of rapid growth and development of Monte Albán. With the borders of their capital secure, religion, art, and innovation rapidly expanded. It also marked a time when the Zapotecs began to incorporate a broader range of areas from the towns and villages near Monte Albán. Much of the expansion was achieved through military might, and not through political savvy. Compared to their previous locations, it was much easier to take control of their neighbors because the towns and villages around Monte Albán were smaller and less militarily stable. With higher numbers and better strategies, the Zapotecs could grow their civilization through the use of military might similar to that of the early days of the Roman Empire.

Also, like the Romans, the Zapotecs allowed those they conquered to retain some level of autonomy. Annexing these territories was meant to be a way of extending their reach, supplies, and power, so the Zapotecs took a more laissez-faire approach to managing their conquered territories. By submitting to the Zapotecs, the annexed areas could retain some of their own laws and power structures. Many of the conquered people lived in areas outside of the valley, but not so far from Monte Albán that they would have been difficult to monitor and trade with.

The signs of the expansion during this time are primarily in the relics discovered in the areas around Monte Albán during this 200-year period. Pottery, jewelry, and other everyday items found in these areas that were conquered indicated roughly when they became part of the larger civilization because the items were significantly different to the works that came from earlier periods It also appeared the changes in style and design were sudden, suggesting the people were being incorporated quickly into the Zapotec civilization. The elegance and intricacies of the Zapotec artisans were well worth imitating as well. As the styles of these items was similar but not identical, archeologists have postured that these items show as much a history of the Zapotecs' expansion as they do about the everyday lives of the people of these smaller territories.

Monte Albán Phase 3

This period lasted from 200 AD to 900 AD, and it proved to be a time of military might and the centralization of power around the capital. Monte Albán was the center of the Zapotec empire, but it was not the capital of their religion. There was not a real separation of their religion and power structures, but these two power structures were each large enough to require their own capitals.

The military strength the Zapotecs had flexed during Monte Albán phase 2 was proven to be highly effective during the third era. Over the 700 years of phase 3, Monte Albán became the largest human settlement in the region. It is estimated the city may have been the home to over 25,000 people during this phase. The Zapotecs also included more than 1,000 settlements as part of their empire, with Monte Albán as its center. This was the time when the rulers were focused on expanding well beyond the valley, conquering areas as far north as Quiotepec and as far south as Chiltepec. Just as other empires found themselves extended too far with inadequate resources to sustain their power structure, the Zapotecs found themselves up against other civilizations with greater military capabilities than their own. The most notable adversary was the Aztec.

However, no central city can sustain the kinds of growth and innovation that Monte Albán experienced during phase 3. By the end of this phase, the city was in decline as the people became complacent and their ideas began to stagnate. While Monte Albán would still be a significant city for the Zapotecs, it ceased to be the capital around 900 AD. Mitla would become the empire's center, although it would never be quite as large or as influential as Monte Albán was at its peak.

Monte Albán Phase 4

Monte Albán still played a significant role in the empire from 900 AD to 1350 AD. However, people from other civilizations began to make it their place of residence. With more people of varied beliefs and backgrounds in a city that relied on people acting in a similar way, the city started to lose itself. Its influence was significantly reduced as Mitla attracted many of the people in the upper echelons of the Zapotec society.

With the loss of some of their influential figures and the introduction of people from other cities and regions, Monte Albán began to lose some of its culture and control. The people who controlled the city were no longer people who necessarily grew up there. This meant that power began to be shared with people who held different beliefs and social focus than the native Zapotec population. The more the power within the city was distributed among other groups, the less power the city had within the empire. Though Monte Albán continued to be important, it was no longer the center of the civilization and its role was less critical.

By this time, the civilization had extended itself too far and had reached a tipping point. Unable to maintain its once dominant capital, the Zapotecs began to lose control over regions on their borders. The losses were not significant at this point, but it was a sign that the once great empire was no longer able to sustain itself as it once had. The people had become too complacent and self-important, a sign that the empire was crumbling. The empire forgot what made it great and internal power struggles became prevalent and its decline was assured. When Rome fell, the Roman Empire ended, and the Byzantine Empire began. Even today, it is easy to see the decline of nations because of how rapidly things deteriorate in their capitals. The fall of Monte Albán signaled the beginning of the end of the Zapotec empire.

Monte Albán Phase 5

The last phase of Monte Albán lasted for less than 200 years from 1350 AD to 1521 AD. By this point, the city no longer enjoyed the power and innovation that had been at its core through much of its existence.

It was also a difficult time for the Zapotec people as they went to war with their more powerful neighbors, the Aztecs. By the time the Aztecs emerged victorious over the Zapotecs, Monte Albán was no longer the mighty city it had once been. Given the location of the city, it is possible that some of the decline could have come from drought and other natural problems that would have devastated the inhabitants of Monte Albán. With power no longer centralized among a few leaders who understood the importance of the structures and irrigation, the people would have been forced to leave, although probably not all at once. The power structure would have been far less resilient than the early structure that had seen the growth of the city. With so many surrounding areas needing attention and protection, it would have been too much to manage internal and external problems. This was the city that the Conquistadors would have discovered, although even then it was still a majestic place.

The Promise of Tomorrow

The Zapotecs had accepted their defeat at the hands of the Aztecs by 1515, but they were still mostly independent. Having successfully negotiated the terms of peace, the Zapotecs were not defeated in quite the same way as those they had conquered earlier.

Then the Conquistadors arrived, and everything changed again. For a few years, while the Aztecs were fighting the invaders, there was hope that the Zapotecs could return to their previous lives from before their loss to the Aztecs. For a short period, they could hope for a return to the power and control they once held. Then the Conquistadors turned their attention to the Zapotecs.

Chapter 3 – Early Agrarian Roots and the Building of a Civilization

The beginnings of one of the most influential civilizations in Mesoamerica were humble. In the early days, there was little to mark the Zapotecs as being any different to their neighbors. They transitioned from being nomads to farmers, then from farmers into small villages. Once they began to live in larger and larger groups though, the shape of the Zapotec society began to differ from those civilizations around them. While they fought, the Zapotecs were also interested in progressing beyond the day to day lives. They sought to record information through writing and design tools to make life easier. Their jewelry, pottery, and other works of art were more distinctive with the addition of writing and images of their gods. At some point, their desire to create clashed with the reality of their lives. The daily routine in a small village or on farms might have been enough if the area had been more peaceful. It was this discontentment with their constant fighting that eventually led to the empire.

It may be that the Zapotecs learned from their early struggles how best to handle more warlike neighbors. Given how they seemed to seek a peaceful resolution later on, despite how powerful they were at their peak, the early days likely formed much of the way they thought about war. The constant state of fighting would have made it difficult to fully implement any tactics because battle was as much a part of their routines as farming. It was only after they moved, that it became clear just how capable the Zapotecs were. Their new capital was one of the most heavily fortified cities in the region.

From Nomad to Villagers

Five thousand years ago, when the Ancient Egyptians were just starting to form their kingdom, the future inhabitants of the Valley of Oaxaca were still roaming across the lands, but they were beginning to take a different outlook on survival. Archeologists cannot say for sure when the nomads finally decided to settle down in one location, but early agriculture gave the people of the region a new way to live. Before 1700 BC, the ancestors to the Zapotecs had become farmers, though they tended only to grow what was needed to survive on their own. Providing enough food to feed an entire community was still not something that most groups of humans practiced. A farmer grew only enough food to feed his family, and others were left to fend for themselves if they could not grow as much food as they needed for themselves.

Then between 1700 BC and 1200 BC, the farmers began to band together to provide support and assistance to an increasingly larger population. Living together provided safety from predators and other humans.

Because of the shift in thinking, the point of agriculture began to shift too. While it is not certain why the early Zapotecs decided to start focusing their agriculture on growing maize (also known as corn), there is adequate evidence the shift occurred after they began to live together in larger groups. This suggests that one of the reasons for the change in farming was a desire to feed more people with less effort. It also provided the farmers with products that they could trade for other goods.

One thing that is known about the shift is that the larger groups recognized that land was difficult to clear, particularly as larger groups of humans joined together. That meant the clearing process needed to be worthwhile. At some point, the early Zapotecs had begun to determine what food would make the most sense for a growing population. Maize was their answer.

As they needed to tend an increasingly larger area of farmed land, people began to take on more specialized jobs. There were still hunters for game, but there were also those who planted, weeded, and harvested the crops. Others stayed with the children and elderly. They would make tools and care for those who where in need.

Over time, the groups became larger, so more people lived in close proximity and worked together to accomplish more in less time. There are remains of the early tools, including pottery, that show that the early Zapotecs had shifted from their early days to the more complex village structure. Their homes were far more basic, with few to no remains of the structures, but the high concentration of artifacts and burials prove the shift to a unified approach to survival had been successful by 3,000 years ago.

The Early Structuring of Society

The ancestors of the Zapotecs did not have lives that were distinctly different from any of the other cultures growing up around them. Their lives evolved from nomadic to farmers to villagers. In the early days, men began to fight each other to run their villages. Called the Big Man, the chief of a village was responsible for raiding other villages, forming alliances with other villages, and inspiring his people against enemies. Once he died, alliances and enemies disappeared because they were based on the Big Man and the people he competed with.

This began to change around 1200 BC when leadership began to solidify around more than just the strongest person in a village. During this time heredity began to play a role in a person's role, and classes of people began to form within villages. It meant a shift in their religion and the way they viewed the world.

To the early Zapotecs, two critical entities were fundamental to their beliefs: Sky and Earth. These were considered to be supernatural entities. Earth was mostly benevolent, but it did not like being treated poorly, including burning and digging on its surface. When it was angered, it would let the Zapotecs know that it was angry by shaking. The result of Earth's rage was an earthquake.

The Sky was removed from the problems of humans and was the home of celestial spirits, particularly their Zapotec ancestors. Being removed from humans did not mean that Sky was not displeased by them though. When Sky was angry about human actions, it would show that anger through lightning.

These entities began to be added to pottery around 1150 BC, indicating that the deities played a more critical role in the life of the people. Around this time, humans began to be shown as descendants of Earth and Sky, and like European royalty, people started to believe the leaders had their positions because of their ancestry. With this subtle shift in thinking, hierarchies began to form. Males began to be depicted as descendants on pottery and other relics from the time and those believed to be related to Earth and Sky were buried with the works that showed their status. The lineage always progressed through males. Women were not depicted as being descendants of the supernatural entities at this point.

A Move to Hierarchies and away from Autonomy

With some people claiming divine ancestry, there was more justification for someone to take control over every aspect of village life. Someone who was not recognized as being divine was not allowed to be in charge. While the Big Man could demand obedience from his people, his words did not hold any sway over other villages. When a leader began to claim divine lineage, it gave his people the right to demand the loyalty and obedience of other villages. If the surrounding villages resisted, violence would ensue. If the village of the divine leader succeeded, it was seen as a sign his words were considered the divine will. Villages were more inclined to accept the new social order and demands of a conquering people when their leader was thought to be related to the gods. The victory was seen as being the will of a greater being, so the conquered people accepted their fate more willingly.

The children of a successful leader claiming divine lineage would automatically be treated with reverence, making it more difficult to deny each successive leader. As the divine leader took wives from new villages, the divine lineage would spread to the other villages, giving them a vested interest in the hierarchy. Over time, people ceased to question the divine claims and accepted this as the proper order of the world.

Signs of the loss of village autonomy were found in the ruins of the city of San José Mogote. The first capital of the Zapotec Empire reflected the hierarchy in a way that the satellite villages did not. The remains of many buildings that were not present in the other villages indicate that San José Mogote was considered to be more important, meaning more effort was placed on creating structures that would last longer. Better materials were used to construct the buildings, and the beginnings of more ornate designs showed the reverence that was given to those who resided in those structures. Many of these materials did not originally come from San José Mogote; rather, they were brought in from the satellite villages. The fact that San José Mogote had such structures and the villages did not suggests the leaders could demand the materials. The satellite villages acquiesced, providing whatever was requested instead of using it for their own structures and products. With San José Mogote being the home of the leaders and the place to which homage was paid, the villages in the surrounding areas were no longer allowed to make their own decisions.

The leader of the Zapotecs lived in San José Mogote, a place that was better fortified and stocked than any of the other villages within the region. Within San José Mogote, there were members of the nobility who were related to the leader or who were related to other, lesser leaders with divine lineage. All members of the nobility were believed to be descended from Earth or Sky, and they were treated accordingly. Some of those of divine descent lived in the surrounding villages. The villages that they lived in were usually larger than most of the other villages, but not as grand as San José Mogote. They were the leaders of these villages, and they took their orders from the central leader. Smaller villages had minor leaders who would follow the orders of the leader of the larger villages. This provided a chain of command that removed the autonomy of all villages that were part of the growing Zapotec civilization.

The Rise of Alliances and Competition

The Zapotecs were not the only civilization taking shape at this time. They had consolidated control of their region under a divine ruler, but other leaders were making the same types of claims and building their hierarchies. Unlike the Big Man who could shame any rivals into following him, leaders were now faced with having to prove they had a superior lineage. To resolve these kinds of disputes, the leader had two possible courses of action: form alliances or compete with their adversary.

The Zapotecs began facing these kinds of challenges around 850 BC to 700 BC And the challenges were not always from external sources.

The people within the villages were part of the hierarchy with their ancestry being easier to track than the ancestry of rulers claiming divine blood without evidence. It was much easier to track lineage from leaders through their offspring, and this resulted in some members of the nobility jockeying for better status when they were of less prestigious descent. The internal hierarchy further solidified during this time.

More interesting than the challenges within the San José Mogote hierarchy were the relationships the growing civilization had with the surrounding neighbors who were too large to force into submission.

Although fighting was indeed an option, it appears the Zapotecs were more inclined to form alliances, a tactic they continued to use throughout most of the duration of the empire. It is supposed that alliances were formed through hypogamy. Hypogamy is the practice of sending a woman of higher rank to a subordinate community leader where they are then wed to solidify the alliance. Given that she was of higher status than the leader she married, this automatically elevated the status of the leader within the hierarchy. It also meant he was indebted to the family who gave him the bride, creating a much closer connection between the subordinate village and the primary noble family in San José Mogote. This same method of forming alliances was common in Europe up until recent centuries. In Europe, it got to the point where royalty was mostly inbred, sometimes with disastrous consequences. For the Zapotecs during this time, that was not as much of a problem because there were far fewer blood relations between the villages and San José Mogote.

Large feasts were another way of building alliances, a method the Zapotecs almost certainly used. However, there is little to indicate how these feasts worked to do more than impress the villages. It could have been a way of showing off how well their harvest had done and their robust stocks of meat. Their primary source of domesticated food appears to have been dog, showing that canines were not held in the same kind of regard in Mesoamerica as they were in Europe where they were more often used as companions.

War and the Beginnings of Writing

While a bit ironic, it is perhaps not unsurprising that the evidence of both war and writing began at around the same time. With pottery being a primary means of seeing how the society changed over time, around this time, words and depictions of wars began to appear on the artifacts that were found at the archeological sites.

When the Zapotec chief fought with the other civilizations, it was usually over resources and goods. At this time, none of the budding civilizations had adequate military or resources to occupy another area, so their primary goal was not conquest. When they could not continue to protect a village or area, chiefs would pull back their military, abandoning the villages to their fate.

It is notable that during this time, none of the growing chiefdoms had any interest in the region where the Zapotec civilization would eventually take root and thrive. As many cultures were unwilling to learn to work the arid region and the mountains and the valleys were considered to be too remote, this area was largely ignored in the struggle to gain more resources.

While the writing at this time was rudimentary, it was still a departure from merely adding images to the pottery and structures. There was more repetition of intricate works similar to the hieroglyphs associated with Ancient Egypt. Of course, the Zapotec hieroglyphs were unique to their civilizations, but it is clear that they were beginning to record thoughts and words in a pattern that aligns with writing. There was less writing found on the structures that have been found in San José Mogote, but the new capital bears many examples of structures with writing following the migration.

Chapter 4 – Religion, Myths, and Power

The Zapotec religion was complex and varied, and they held their ancestors in reverence in a way that is commonly associated with Native Americans. With the development of the civilization through leaders who claimed divine heritage, there was no separation of church and state. The social structure that a person was born into was the one they would be in until the day they died. Politics were equally complicated, although the Zapotecs believed that their rulers were descended from supernatural beings.

The Zapotec Pantheon

There were two primary supernatural beings the Zapotecs believed in: Sky and Earth. These two beings were mostly benevolent, but when they were angry, they would let the Zapotecs know about their anger through earthquakes and lightning. These beings were given names and were depicted on many of their artworks and stories. The rain god, Cocijo, ensured they had adequate precipitation in the less arid areas, although he was not crucial in the capital, Monte Albán, because it was dry and received only about two inches of rainfall a year. However, they did rely on the deity to keep their water sources full. Coquihani was their god of light.

Lesser gods were responsible for the more common aspects of life, such as fertility and agriculture. These gods were both male and female. In looking over their writings, you can tell a deity's gender because it is reflected in the clothing worn: men wear capes and women wear skirts. Very little is known about them, apart from the fact that there were minor gods.

The pantheon is not nearly as extensive as the Conquistadors initially believed. Where they had interpreted many of the prayers and sacrifices to deities, it appears that many of these were actually to ancestors, and not deities. No human could talk directly to Cocijo or Coquihani, so they had to ask their ancestors to intercede on their behalf. It appears that mainly only the members of the nobility had ancestors who could interact with the gods because commoners returned to the Earth when they died, and not to the sky. However, it is possible that commoners prayed to their own families as well, particularly if they needed to communicate with Cocijo.

Rituals, Sacrifices, and Myths

While they did acknowledge the Zapotec king, the priests had their own internal structure with class being less relevant for interactions. Since the Zapotecs were firm believers in their religion, the priests and other religious figures were held in high regard and wielded their own power. While they never tried to rival the king, they were obeyed by the people. As the king consolidated his power, so too did the priests, and they spread their decisions to the priests of the other villages and settlements.

The deities required regular sacrifices, and these were given based on the time of year and current events. For example, the first warrior caught in battle was sacrificed to the gods as a way of thanking them. Others captured in the fight would become slaves or sacrifices depending on their usefulness. Officers of the opposition military were usually eaten. It is not entirely clear why officers were eaten; however, it is probable that the Zapotecs believed that other civilizations derived from different gods. Since everything that moved had a spirit and the Zapotecs believed that officers were descended from the gods, eating the officers might have been a way of getting closer to their gods. Sacrifices, including humans, were made on religious holidays.

Small animals and harvests were also offered up to the gods and made up a larger percentage of the sacrifices. However, the priests made the most frequent sacrifices, cutting themselves and adding their blood to the ceremonies. Special tools were made for the priests to cut their own tongues and pierce their ears. While it is not known exactly why their own blood was considered essential, priests would often cut or pierce themselves during ceremonies, giving up a little bit of themselves. It was likely one of the reasons why they were held in high regard. Since the priests had dedicated their lives to the gods they worshipped, it is likely they gave their own blood as a way of returning some of their spirits back to their gods. Little is known about the reasons for the bloody tradition, and it is particularly interesting because many of the ceremonies seemed to demand so much from the priests. While there were other kinds of sacrifices, it appears that priests frequently gave more of themselves than they took from others. The number of obsidian knives and stingray spines in the remains of temples shows just how important it was for the priests to give of themselves since these tools were not used on the sacrifices.

The Zapotecs had their own myths about how the world began. It is perhaps surprising that they believed in a superior being who created the world, but whom no one could talk to. This being did not appear to play a role in their worship because no human was able to interact; not even their ancestors who resided in the clouds. According to the Zapotecs, the creator had allowed for humans to be born of the rocks in the Valley of Oaxaca. This not only gave them a history, but it proved the region rightfully belonged to the Zapotecs. There were other versions of the creation myth though. Some taught that humans descended from the animals who lived in the region. Ocelots and jaguars were considered to be the most common sources for humans.

However, the most common myth was that the leaders of the Zapotecs were direct descendants of supernatural beings. Once they died, the leaders would return to the clouds, where they would communicate with the gods. Commoners would continue to show reverence to their ancestors, but the ancestors of the noble class were revered by all. This myth is the source of the people's name, "Cloud People."

Distribution of Power

In the larger areas, such as Monte Albán, power was centered around the nobility, particularly the ruler of the civilization. The Conquistadors noted that the social structure and power were tied together, and they even compared it to the social and power structures that were common in Europe at the time. Some positions were comparable to those of counts, dukes, earls, princes, and other strata of the power hierarchy.

However, the further from these populous regions archeologists go, the more evidence they find of levels of autonomy. During the Monte Albán Phases 1 and 2, there was a high level of autonomy and independent states within the civilization. It was only during the Monte Albán Phase 3 that a more rigid system was put in place, and power was removed from these areas. With Monte Albán as its seat of power, the Zapotecs at their peak had one of the largest domains in Mesoamerica.

During Monte Albán Phase 3, the Zapotec king was the sole seat of power, and his word was law. The king made all critical decisions, and his word was spread to the villages.

Monte Albán was the center of political power over the majority of the civilization. While the political will and power came from the capital, the city of Mitla was the seat of the religious authority. Toward the end of the civilization, the political power also shifted toward Mitla, but it had long been accustomed to a different kind of power by that time. Part of the remains of this one formidable population center was a palace. Made mostly of mud and stone, the palace still has elegant carvings and decorations that indicate it was an important structure.

There are many remnants of the buildings where the powerful lived, including the palace in Mitla. However, the temples where the people worshipped are rarely found in good condition. Archaeologists often have to search hard the find the ruins of these structures because during battles and wars the Zapotecs and their neighbors would always burn the temples of their opponents. This was meant to anger the gods against the people for failing to protect their temples. With many of the civilizations long gone, their temples rarely remain as those would have been the first things destroyed by the people who came after them. The temples were as extravagant as the palaces. Like many other civilizations in the area, the Zapotecs favored pyramids for their temples, and the tops were adorned with the deities that the temples were dedicated to worshiping.

Some ruins offer information about other aspects of life. From sports and competitions to government buildings, archeologists can get an idea of how power was distributed over the civilization. There are signs that the further from Monte Albán they explore, the more unique the pottery and buildings are. Toward the borders, the buildings and facades were blended with the neighboring civilizations, showing there were times of alliances and a symbiotic relationship between the Zapotecs and many of their neighbors. People today think of the natives of the continents as being warlike and barbaric, but the reality is that they were not so different from the Europeans. The Zapotecs, in particular, tended to prefer alliances and politics over fighting and war, probably because they remembered their early days of constant fighting. They were also skillful negotiators, so relying on politics to resolve conflicts would have been far easier for them.

Determining the Next Leader

While it was not possible for a commoner to gain a position of power, the children of the leader could vie for the position following the death of the leader. Archeologists can identify the position of the princes from the objects buried with them. Many of the items included writings that signified the son's place within the noble family. The position of the sons was indicated on their tombs, with the extended fingers of the depicted prince indicating his status and birth order. The first-born son was depicted as having an extended thumb, showing that he was the likely heir to the nation. If the depiction showed the prince's index finger extended, it indicated he was the second son of the king. Each consecutive extended finger showed the birth order of the child depicted.

The first-born son to the king's first wife usually became the next leader, but it was not always guaranteed. To become king, the sons would have to prove they were capable leaders. They had to meet five obligations.

1. The future king would need to take captives who would be sacrificed when he was elevated to the kingship. This proved that he was capable of taking control and he was strong enough to lead.

2. His blood had to be sacrificed to the gods, showing he was willing to give himself to the people and their gods at his own personal cost.

3. The heir had to sponsor the building of a new facility. These buildings were usually some of the most varied, and some of the most remarkable structures stem from this requirement. The type of building and its intricacies provided a look into what the princes considered significant.

4. The heir also needed to commission a monument that would be dedicated to one of his ancestors. Like the facility, this monument provided a unique look into the minds of the princes.

5. He also had to seek the support and approval from others in power. Rulers in neighboring areas had to agree to his ascension. This helped to reduce the risk of wars and problems as it established a level of trust between the Zapotec ruler and others.

One of the most notable buildings that remains in Monte Albán was a result of a prince proving his worth. Each potential king contributed to the society in a way that was unique. Some focused on the buildings while others concentrated on relationships. Whichever approach they took, the future king could not simply relax knowing his place was secure. By ensuring that the prince would take care of his people, the Zapotecs looked to ensure their civilization would continue to grow and thrive instead of becoming complacent. This is perhaps one of the reasons why they could continue with their innovations for so long.

The Dead

The Zapotecs treated their dead with as much respect as any other advanced civilization. There were entire structures dedicated to the deceased, and they were buried with gifts and treasures to ensure they had their things in the afterlife. Many of the items with which they were buried left hints about who they were, as well as the way they were buried.

Entire areas of cities and villages were dedicated to taking care of the deceased. Rituals were long and complicated, particularly for the leaders and people with power. The complexes within cities were large, allowing for the increased number of dead who had to be tended to on a regular basis. Elegant and elaborate tombs were covered in delicate motifs that told the stories of the people who were buried. The stories were varied, including telling of a brave warrior who met his end in battle, priests who carried out the will of the gods, and rulers who contributed to the civilization in their own ways. Tombs were built underground, providing a more stable resting place in the mountains.

Chapter 5 – A Familiar, Tiered Society

Once the Zapotecs had settled on the top of Monte Albán, they already had a relatively rigid hierarchy that determined a person's potential positions in life. There were two distinct classes, and it was impossible to cross from one to the other, with one exception – there was less class distinction among the members of their religious hierarchy. And the priests wielded their own kind of power, just as they did in Europe.

The Royal Family and Class

As the Conquistadors noted during the years when they observed and questioned the Zapotecs, the social structure for the ruling class was similar to that of the ruling classes that the Conquistadors were familiar with in Europe. A person was either born into the class, or they weren't – there was no way to transition between the two. They practiced strict class endogamy; they only married within their own class.

At the top of this class was the king and his primary wife. Other members of their family had titles to distinguish where they were in the ranking. The upper class did have different levels, with people in the highest strata being the ones most closely related to the ruler, but they could marry anyone else within the upper class. Some marriages were arranged to forge closer bonds between the ruling class, their neighbors, and other villages within the civilization.

The homes of the upper class were far nicer and located in places that offered a better view of the people. Families often continued to live together even after marriage. They had locations called royal houses for large families that were of a more distant relation to the king. The royal palace was for the king and his immediate family. These structures were built on a stone foundation and the walls made of adobe brick to provide the sturdiest buildings for the nobles.

The upper class commissioned many of the structures in the cities as a way of contributing to the society. When Monte Albán was first settled, the rulers had the entire top of the mountain flattened so the city could be built on it. This also gave them a strategic advantage over any invaders because they could see anyone advancing while they were still far away. Such innovation was part of the foundation of the requirements for the ruling class to push the civilization to strive beyond the norms that were established elsewhere. One of the largest areas in the city was atop where the mountain was leveled, and it was known as the Great Plaza. This area likely served as a place for entertainment and commerce. Other facilities and buildings surrounded it. There was also a stadium nearby, as well as several temples.

One of the remaining structures that is the most impressive is The Conquest Slab in Monte Albán. The facility is designed in the shape of an arrowhead, and the walls are scrawled with hieroglyphs that extend nearly all the way around the facility. Archaeologists believe the stories carved into the walls detailed the provinces the Zapotecs conquered, based on the figures carved into each of the 40 stones. The hieroglyphs on each of the stones include a carved head believed to be the ruler of that province because of the elaborate headdress they wore in the image.

The royal Zapotecs were the rulers of the people and held the offices. All official government employees were from this class, and it does not appear they held other types of positions within the society.

Apart from their homes, the noble class was allowed to wear better clothing than commoners. They had colorful mantles and loincloths that let people know their status which made it easier to show proper respect to those in the upper class. Their clothing was also made of cotton, which was more comfortable in the temperate region. In addition to more colorful cotton, members of the royal class could also wear feathers in their clothing and feather headdresses. Their jewelry was typically made of jade, as was their lip plug and ear ornaments. These accessories were not available for use by commoners. When they were called to war, nobles were given a quilted cotton armor that offered better protection than the clothing the commoners usually wore. However, it also marked the nobles for their enemies to recognize when they had captured someone of the higher class. This could mean that the nobles would be traded or purchased, or it could also mean their enemies would eat them.

Nobles also had a different diet. They received some of the best of the crops, and their meats included large game, such as deer and elk. Commoners joined them for their hunts, working to scare the prey out of their hiding place while the nobles killed the animals. Nobles also have the privilege of eating chocolate, something else that was denied to commoners.

The Commoner Class and Its Layers

The second class belonged to the commoners, and it included everyone who was not a part of the noble family. This class was far more varied than the noble class as it contained anyone who was not considered to be related to the gods. At the bottom of this class were the slaves who came from the conquered nations. At the top of the commoner class were the successful merchants who could have more wealth than some of the minor noble family members. However, they were not allowed to marry members of the upper class, even for financial gain because the Zapotecs did not believe the two classes were equal. When the member of one of the noble families died, they would become ancestors who could speak to the gods for the people. No matter how much wealth or prestige the merchants earned, they would return to the Earth once they died. This belief in the afterlife kept the Zapotecs from intermarrying outside of their class.

Slaves could earn their freedom and become productive members of the society. Some slaves would be given to the nobles to be concubines, and others became sacrifices to the Zapotec gods. Those who earned their freedom would be allowed to marry anyone within the commoner class because there was no real distinction made between the wealthiest merchants and slaves. Those who were used as concubines would provide descendants to the nobles, but it is unclear what the place of those offspring was within the society.

The homes for commoners were far simpler than the homes of nobles. Homes were small, although large families probably lived in them. The occupations of the common class were diverse. The merchants provided a bridge between the Zapotecs and other civilizations since they would travel farther than nearly any other member of the civilization to complete their work. Many of the commoners who lived in cities were artisans and entertainers. Some were weavers who made beautiful clothing for the nobles and less costly and elaborate garb for the successful merchants. Musicians, dancers, and sculptors stayed employed in building the culture, and it is their work that has survived for archaeologists to find today. There were peddlers who were different from merchants because they operated on a much smaller scale. Some peddlers traveled long distances and brought much-needed goods to more remote areas, and others who worked solely within the cities or a small group of villages. Diviners and healers provided help for determining a person's future and for curing ailments.

There were also those who were innovators that worked for the betterment and advancement of the society. Engineers developed new ways to accomplish difficult or repetitive tasks, and they ensured the development and maintenance of the irrigation system, so there were no issues within the cities and large villages about water. From developing the first written language in Mesoamerica to creating the first irrigation system to improving the products such as pottery, jewelry and buildings that were used every day, the Zapotecs made good use of those who sought to further the culture.

The occupations of commoners were similar to those of other societies of the period, although they were not as oppressed as commoners were in some nations. They were free to act according to their own needs and whims as long as it did not harm the society. This level of freedom is one of the reasons why the Zapotecs could advance their civilization and technology so much further and faster than their neighbors. Many nations based their advancement on conquering and expanding their reach. The Zapotecs created a comfortable world for themselves and ensured that it could be sustained before they began their expansion. Because they had a strong commoner class, the Zapotecs could encourage people to do more and strive harder. By keeping the commoner class from being further divided into rigid subgroups, it gave people who had less wealth the hope that they could work towards getting more. With a marriage pool that was much larger than the limited choices of marriage partners from rigid class subsets possible in Europe, it allowed people to choose their own path and find more suitable partners for their lives.

Men of all social levels could marry more than one woman, but most commoners could not afford to have multiple wives. Mostly wealthy merchants were the only men who could afford to have more than one wife and numerous children. They had larger homes, but the homes were not nearly as elegant or sturdy as the homes of the nobles. Nor were they eligible for higher office.

The clothing of commoners was also significantly different to the clothing of the nobles. The commoners used agave fibers in plain colors for their mantles and loincloths. Their jewelry was also less noticeable and ornate and were not made from precious metals or gems.

The Religious Order

Technically, the religious order was not a separate class, but the strict hierarchy prevalent in society was far less noticeable among the priests. The noble classes held higher stations within the religious chain of command, but the nobles were harder to distinguish from commoners within the temples because they were much more similarly adorned. All priests were expected to hold religious ceremonies and perform rituals, so that the roles of nobles and commoners within the Zapotec religious order were far less rigid than it was in society. Priests of noble blood were also expected to give more blood during ceremonies, as well as consume more hallucinogenic plants than the priests who were commoners. The roles of the upper-class priests were more important than a commoner priest's role, but they did perform many of the same tasks and duties. A commoner in society could never be confused for a noble person because they did not hold the same jobs or even similar jobs; but within the religion orders, lineage was less important than duty to the gods.

The king received religious training, giving him a better understanding of the religion he was to represent during his reign. Typically his religious training would last for a few years.

At the top of the religious hierarchy was the high priest, and the Conquistadors considered him to be comparable to the Pope. His role was largely fulfilled from the temple in Milta, and it was likened to the Vatican in Rome. The home of the high priest was beautifully crafted and well maintained over the years. With two pillars flanking the front door to the outer room of the temple, it was imposing and helped put people in the right frame of mind as they stepped into the temple.

While nobles were placed in higher positions within the religious order, many commoners were instrumental in performing some of the most important ceremonies. It is perhaps a result of the members of the religious orders being held in such high regard that a commoner who chose to join the priesthood was considered to be nearly as valuable of those born of noble blood. In the Zapotec religious structure, there was equality for men.

The rituals that commoners could perform included adding their blood to the ceremonies when it was required. Their blood was considered an acceptable part of the sacrifice. They also participated in mind-altering parts of the ceremonies, eating hallucinogenic mushrooms and jimson weed to induce the right state of mind for the ceremonies. Fasting was practiced for long periods of time to keep the spirit clear, and the commoners could sacrifice slaves, children, and dogs just like the priests who had higher lineage. Apart from the most notable ceremonies, there were very few distinctions between noble and commoner priests, something that even the Conquistadors found unexpected. The blurring of social structure within religion demonstrated that birth status was less instrumental than a willingness to serve.

Chapter 6 – A Day in the Life of the Zapotecs

Trying to decipher what a day looked like for one of the Zapotec people is a unique challenge. The way the world looked changed based on the social structure that a person was born into and where they lived within the civilization. Just as the experiences of someone living in Mexico City today are significantly different from someone, who lives in Catalina or a small unknown village in modern-day Mexico, a typical day in the Zapotec civilization depended on a person's location and status.

Wide Variety of Living Standards

The Zapotec cities were in the most populous regions of the civilization, and the days of the people who lived in the city were far more varied than those who lived outside of them. In the cities, there were people who had never worked a field of crops because they had more specialized jobs. Naturally, there were priests and other religious figures who spent their days in prayer and sacrifice. There were artisans and warriors who focused on their tasks. Still, they could live more comfortably than lower nobles who did not have the same resources. There were beggars and poor people within the cities too, and their experience was significantly different than many of the other citizens because they did not have the resources to contribute or improve their situation. Slaves were also common in cities, but depending on the tasks they were assigned, they could earn their freedom and become part of the society. Concubines typically did not leave their role, but a slave for a merchant or other commoner could often work to earn their freedom.

In the areas away from the cities, the primary occupation was farming. They lived in large and small villages of varying levels of wealth and comfort. They lived in mountain settlements acting as a stopping point for travelers and merchants while eking out a living in less than ideal circumstances. There were ranches and rural areas where farming occupied the vast majority of the day for the people who lived and worked there.

Hunters were still common across every area and in every region. The nobles would go out to hunt large game, taking commoners out with them to beat bushes to drive the wildlife into the open. Commoners could hunt anything that wasn't big game, such as jackrabbits, squirrels, and other small animals.

As you can see, the experience of each Zapotec was unique to their environment and status. It was easy to recognize someone of the higher status just by looking at them. The commoners may have had less brilliant clothing, but they were free to live as they pleased. The only restrictions were that they could not intermarry with the nobles, and they could not hold higher government positions. However, commoners could hold minor government positions. They could also join the priests and serve the Zapotec gods. It is certainly a different image of life than the members of many of the other civilizations at the time had because it seemed to offer a lot more freedom of movement within the commoner class. The noble class seemed to have less freedom and mobility because a lower noble could not become king. However, a slave who earned freedom could become a wealthy merchant over time.

At Home

The remnants of the different structures provide a look into the types of homes and buildings that were common. These structures were as impressive as the resident could make them. Their religious structures saw regular ceremonies and sacrifices as they tried to appease Sky and Earth, and beg for their ancestors to intercede during times of crisis and problems. Each village also had its own government building, although the type of governance that was conducted in them is largely left up to the imagination. There were also schools and dry-goods stores where education and commerce were conducted. Most villages even had a medical facility where the sick and wounded were tended to on a regular basis.

The average home was made of stone and mortar, and archeologists can still find them today. They were noticeably smaller than the homes of the nobles, but they were still adequate for the families who lived in them. Nobles required larger homes because the males typically had between 10 and 15 wives. With such a large family, they needed a much larger residence than a farmer who only had one wife. Outside of the noble class, the only men who were able to keep multiple wives were the men who were wealthy. This was often the merchants, although some of the innovators were also successful enough to have more than one wife.

Early Astronomers and the Passage of Time

The Zapotecs were one of the first civilizations to look to the stars, which is not surprising given the fact that they believed they descended from the clouds. However, they did much more than just admire the stars. The Zapotecs created a calendar that was not too different from the European calendar, although they dealt with the extra days a little differently than the Europeans did.

Unlike the Europeans, the Zapotecs believed that time was part of a repetitive cycle. Instead of constantly progressing forward, time would return to the same point over the years, and it would move through the same cycle over and over again.

Like the European calendar, the Zapotec calendar based their timeline on their religion. According to their calendar, a year had 260 days and was divided into four months. Months were more closely aligned to the seasons because the Zapotec civilization was based on agriculture. The seasons of the year played a vital role in the activities and the decisions of the Zapotecs. Each month was 65 days long, and contained five weeks. Each week had 13 days. This calendar dictated the activities based on the rituals. The division of the calendar into four parts represented the movement of time in its repetitive cycle.

The Zapotecs had a second calendar that was based on the sun's cycles. This calendar was distinctly different from the ritual calendar, dividing the year into much finer sections to better plan for the agrarian needs based on the specific movements of the sun. Structuring their lives around a calendar that reflected this made it easier to track the needs of the farmers. This calendar had 18 months that were 20 days each. An additional five days were added to the year to keep the calendar current with the seasons. This offered a more regular structure to their months instead of varying the number of days in each month.

It is interesting to note that many of the artifacts and relics found in the Zapotec ruins include the names of the people whose remains were discovered. Archeologists have noted that the Zapotecs tended to name their children after the days of the calendar, and it is believed that the name reflects the day the child was born. The Zapotecs believed in luck, and certain days were considered lucky. Children of the members of the nobility tended to be named after the lucky days closest to when they were born instead of being named for the day they were born. It was common that the remains of nobles would have names like "9 Flower" or "8 Deer" to reflect their place in society as well as providing a rough estimate of when they were born. They also received nicknames that reflected days, although it is difficult to say where those nicknames originated. Men were often nicknamed "Lightning Creator" or "Great Eagle" and the names may have stemmed from accomplishments or close ties to the ruler.

Bumper Crop

Maize, or corn as it is also known, was an early favorite crop of the Zapotecs as it provided the greatest return for the least amount of work. Not that maize was easy to farm, but it was far simpler and more stable than other crops that were grown in the early days. The Zapotecs continued to grow other foods, but maize was the staple on which their culture relied to sustain itself.

Outside of Monte Albán, the land was largely fertile and very conducive to regular bumper crops to support the growing civilization. It was an ideal place to grow maize without having to spend as much time defending their work from neighbors because they were more removed from those warlike neighbors. This played a large role in the civilization's ability to grow and thrive. Without maize, it would have been far more difficult for the Zapotecs to have established such a large and cultured nation that helped to change the mentality and path of the peoples in Mesoamerica.

It is perhaps ironic that while the Zapotecs relied on the crop and those who farmed it, farmers were not as highly regarded as the leaders and the priests who served largely auxiliary functions. Without the farmers and their regular production of maize, there would not have been a Zapotec nation.

Other Crops and Food

Maize was the most important crop, but it was far from the only one that the Zapotecs grew. Although the capital was located in an arid place, many places within the empire offered ideal conditions for growing many different crops. There were three distinct types of soil and regions for farming, and various types of agriculture were practiced based on the type of irrigation required to sustain the plants. The ability to innovate and develop the various methods of farming was a large part of the reason for the ability of the Zapotecs to survive.

1. The lands in and around Monte Albán were stony. However, evaporation was slower than in some other areas.

2. The land in the valley was much richer and better for growing crops. The evaporation rate was much faster than it was in the mountains.

3. The Piedmont area was the most varied as it sloped and dipped, making the land more difficult to till, but easier to ensure the water required was available.

Tailoring the agricultural needs to the specific region, the Zapotec had five distinctive methods of farming.

1. Rainfall farming was carried out in areas where rain was common and plentiful. These areas required less robust irrigation and had more reliable crop growth.

2. Well irrigation was required for areas where the water was further underground.

3. Canal irrigation was used to provide water to areas where rain and water were less frequent. This was one of the most advanced types of supplying water to those areas.

4. Floodwater farming was used in areas where there was a lot of water, but the rain tended to be dumped all at once.

5. Hillside terracing provided a way of delivering water to piedmont areas and higher regions where water was more difficult to find.

Different plants were planted and harvested across the regions depending on the needs of the crops. In addition to maize, the Zapotecs relied on beans, avocados, tomatoes, squash, chili peppers, prickly pear cactuses, and agaves to keep their people fed. There were also special foods grown for the nobility, such as cocoa beans for chocolate.

In addition to farming, they continued to forage for foods like herbs and acorns. Although dogs were raised for food, hunting was prevalent. Large game was restricted to the noble class, but there were plenty of other small game animals that commoners could eat, including turtles, gophers, lizards, and doves. Although commoners were not allowed to eat the bigger game, they frequently hunted with the nobles. This helped to bring the community together as they worked toward a common goal.

The Role of Tributes

The Zapotecs tended to expand through peaceful means, but there were times when they extended their borders through war. When they conquered a people who were not willing to join them peacefully, the people of the defeated areas were required to pay tribute to the conquering Zapotecs. This reminded them that they were part of a new culture. The leaders of larger regions operated the military and provided the necessary support as determined by the king.

The only regular members of this military were the noblemen who were assigned to a particular position. The commoners required to do most of the fighting were called to serve as needed. Soldiers who distinguished themselves in battle were rewarded with special outfits and indicators that marked them as being superior to the average fighter.

Although this type of military proved to be more advanced than that of their neighbors and the their fortifications provided much better protection from invaders, the Zapotecs were still inclined to settle disputes through diplomacy whenever possible. The method used by the Zapotecs to command and fill the military ranks and the use of diplomacy were also innovations that they used to their advantage.

Chapter 7 – The Arts, Athletics, and Technology

Perhaps one of the fascinating things about the Zapotecs was how much more advanced they were in terms of the arts and sports. Writing began early in their civilization and continued to play a crucial role over the course of the empire's existence. Their language was intricate, and that was reflected in the hieroglyphs they used to express themselves. Zapotec artisans created delicate works of jewelry and pottery that helped to distinguish which works were from their society and which artifacts belonged to other nations. They were also excellent sportsmen, and there were times when those sports were played with neighboring civilizations.

A Highly Developed Language

One of the most notable aspects of the Zapotecs was their language. It was part of the ancient Mesoamerican family group called Oto-Manguean. When different people who used the Oto-Manguean language began to splinter and scatter around 1,500 BC, the Zapotecs were quick to change the language to meet their own needs. The meaning of words was reflected in the tone used when the word was spoken. Languages today like Italian and Spanish are tonal as well, with the tone of the speaker's voice being an indication of what is meant.

Although it is impossible to know exactly how the language sounded in the early phases of the empire, Zapotec is still spoken in parts of Mexico today, including the areas around Northern and Southern Sierra, the Central Valleys, and the Isthmus of Tehuantepec. Although it has certainly changed since the peak of the civilization, there are hints of how the language was used during the time of the Zapotecs.

The Intricacies of the Written Word

The Zapotecs were among the first to begin recording information in the region. Their writing system would be mimicked by the other major cultures in Mesoamerica, including the Mayans, the Mixtecs, and the Aztecs. Most of the writing told stories about their conquests and leaders. Some of the remaining artifacts tell stories that would have otherwise been lost to time, although the stories are usually fragmented and incomplete.

Their writing was similar to the Ancient Egyptians as stories were told in pictures that told a story based on the positioning of the figure. The writing was logo syllabic, meaning that a symbol was dedicated to each syllable of the words they spoke. Reading was more akin to the eastern tradition, reading columns of text from top to bottom instead of left to right. Despite what archaeologists have been able to decipher of their writing, there is still much that remains a mystery because the language is so complicated.

Writing appeared during the early days of the civilization, and much of it focused on the vanquishing of enemies. The leader of San José Mogote had art made that depicted him conquering his enemies and sacrificing them to show his dominance and superiority. It is currently the oldest instance of Zapotec writing, but it is not a surprise that it was used to indicate the successes of the ruler. Given that the people were always struggling against their neighbors, this would have been something everyone knew was necessary to ensure their survival. By focusing on competition and being successful in their struggles, the Zapotecs were validating their abilities and the superiority of their gods. Many works in early human writing reflect a similar struggle and overcoming of others.

One of the primary locations where archeologists have encountered writing is among the burial places of the dead. The Zapotecs buried their people with items that spoke of who they were. The writing reflects their station and accomplishments that are still being deciphered by archeologists. Writing appeared to be used primarily as a way of recording genealogical information by the time the civilization was thriving in the Valley of Oaxaca. This was quite a shift from the early days when it was primarily used to show dominance and justify the deeds of Zapotec leaders. Inscriptions have been found at all known burial sites from the time the Zapotec civilization was established. Unlike today, writing was a way of recording history so it would not be forgotten, and not as a source of entertainment or news. However, the inscriptions do tell elaborate tales that are probably enhancements of the facts.

Many remains are also marked with writings that tell stories and details about what the objects were used for. In the case of tombs, the writing tells stories of the accomplishments and history of the people buried within them. Powerful animals were used to represent powerful rulers, with big cats being one of the most popular representations. Flying animals were used to represent other members of the noble family who would one day return to the skies in the form of clouds. Warriors were denoted by the use of dangerous predators that were not used to represent the king.

The Zapotecs believed speech was different between the two classes. Over time, they came to have different speech patterns and images. Members of the nobility were thought to have a more elegant manner of speech, and commoners were considered to have speech that was filled with lies and inaccuracies. Although it is unlikely that the speech was significantly different, it was undoubtedly portrayed differently in writing. Nobles were written about using more elegant scrawling language. It is the language of the nobility that is represented today in the various edifices and structures that remain. This was likely due in part to the possibility that the leaders were using the speech as propaganda for their people. By showing themselves as stronger and more honest, the nobles would be kept in awe by the commoners.

Intricate Artifacts

Among their many accomplishments, the Zapotecs were experts at working with gold and silver to make amazing pieces of jewelry. They could make incredibly detailed designs and embellished larger pieces, resulting in some of the most artistic pieces in Mesoamerica. Many of these pieces were given to the rulers, and it was an honor for an artist when a ruler wore a particular piece of an artist's work.

Jade was used exclusively for the nobles, and it was added to many of their accessories. From their ear ornaments to decorations placed in their lips, jade highlighted the place in society that someone held. It was one of the few precious minerals that was used by the Zapotecs. Remains of the Zapotecs who have jade ornaments make it easier to identify them as important people within their communities.

Much of what archaeologists have learned about the Zapotecs is through examining their pottery. While pots and ceramics had functional purposes, such as storing water, eating, and during ceremonies, they also played a role in burials and decoration of homes. Doubling as a tool and a symbol, pottery provides some insight into the lives of the Zapotecs. The pots and ceramics that were functional were usually worn and largely undecorated. Other pots and ceramics were very detailed, telling a story or providing an aesthetically pleasing appearance. Most of the people discovered in the Zapotec regions were buried with pots, which they could use in the afterlife. The more intricate the pot, usually the higher the status of the person with whom it was buried.

A Healthy Sense of Competition

As a people who preferred diplomacy to fighting, the Zapotecs tended to hold friendly competitions with their neighbors. During Monte Albán phase 2, ball courts became common. The ball courts look similar to the shape of the Roman numeral for one (I), and it was a place for the Zapotecs to play and exercise. The game itself has been lost to time; even the descendants of the Zapotecs do not know how the ball game was played or what the rules were.

Based on the number of ball courts in the cities and villages, it is clear that it was one of the favorite pastimes of the people, perhaps like soccer is today. Some places have large rectangular areas that archeologists assume were used for the sport because there are no other locations that could have be used for playing the game. Looking over the hieroglyphs at the courts, it appears the game required participants to wear knee guards, gloves, and other protective gear as they played the sport. The ball was made from the rubber tree, giving it more bounce than if it had been made of animal skin or other materials.

The city of Dainzu has the most famous ball court. Located at the base of an easily defensible hill, it was the ideal location to play sports. Since the location was easy to protect, it was difficult for enemies to sneak up on the Zapotecs while they were relaxing and playing. On the lowest terrace of the Dainzu complex are carved walls that display details not of slain enemies, but of competitors in the sport. It is an intricately carved wall that is unlike anything else in the Zapotec ruins, and it has captured the attention and imagination of many who have seen it. The ball court is not shaped like many of the other courts. The court that has been most studied is rectangular in shape instead of being shaped like the Roman numeral I. However, there is another ball court in Dainzu that does conform to the type of court found in the capitals of the Zapotecs. The writing on the first ball court provides just enough details to encourage archeologists to make guesses about the game. However, there is not enough information or detail to help archaeologists to ever be fully confident they know how the sport was played or exactly what its role was in the Zapotec society. They are continually revising their ideas of the game based on the latest findings.

A Look into Technology's Roots

The Zapotecs were able to turn an arid, apparently uninhabitable mountain into their thriving capital city of Monte Albán, and proved that they were more advanced and logical than many of the other civilizations around them. They were able to adapt and build their environment to suit their needs instead of learning to work within the limitations of a particular area.

Easily one of their greatest accomplishments, the Zapotecs were able to grow their civilization and thrive in areas where other civilizations could not because they had their own form of irrigation. Using a series of canals, they could ensure that water was free-flowing and available regardless of the limited amount of rainfall that fell in the region.

One of the main sources of water came from the Atoyac River, the river that flowed through the Valley of Oaxaca. It provided the water needed to sustain the crops and population when there was no rain. From this river and small streams that fed into it, the Zapotecs created irrigation systems and directed the water up to higher regions. This meant the water was distributed without taking any away from the crops. There is also evidence they created a dam to increase and store a large amount of water where it was needed.

Architecture in the Zapotec civilization was also different from many of their neighbors. While they also built pyramids, many of the remaining structures appear similar to the kinds of structures found in Europe at the time. For example, the most studied ball court in Dainzu had intricately designed walls. The more common types of ball courts were lined with stands that were probably for the spectators to watch the game. Looking at these remains calls to mind bleachers and stages where people could sit to be entertained.

However, it is the burials that have the most intriguing architecture. The dead were buried underground in tombs, regardless of the station and class of the deceased. These tombs were located below the floors of the homes where they lived. Stairs led down from the home into the vestibule outside of the tomb. It is probable that this was symbolic of the passing from this world into the next. Though only the members of the noble class had ancestors who could intercede, commoners still held their ancestors in reverence, as is made clear by the structures where the dead are buried. The tombs also had intricate designs and decorations added to them to tell the stories of the dead.

Chapter 8 – Two Worlds Collide

The Zapotecs had been a well-established civilization long before the arrival of the Conquistadors. The capital that had been the center of their growth for centuries was already in decline and was no longer the center of arts and innovation. There were clear signs the civilization was in decline, both because of internal and external forces.

While there is no way to know what the internal politics were at the time of the arrival of the Spanish, it was a civilization that was apparently past its peak. The transfer of power from Monte Albán to the religious center of Milta was a sign that things were shifting. Had the Conquistadors not invaded, it is possible that an entirely new civilization would have risen from the decay. However, this was a period in Mesoamerican history where an outside force altered the trajectory.

The End of a War

The Zapotecs had warred with the Aztecs for nearly a year before the arrival of the Conquistadors. The Zapotecs had not been the victors. Given the way they had dominated their neighbors for so long, or found diplomatic solutions to power struggles, the battle with the Aztecs must have taken a much harsher toll on the aging Zapotec civilization. It is not certain exactly what happened or how the Aztecs had won the war. The Aztecs were at the peak of their civilization, and they dominated their area. Had the Conquistadors not arrived, it is possible they would have ended up incorporating the Zapotecs into the Aztec Empire.

Innovation and new ideas had become less frequent, and they had not undergone any substantial changes in several hundred years. The Aztecs were more warlike than the Zapotecs, so it is probable that the growing nation would have wholly consumed the Zapotecs into their society.

Before the Conquistadors arrived, a war ended with minimal loss to the Zapotecs. Although the war had been longer and bloodier than the Zapotecs were accustomed to, they had negotiated favorable terms with the Aztecs. With the king of the Zapotecs accepting a bride from the Aztecs, annual tributes to the Aztecs, and small Aztec garrisons within the realm of the Zapotecs, it appears that the shift of power towards the Aztecs was in progress. If not for the interference of the Europeans at this point, the civilization of the Zapotecs may have been long lost to time. It is possible their extensive history would have been all but wiped out by the Aztecs.

There is no way to know how the strained relationship would have worked out had it taken its natural course. What is known is that the relationship between the Aztecs and Zapotecs was not ideal for the future of the Zapotec civilization.

The Conquistadors' Arrival

The Conquistadors arrived before the Zapotecs had disappeared and their existence was of interest to the Spanish. Having been around far longer than the Aztecs, the Zapotecs had a much more structured society; one that was familiar to the Spanish. They could draw comparisons between the aging empire and their own experiences, something that was difficult to do with the Aztecs.

Although the arrival of the Conquistadors resulted in a record of the existence of the Zapotecs and kept the civilization from disappearing into oblivion, there is no doubt that the arrival of the Spanish also signaled the end of the declining civilization.

Hernán Cortés arrived in Mexico in the early 1500s, soon after the end of the war between the Zapotec and Aztec Empires. This mission was one that he had set out for himself and one that he was ordered by his superior, the governor of Cuba, not to begin. Initially, Cortés was interested in taking over the Aztec empire. Cortés operated in a way that was very opportunistic. By making friends with the enemies of the Aztecs, and eliminating some of the their allies, Cortés was able to maneuver his men into a better position, both physically and militarily. He succeeded in taking over the Aztec capital, but he soon left when he heard that the Spanish were coming to arrest him since he had followed through with a mission they had specifically ordered him not to undertake.

Following the conquering of the Aztecs, the Zapotecs were hopeful it would mean a return to their original way of life. Without the Aztecs dominating the region, this seemed possible, although the threat of the Conquistadors should also have been clear at that point. The Spanish were more interested in dominating and forcing their way of life on the people, claiming the land for their country. The warning signs were there, but the Zapotecs were more optimistic. That was probably because no one in Mesoamerica had ever seen anything quite like the Conquistadors before their arrival.

A Tentative Peace

The Spanish were very interested in learning more about the Zapotecs, and they probably realized just how different the Zapotec outlook on life was compared to the other natives they had encountered. The Zapotec society was far more familiar than dissimilar to the one that the Spanish knew. While they viewed the cannibalism and sacrificing of humans to the gods as barbaric, even this was not too different compared to the history of Spain. The Spanish Inquisition was still prevalent in Spain at the time that the Conquistadors were invading the civilizations in Mesoamerica. This meant they were not entirely unsympathetic to the idea of sacrificing humans for a religious cause. It was perhaps hypocritical they viewed the Zapotec sacrificial rituals as barbaric without condemning the violence and atrocities that were occurring in Spain at that time.

Whatever their personal feelings were about the Zapotecs, it was certain that the Spanish Conquistadors were impressed by the organization of the society and religion. This is evident from the way that they frequently compare the Zapotecs to their own royal lines and the Roman Catholic Church in their writings.

The Conquistadors began to ask questions of the Zapotecs. The interrogations were meant as a way of gathering information and learning about the natives of the land they would eventually conquer (although they may not have been aware of that at the time). The Spanish had two periods when they questioned the Zapotecs, in 1578 and 1581. The reflections of the people that they questioned offer a glimpse into the way the Zapotecs viewed themselves, even if the information was a little skewed by the lack of full understanding of the information the Zapotecs were trying to impart. Much of the information that was provided has been studied and learned by archeologists as a starting point for better understanding the ruins and artifacts that they encounter at archeological sites. Of course, skepticism should be employed when reading the writings as they are not perfect representations of the lives of the Zapotecs. However, it does provide valuable information about these people since archeologists are still working to unravel the meanings of most of the hieroglyphs left by the once great civilization.

The Conquistadors questioned the Zapotec king, Cociyopii, the last ruler of his dynasty. They inquired about his "idolatrous" religion and their practices. Later, he would be baptized and renamed Don Juan Cortés. The way the Spanish understood, or perhaps misunderstood, the ideas and descriptions that Cociyopii relayed created nearly as many questions as they resolved: however, the imperfect records do provide details that would likely have been lost to time had the Spanish not attempted to understand and write about the Zapotecs.

There is no way to know exactly how many people were living in the Zapotec nation when the Conquistadors arrived. The borders of the different civilizations changed often, and the Mesoamericans did not take a census of how many people there were in their empires. At the time, the Zapotecs still ruled over a large area, well beyond the Valley of Oaxaca.

The Fall of an Empire

One of the few things on which archeologists can agree about the fall of the empire is that it happened after the arrival of the Conquistadors. There are different theories on what caused the decline. The diseases brought by the Spanish took a significant toll on the Zapotecs, just as European diseases negatively affected natives in North and South America. Given the size of the Zapotec empire, it is inconceivable that disease wiped out the entire nation. However, the diseases probably did cause serious problems for the areas that were more populous because there may not have been enough people left to continue with vital functions within the society, such as food production.

Despite the initial hope following the fall of the Aztec empire, the Zapotecs did not fare any better under the rule of the Conquistadors. They had a proud heritage and religion that were completely contrary to the government and religion the Spanish forced on every nation they conquered. Although the last ruler did give in and allow himself to be baptized into the Christian religion, this was more likely a sign that the nation would not survive the invasion, even if illness had not devastated the people from the different regions.

After this, the nation began to break apart much more rapidly. With the loss and conversion of the king from the religion they had practiced for more than 1,000 years, many villages and regions probably saw this as their opportunity to become autonomous. Some historians and archaeologists believe the empire fell to infighting as different pieces broke away to rule themselves. It would have become impossible for the nation to re-emerge after losing so many areas that had been crucial to maintaining the kind of social structure they had before that period. Also, the loss of the king would have been a serious blow to their religion. If he was the descendant of the gods and he chose to turn away from them that meant the people of the civilization no longer had the foundation for the hierarchical society that had dominated their lives. The loss of their religion would have been a significant blow to the whole civilization. Without their religion, chiefs and other leaders would have seen an opportunity to gain power they could not have held under the king. Commoners may also have seen a chance to reach well above their station.

Mitla continued to be a center for the remaining Zapotecs who clung to their old way of life. They continued to live and work there, even after the Conquistadors conquered their nation.

However, many of the former Zapotec people moved on and started new lives under a new structure. Some of them disappeared, either being added to other cultures or trying to live in areas where they could not survive. Some moved on and created little pockets that kept some of the ways of their ancestors. These people survived through the centuries and still speak a dialect that is descended from the Zapotec language. Some of the knowledge of their ancestors has been recorded, but much of it has been lost. Myths and stories have survived, but they have changed over time, so they do not entirely align with the recordings of the Conquistadors. They are the only link to a people who once ruled a large portion of Mesoamerica. When most of the rest of the world around them sought to force ideas and beliefs on their neighbors, the Zapotecs offered other solutions that meant entirely avoiding war when possible. With their ever-growing reach, many of the smaller civilizations saw an opportunity for a better life by joining the Zapotec people. The fact that the Zapotecs were adept at war was another reason to join them peacefully. They were one of the few civilizations in the area who sought other means of expanding, and their influence is impossible to overstate for the region.

Conclusion

The Zapotec civilization was one of the earliest and most influential civilizations in Mesoamerica. While many budding civilizations looked to expand through conquering, the Zapotecs were more interested in innovation and technology. Their first capital in San José Mogote shows many of the early hallmarks of the civilization they would become. As their neighbors focused on resources and growth, the Zapotecs were beginning to form their own language and writing. The hieroglyphs they used during this time were later changed and incorporated into more intricate works. Even before they left San José Mogote, the Zapotecs demonstrated a much different interest in the world around them. They revered the food they killed because it contained a spirit from the gods, and sought to find balance with their world. It was this interest that ultimately led to the founding of a completely unique civilization in Mesoamerica.

When resources were scarce and constant battles began to wear on the Zapotecs, they moved. Opting to take a less traditional and easy path, the Zapotecs moved to an area that others had avoided. Leveling the top of a mountain for a new city, they began to build an empire that would be unlike any other in the region for several hundred years. They created irrigation systems that allowed them to live in dry areas where no other people would settle. Because of their innovation and intelligence, they established themselves in areas that were much easier to defend from other, warlike nations. The new city at Monte Albán was heavily fortified in addition to being difficult to reach. This ensured the population could pursue other interest rather than having to focus on war.

The Zapotec civilization found its footing and established itself as a people more interested in diplomacy than war for their early days. Even after they began to expand beyond their early boundaries, the Zapotecs tended to pursue peaceful resolutions. However, when forced to fight, they proved to be adept at waging war.

The people living within this ancient Mesoamerican civilization were free to live their lives in a way that was largely unfamiliar in Europe where slaves were usually slaves for the rest of their lives and the classes were rigidly defined into subsets. While the society was strictly divided between those who were believed to be descended from their gods and everyone else, the commoners were not limited in their potential as long as they did not aspire to marry members of the nobility or hold positions of power. Commoners could pursue their interests and abilities to add to the reputation of the Zapotecs. There were many positions within the nation as well. Farming was one of the primary jobs, but within cities and large villages, there was a wealth of artists and innovators who made beautiful and intricate works that established these people as being among the most refined for their time.

With a history that was over 1,000 years long and a way of thinking that was dissimilar to many of their neighbors at the time, the Zapotecs will always provide a completely new perspective for archaeologists and historians to explore.

If you enjoyed this individual book on the Zapotecs, can you please leave a review for it?

Thanks for your support!

Part 3: Maya History

A Captivating Guide to the Maya Civilization, Culture, Mythology, and the Maya Peoples' Impact on Mesoamerican History

Introduction

In the past decade or two, there has been an upsurge of interest about the Maya, their history, civilization, and culture. There have been more documentaries and fiction movies, books and stories about them. This was partly fueled by the mythical Maya prediction of the end of the world in 2012, which for a short period of time put this civilization under the media spotlight. But there is much more to their culture than the common misconception about their calendar. And for a long time before the Maya caught the eyes of the wider population, archeologists and historians did their best to uncover and piece together the complete story about the Maya civilization.

Those scientists wondered how the Maya built those magnificent cities and temples; how did they create such stunning pieces of art and jewelry? They tried to understand what the Maya drew, carved, and wrote on their walls and books. Every aspect of Maya life was interesting to them. As their research progressed and understanding and knowledge of the Maya civilization accumulated, one thing became clear to historians. The Maya were one of the most important and most influential civilizations of the whole Mesoamerican region. A simple illustration of that point is that if you were to close your eyes and try to imagine a general picture of Mesoamerican life prior to Columbus' so-called discovery of Americas, you would most likely see the quintessential representation of the Maya civilization. You might envision people walking around dressed in jaguar skins, or ones with brightly-colored headdresses made from feathers, or huge step pyramid temples adorned with strange hieroglyphic carvings, maybe people with painted faces and pierced noses and ears, human sacrifices in front of the masses, or warriors with wooden clubs sneaking across the jungle. We can't even imagine Mesoamerican history and culture without the Maya. And that is why it is rather important to know as much as we can about them.

In this book we will try to shine a bit of light on the Maya civilization, from its origins and history, through the everyday life of the Maya people, with the unavoidable topic of their religion and mythology, ending with the usually forgotten subject of what happened to the Maya after the Spaniards came and where are they now. And at the same time, with getting to know more about this important civilization, another important part of this book is to debunk some of the myths and misconceptions that, like with all other great civilizations, became synonymous with the Maya. So, get ready to learn and enjoy on this guided tour through Maya civilization.

Chapter 1 – Meet the Maya

Every story about the civilizations of the American continent begins around 40.000 to 20.000 years B.C.E., when during the last great Ice Age, a land bridge connected Alaska and Siberia. During that long period, small groups gradually started moving to what would be later named the New World by the European explorers. Although there have been some other theories about how and when the humans first migrated to the Americas, this theory is currently predominant thanks to abundant evidence that supports it. First, archeologists found similarity between the tools that were used by the people living in Siberia during that period and the tools of the first settlers across the Pacific Ocean. Then the linguists found core similarities and relations of the Siberian languages with the languages spoken by the Native Americans. The last and probably most conclusive piece of evidence came from geneticists, who compared DNA from both groups of people and found common ancestry. They confirmed that most of the indigenous people of the Americas came from what is today southeastern Siberia.

Of course, that migration didn't happen in one huge wave, but slowly, over time, small bands and tribes crossed over from Asia. And from Alaska and northern parts of America, they started migrating south. They did that as they searched for better places to live, with warmer climates with more diverse plant life and better hunting grounds. Over hundreds and thousands of years, these bands of hunters and gatherers roamed across the continent and started to adapt, inventing new more unique stone tools. Archeologists found those tools on the Yucatan peninsula, which is the Maya homeland, and they have dated it to around 10.000-8.000 B.C.E. That is probably when the first people, most likely Maya ancestors, came to the region. But before moving on to how those early hunter-gatherers rose to become the fabled Maya, we have to understand where they lived and how it affected the development of their early civilization.

So-called Maya homeland covered the southeastern parts of present-day Mexico, including the already mentioned Yucatan peninsula, and northwestern part of Central America, on territories of modern-day Belize and Guatemala, and parts of El Salvador and Honduras. From that, we can see that the Maya covered a relatively large area, around 320.000 km² (123.000 mi²), which can be divided into three geographical and climate zones. To the north, covering pretty much the entire Yucatan peninsula are the Lowlands, then in the center of the Maya region are the Highlands, and in the south is the Pacific Coastal Plain. The Pacific coast region was a dense rainforest area, with the highest amounts of annual rainfall of the entire Maya homeland. Some of the first Maya settlements were founded in this region, along the lagoons on the coast. With plentiful forest wildlife and plants, sea and freshwater creatures it was a perfect place for early settlers, while the rich soils along the river banks made it a good place for agricultural societies that came later. It was also an important trade route in later periods when more complex communities arose, connecting Mexico and Central America.

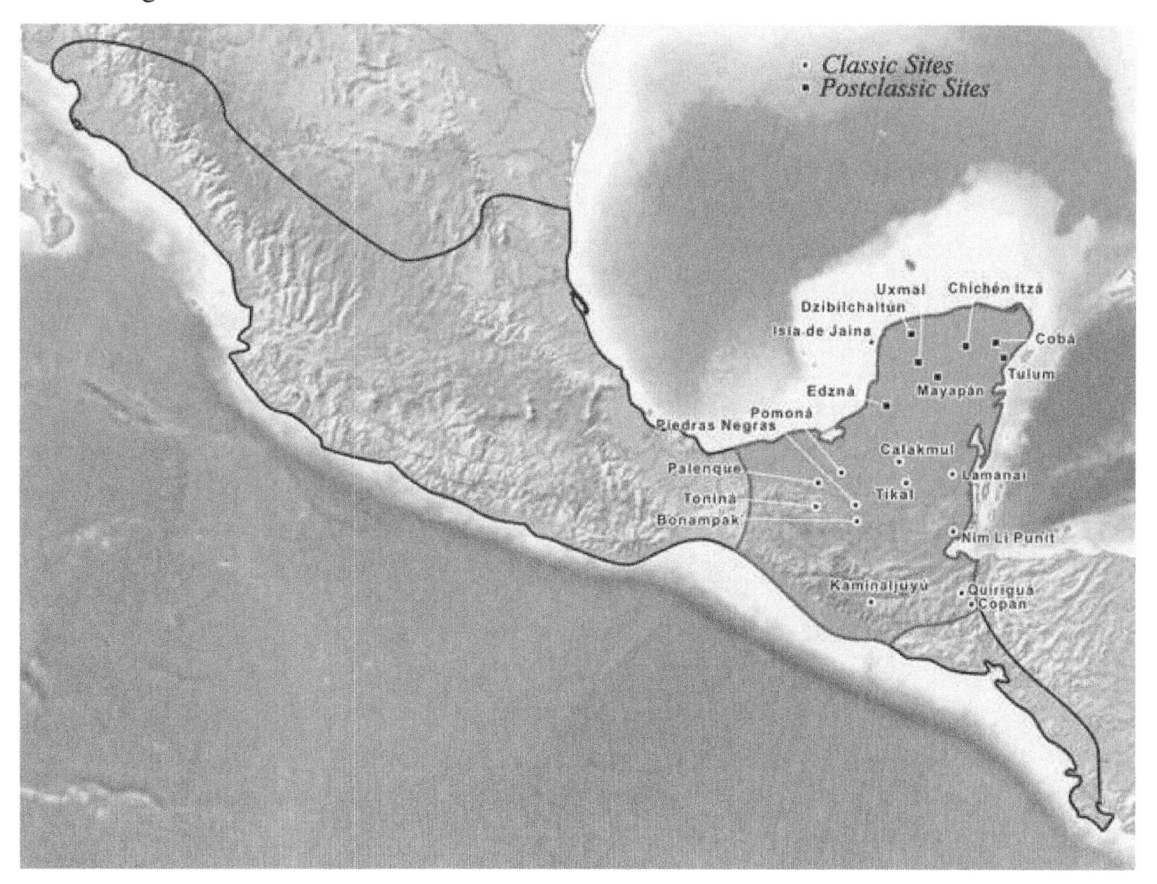

The Maya homeland. Source: https://commons.wikimedia.org

To the northeast of the Pacific coast region is the Highland region, aptly named for its high mountains of an average elevation of over 760m (2500ft), with highest peaks reaching up to about 3000m (9850ft). With higher altitude came lower temperatures as well as less rainfall. Yet the volcanic activity of the mountains provided important stone resources for the Maya like obsidian (also known as volcanic glass) and volcanic basalt. Volcanoes also made the surrounding soil quite fertile, and certain valleys climate was perfect for farming. Beside volcanic stones, the Highlands were also rich with other precious minerals like jade and serpentine. All that combined made this area favorable for settling despite the danger from volcanic eruptions and earthquakes. Quite different from that area are the Lowlands, which are mostly flat, and were in the past covered with thick forest. This region is rich with limestone and chert, important building materials for the Maya, as well with areas of fertile soil and abundant wildlife. Southern parts of the Lowlands are filled with lakes and rivers, which provided fish for the inhabitants, and at the same time facilitated communication throughout the dense forest. In northern areas, which are richer with limestone, water is more scarce, and the only sources of it were the sinkholes, also known as cenotes in that region. And the coast of the Atlantic Ocean on the Yucatan Peninsula provided this region with both saltwater fish and shellfish. When all things are considered, even if at the first glance it doesn't seem so, the whole Maya homeland was rather rich with food, water, and building materials, which explains why exactly the Maya ancestors chose to settle there.

But probably more important than that was the abundance of fertile soil. Around 6.000 B.C.E., agriculture spread around Mesoamerica, which marked a vital step in the development of the Maya culture. Their ancestors were already living somewhat sedentary lives, with an abundance of food in the forests around them. But with the rise of farming around 2000 B.C.E., they had more food surpluses, which meant the population grew faster and was more prosperous. And in search of the more fertile soils, the Maya ancestors started spreading from the coastal part of the Maya homeland inward, which explains why the Highlands were at first a bit slower in their development. As their societies became more complex, thanks partially to more excess food but also due to connections with other Mesoamerican civilizations, their cultures started to evolve, and around 1500 B.C.E. an early Maya civilization was beginning to form. Though it should be mentioned that linguists today believe that Proto-Mayan language, from which all modern Mayan languages evolved, formed as early as 2200 B.C.E., which meant that the Maya people had differentiated from other Mesoamerican tribes even before they rose to a level of civilization.

Of course, in the early stages of their development, the Maya were not as dominant as we usually depict them. From 1500 B.C.E. to around 250 C.E. there existed the early Maya civilization, known by historians as the Preclassic period. During this time, the Maya learned, adopting new technologies and ideas from their neighbors who were, at the time, more developed. Then came the Maya golden age, the Classic period, which lasted from about 250 to 950 C.E. In that era, also known as middle Maya civilization, they were the most dominant culture in Mesoamerica, with huge cities, a strong economy, advanced technology compared to others. But that golden age came quite abruptly to an end during the 10th century A.D., which led to the third era of the Maya – the late Maya civilization, or Postclassic period, which lasted until the Spaniards came to Mesoamerica in the early 16th century. That period is marked by a slow fall of the Maya, who were still an important civilization, but no longer as dominant as before. Of course, all that changed with the arrival of the Spaniards who had demonstrated little understanding of any culture, religion, or idea that didn't agree with their Christian view of the world. So, with great dedication, they worked on crushing the Maya people and their civilization, which led them to be mostly forgotten for a few centuries. They became just one more "savage" tribe from the so-called New World.

That attitude slowly started to change in the early 19th century when Mexico and other Central American countries gained independence from the crumbling Spanish Empire. Many became interested in the history of these lands, with their curiosity being sparked by some of the fine Maya artifacts that had been circulating in the art markets. Of course, at the time, the art collectors weren't aware that these were actually Maya artifacts. Yet some daring explorers started to roam the thick Mexican jungles, some in search of knowledge, others in search of material gain. Over the decades they found many sites covered with jungle trees and vines, gathering more attention which culminated in the 1890's when the first major archeological excavation and examination of the Maya sites began. By then archeologists and historians were sure that pre-Columbian civilizations, of which the Maya were probably the most famous one, were more than mere "barbarians," but now their task was to understand those cultures and uncover the past. Although many Maya sites were found and researched in the late 19th and early 20th century, not much was yet known about this mysterious civilization.

The 1950s marked a turning point in understanding the Maya past. Firstly, new technologies and new archeological sites allowed researchers to attain a more complex grasp of how the Maya civilization looked and evolved. But more important were the first breakthroughs in deciphering the Maya writing, which meant that researchers could gain a new level of comprehension of the Maya past. Understanding text written on monuments, in books, and on temple walls gave far more details about the Maya than any other artifact could. That groundbreaking discovery also ignited a new interest in the scholars about Maya history, making it one of the most dynamic fields of historic research at that time. Even today, new archeological findings are being uncovered and scholars have an even better understanding of Maya script, widening our knowledge and understanding of the Maya civilization. And today, as the interdisciplinary approach has become the norm in the discovery of the past, archeologists and historians are now working together with scientists from other fields, such as linguists, anthropologists, geneticists, which is important for getting a better, more detailed picture of the Maya civilization.

One of those details about the Maya that is rather important to know is that they aren't as unified as a group as most people imagine. When thinking about them, most people assume it is one big homogenous tribe that formed a civilization, perhaps similar to the ancient Greeks. But in reality, the Maya were more divided in smaller groups. This is most evident in their language, which from the early Proto-Mayan and over the course of thousands of years has split into many smaller regional language groups. By the time of the classical era of the Maya civilization, there were six large language subgroups of the Mayan; Yucatecan, Huastecan, Ch'olan-Tzeltalan, Q'anjob'alan, Mamean, and K'ichean. But despite those divisions among the Maya population, they surprisingly managed to keep a tight cultural and civilizational cohesion, similar to ancient Mesopotamian civilization. Of course, since the times of the classical Maya, much has changed, and today linguists have differentiated about 30 variations of the Mayan language. Of those languages most used is K'iche' (Quiché), with approximately 1 million speakers, concentrated in Guatemala. Also important is the Yucatec Maya language, which covers the largest area, the Yucatan peninsula, and has about 800,000 present-day speakers. Overall, there are more than 6 million people still speaking one of the many Mayan languages, although it should be mentioned that not all of them consider Mayan to be their first language.

A present-day Maya family from Yucatan, Mexico. Source: https://commons.wikimedia.org

That leads us to another truth that is often overlooked when talking about the Maya; their history doesn't end in the 16th century, nor did they disappear as a unique ethnic group. Although Spanish rule heavily influenced them, they managed to keep their identity intact, preserving their language, traditions, and culture to the present day. Most of the Maya today live in Guatemala, where they constitute about 40% of the entire population. They also form a significant minority in southern Mexico and the Yucatan Peninsula. Honduras, Belize, and El Salvador also still have some indigenous Maya, but in much smaller numbers. Altogether there are somewhere between 6 and 7 million Maya people today, making them one of the larger native ethnic groups in Americas, which is another important reason for us to get to know more about their past, their culture, and their civilization.

Chapter 2 – From tribal villages to early states

Before going into the finer details about the Maya civilization we first must take a look at how it developed through history, starting with the earliest era, the Preclassic period. It is during this time that the Maya created the base of their culture, making their society more complex and changing their economy, warfare, and politics. Their civilization evolved from tribal villages, through more complex chiefdoms and resulted in the early Maya states. Those changes first began on the Pacific Coast region where, most likely thanks to the improvement of agriculture, the Maya first came to have food surpluses. By 1700 B.C.E., there were already some larger villages showing clear signs of a completely sedentary lifestyle, although rather primitive and uncivilized. But in the next century or so another great and important improvement began to appear. That improvement was pottery. As a cultural expression, it was used to make figurines which were mostly representations of females, as in most early societies around the world. In more practical forms, the Maya started making pottery vessels for storing and transporting food. It is important to note that this rise of sedentary agricultural life was happening at the similar time across Mesoamerica, which allowed for the development of trade. And, luckily for the Pacific coast Maya, they were in perfect position for it.

The easiest and quickest trade route from Central America to present-day Mexico crossed the Maya territory in the far south. And with pottery, it was easier to transport and trade food, which was most likely the first trading item of the region. For the Maya, like for many early civilizations, it was a crucial step in evolution. Trade sparked the stratification of the society, and the birth of the elite class among the Maya. Due to the gathering of wealth and power, the ruling strata started to exert increasing levels of control over the lower classes. This led to forming of the first so-called petty chiefdoms during 1400 B.C.E., in which a central village ruled small hamlets. These signs of hierarchical society meant that the early Maya chiefs were also able to force the commoners to take part in public works needed to create communal projects like building temples or other ritual buildings, which were the cornerstones of early civilizations. Further, trade pushed the Maya society to develop better craftsmanship and new tools, both to improve farming, for even more food surpluses, and also to be traded. That meant that besides farming, part of the Maya population focused on developing craftsmanship skills. And that social diversification is considered to be another important step in the creation of early civilizations.

Not long after, by the 1200s, the Maya villages on the Pacific coast became rich and powerful, with populations of more than 1000 for the first time. They improved their pottery to the artisanal levels, while large amounts of obsidian in some of those villages shows us that their wealth and power came from the control of that valuable resource. Yet trade remained the most important thing that drove the Maya civilization forward. At this point, the most developed Maya villages became powerful enough to evolve from local to regional trade, which meant the Maya came in contact with other higher developed societies. Of these, the most significant was probably the Olmecs that lived on the Gulf Coast of south-central Mexico. The Olmecs were at the time the most developed civilization, with structured religion, trade, urban centers, and highly sophisticated art; they are considered to have influenced the development of the entire family of Mesoamerican cultures and civilizations. The Maya were no exception. From the Olmecs, the Maya adopted the base of their future civilization, from the pantheon of gods and monumental buildings to urbanism and rituals, and to art style and veneration of rulers.

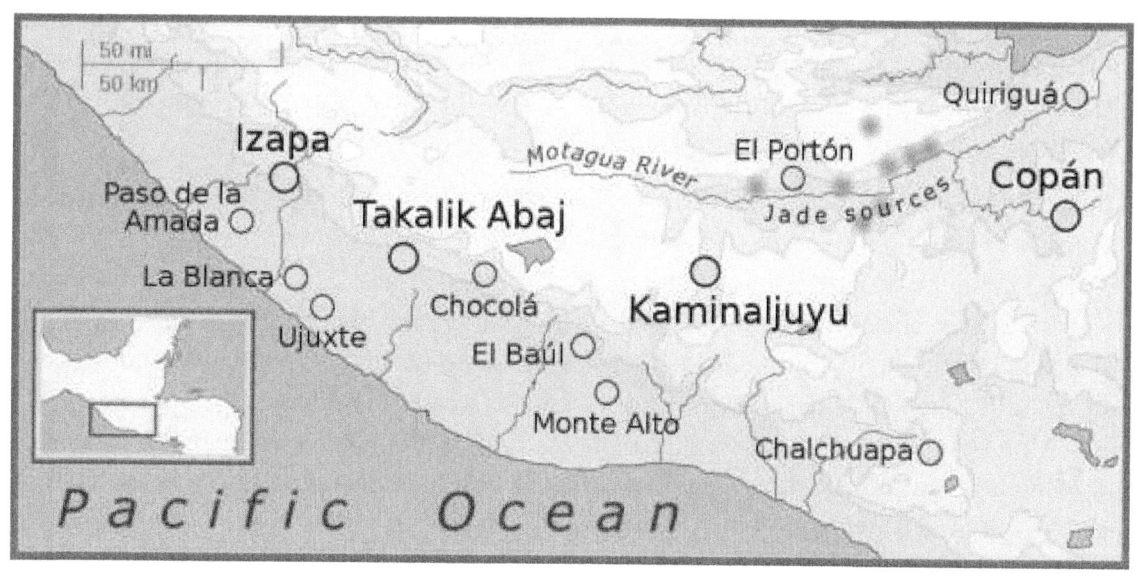

Pacific coast region of the Maya homeland. Source: https://commons.wikimedia.org

But even though the signs of cultural interaction of the Olmecs with a large part of Mesoamerica is certain, in recent years there have been some historians that tend to disagree with the notion of the Olmec civilization being mother culture of the entire region. They believe that the cultural exchange happened so quickly it is impossible to be sure if all the traits mentioned actually originate from the Olmecs. They argue that this civilizational leap is work of the entire network of the Mesoamerican cultures, connected through trade. But no one can deny that during that early era of Mesoamerican history the Olmec cities were the biggest and most powerful, and many of their neighbors and trading partners copied from them. Among those mimicking the Olmecs were clearly at least some of the Maya villages. By 1000 B.C.E., Olmec-styled art began to replace earlier forms of the Maya figurines and vessels, while jade became an important precious material coveted by the Maya elite. Later on, from around 850 B.C.E., when those villages started to grow into urban centers, they also mimicked the configuration of La Venta, the most important and the mightiest Olmec city from 900 to 300 B.C.E.

That leap from villages to early cities is important; it indicates that by the time Maya civilization had become richer and more powerful, it was at least in part thanks to their increased trade with the Olmecs and other cultures. But this was only the state of affairs in the Pacific Coast region of the Maya homeland. In the north, in the Lowlands, things were slightly different. During the time the southern Maya started to get involved in the regional trade, around 1200 B.C.E., their northern brethren remained at the low level of simple agricultural villages and still lived in egalitarian society. The lowland Maya started to catch up with the Pacific Coast around 1000 B.C.E., as the first signs of public architecture show us. This meant that society was getting stratified, while the Olmec-style jade artwork shows us that they slowly started to get involved in the trade as well. By 700 B.C.E., the changes in the lowland Maya societies started to pick up the pace as their population started to grow faster. They started to create monumental public complexes, while they also worked on making ridged and drained fields for farming. And trade became a more vital part of their lives, similar to the southern Maya. The artifacts found in the lowland Maya centers are mostly of Olmec origin, which shows that they were one of the most important trade partners of the lowland area as well.

As both southern and northern parts regions of the Maya homeland experienced a period of growth, accumulation of wealth and power, the strongest cities started to evolve from previously mentioned petty chiefdoms to proto-states. One of the earliest and best examples of this is the La Blanca site, which flourished roughly from 900 to 600 B.C.E., in the Pacific Coast region. It managed to gain control of 300km^2 (115mi^2) of the territory around it, with two more urban centers apart from the capital. Those centers were of course smaller, and hierarchically secondary to the capital. Alongside these urban centers, La Blanca inhabitants controlled at least 60 smaller villages and hamlets in the surrounding area. That kind of power granted La Blanca a lot of labor power, which was used in monumental public works. One of the examples of that mobilization of the workforce was a platform temple that was 24m (78ft) high and is considered to be one of the largest in Mesoamerica of that era. Apart from La Blanca, many other similar larger urban centers spawned in the southernmost parts of the Maya region, with a more complex site hierarchy and influence than in earlier times.

One of the most illuminating examples of this power comes from the ruler tombs in these capitals. The biggest tomb, dated to about 500 B.C.E., was a stone crypt, that was filled with precious goods like jade and shells, a carved stone scepter and three trophy heads which were a clear indicator of status and wealth of the male buried in it. But more than that, the true power wielded by the dead king was demonstrated by the 12 human sacrifices found around him. They, unlike the king, were buried with their faces down. Their role in this burial ritual was most likely to be servants to the ruler in his afterlife. Human sacrifices and trophy heads also show us, together with other carvings and findings of projectile heads, that warfare was becoming a more important and regular part of the Maya life. The Maya rulers found that small-scale raids were a good way to both gain wealth and labor force, but also to eliminate their rivals. Besides that, war captives were used for religious sacrifices, and with that rituals rulers also reinforced authority over their subordinates, proving that they are more than capable of taking care of them in both religious and material aspects of life.

The prosperity of the material and religious life was also evident in the Lowland region, although not as much as on the Pacific Coast. They erected even larger temples than before, like ones in the south Lowland site of El Mirador, which rivaled in size the Egyptian pyramids. They also built ritual ball courts as well as *sacbeob,* singular *sacbe,* which were elevated roadways connecting temples, plazas, and other structures in ceremonial sites which most likely had some religious significance. Yet at this time it seems that the most important process in the Lowlands was the expansion of the Maya from riversides and lakes into the much densely forested interior of the region. This was made possible by development of swidden agriculture, more widely known as the slash-and-burn technique, which made it possible to clear parts of the forest for farming, then leaving it to replenish so the process could be repeated. With that expansion, nearly all of the entire Lowland region was now settled by the Maya people.

The expansion of Maya civilization was not only limited to the Lowlands. As both northern and southern areas of Maya territory got wealthier and more involved in trade, they also spread their influence to the Highlands. Of course, this mountain region was settled as early as 1000 B.C.E., but it remained fairly sparsely developed. Their growth and expansion only stated around 800 B.C.E., most likely influenced by the development of trade between the Lowlands and the Pacific Coast, which meant traders had to cross over the Highlands. This meant the Highland Maya started to learn and adopt advances made by their kinfolk. By 600 B.C.E., they started to use irrigation to make the valleys they lived in more fertile, and this with other signs of public works like monuments and temples show that by that time they had managed to develop stratified societies where elites were able to mobilize the labor force for common projects. The best example of that is Kaminaljuyu, an urban center located in present-day central Guatemala, near Guatemala City, which managed to use the control of irrigation to enforce its direct rule over the entire valley in which it was built. Carvings show that the rulers of this city exerted strong authority thanks to their religious roles as well as their success in warfare. And, as they were located on an important trade route that connected the south and north Maya regions, they got quite wealthy by controlling it.

Of course, that wealth was going mostly to the ruling elite, or to be more precise to the rulers, as was the case in nearly all Mesoamerican cities at the time. This accumulation of wealth and power in the hands of the rulers was the key for the next step of development in the Maya society, which was forming of the early states. But by 400 B.C.E., cities like previously mentioned Kaminaljuyu and El Mirador, as well as many others, grew considerably, covering up to a 4km^2 (1.5mi^2), which made these urban centers as big, if not bigger than, cities of Ancient Greece like Athens. That growth was a direct consequence of their success in trade, as the previously dominant Olmecs were in steady decline, slowly disappearing from the historical stage. With more wealth, the Maya society became more stratified, with more than just two classes-the ruling elites and the commoners. All that culminated with the creation of a strong ruler cult, possibly influenced by the Olmecs, which was partially based on their religious role in the society. With the unquestionable authority of the rulers, which can by now be even called kings, the transformation of the Maya polities from chiefdoms to states was complete.

An excavated portion of the Kaminaljuyu acropolis. Source: https://commons.wikimedia.org

A good example of this transformation is El Ujuxte, a city that can in a way be considered a successor of La Blanca as the most important urban center of the Pacific Coast region. That power center managed to form a state that covered a 600km^2 (230mi^2) area, with four levels of administrative hierarchy, ranging from a few dozen simple, smaller villages, to secondary city centers that copied the capital. And as the capital, El Ujuxte itself was centrally-organized with large monumental buildings at the city core, which most likely filled ceremonial and religious roles that were also important for the authority of the ruler. That center was surrounded by the residential area, which meant that this city was a busy urban center with a lively economy. The archeologists think that this state, besides controlling trade routes on the coast, which was certainly a huge part of its success, relied on cacao and rubber as main resources that made it wealthy. Of course, the riches that were flowing into the city were mostly going to the ruler and the elite around him, which is evidenced by the numerous grand public works, tombs, and monuments the kings built as signs of their power. Of course, El Ujuxte wasn't a lone example for this, there were many states and cities on the Pacific Coast that went through similar growth and advance in the last centuries before the common era.

The northern Maya of the Lowlands also followed similar development, which is probably most evident at the El Mirador archeological site. The city of El Mirador was slightly smaller than El Ujuxte, but its true power is clearly shown through the scale of its monumental buildings. La Danta pyramid temple, which was part of this urban center, wasn't only the biggest pyramid in the history of the entire Maya civilization, but it also holds the title of the biggest known pyramid in all of Mesoamerica. Furthermore, being 72m (236ft) high with an estimated volume of 2,800,000 cubic meters, it is one of the biggest pyramids in the whole world. And, even though the majestic temple remains impressive for its time as well as our own, it is worth noting that much more labor in the form of construction and maintenance went to the network of roads and causeways that connected El Mirador with its subordinate centers. Those pathways made trade much easier and allowed the rulers of this state to control it better. Similarly to El Ujuxte, that control was the backbone of El Mirador's power and wealth. But unfortunately, even though there are clear signs that some of the surrounding towns and villages were under control of El Mirador, archeologists cannot be exactly sure how far and wide its political dominance reached. What is certain is that the authority of the El Mirador kings was enormous, especially for that time, commanding thousands of laborers and ruling over a population that measured in tens of thousands. Without a doubt, they ruled over the most powerful state in the Lowlands.

The kings of Kaminaljuyu were in a rather similar position to their peers of El Mirador and El Ujuxte, ruling over a state that was the most powerful in the Highland region. Exact hierarchy and reach of its direct rule are today uncertain, due to the fact that the present-day Guatemala City lies on a large portion of that ancient metropolis. Yet, with signs of control over important obsidian quarries located about 19km (11mi) northeast of Kaminaljuyu, it can be seen clearly that its political dominance covered a rather large area. But, the control of those quarries also reveals that this city was an important producing center of cutting tools, which were exported to other areas of the Maya homeland. Besides its own exports, the economy of the Kaminaljuyu was also dependent on the trade connection between the Lowlands and the Pacific Coast which went over its territory. With the rising economy, the rulers of that city were able to expand earlier irrigation systems with two new large canals, which was important for advancing the agriculture in the area not so well suited for it. That kind of public projects also clearly shows that the Kaminaljuyu kings also excreted rather strong authority over their subordinates, as manpower needed to build and later maintain that irrigation systems, as well as other monumental building, was equal to manpower used by El Mirador rulers needed for their public works. Beside that indirect evidence of their power and wealth, numerous monuments and richly filled tombs also stand as testimony to that.

But those monuments tell more than just how mighty various rulers and kings were. They also give a glimpse of how with the development of states the Maya society also became more complex. Looking at those monuments, as well as other pieces of art, it is clear there were more specialized artisans, who focused more on honing their skills to new levels. That kind of horizontal stratification of the society is the result of a more diverse division of labor and developed economy. One of the products of that the evolved Maya society was cultural and civilizational development, which led to some significant innovations. The most influential and most important of those were certainly the development of writing systems and now so-called Mayan calendar. Though it is true both of those innovations were actually adopted from other Mesoamerican civilizations, with them the Maya developed all the hallmarks of what we today consider to be their classical civilization. Some historians even consider this period, around 1st century B.C.E. and 1st century C.E. should be seen more as an early Classic period rather than late Preclassic, but the old division remains. But no matter how scientists label this period, it is clear that the Maya society achieved rather high levels of sophistication.

Unfortunately, that sophistication doesn't mean the Maya were peaceful, neither among themselves nor towards their neighbors. This is clearly evident from scenes of conquests and victories of the Maya kings and warriors, which were a common topic of carvings on monuments, as well as some other types of arts. Human sacrifices and trophy heads show not only the militant side of the Maya society, but also that prowess in war was important for cementing authority of the Maya kings. And if all that seems like circumstantial evidence, the fact that some of those rulers built fortified ditches and walls around their cities undoubtedly confirms that war was an important part of Maya society. And it seems none were safe from the dangers of war, no matter how strong and big their states were, as even El Mirador, one of the most powerful cities at the time, was fortified. Archeologists have also found signs of struggle on some sites, which have signs of deliberate destruction, showing that warfare didn't consist only consist of simple plundering raids, but was actually aimed at destroying the enemy at times. But wars didn't only affect the two, or more, sides that were involved directly in fighting. Some cities suffered greatly when clashes for power disrupted important trade, which obviously was an important part of the Maya economy.

Some historians even argue that it was war that was the root cause of the decline of the early Maya civilization that began around 150 C.E. They think that competition for power and control of trade actually disrupted it so much that many cities were abandoned and destroyed, leading to a so-called cultural hiatus that approximately lasted from 150 to 250 C.E. But although war clearly played an important part in demise of the preclassic Maya, it is more likely that this was brought about by a set of interconnected circumstances. For one, there is evidence of droughts in nearly the entire Maya homeland. It is thought that the humans themselves played a crucial part in causing that with overpopulation, deforestation, and the overuse of fertile soil. This led to drying out of lakes around Kaminaljuyu, while El Mirador surroundings turned into a swampy area. And as if that wasn't enough, Ilopango volcano in El Salvador erupted on the edges of the southern region around 200 C.E. Many sites on the southeast were abandoned; ones which were important producers of obsidian tools, vital for the Maya economy, and which cut off the trade routes to Pacific Coast cities and the rest of Central America. And volcanic ash that spread around the region made farming much more difficult, clogging the rivers and changing their courses.

Those natural disasters more largely affected the Pacific Coast region, which led to the fact that it lost its place as the most developed region of the Maya civilization, ceding that role to the Lowlands. Disruption of trade in the south yielded new possibilities for the northern Maya, which they took. Yet these weren't enough to save all of them, and El Mirador fell since the swampland wasn't fertile enough to maintain its large population. Kaminaljuyu was of a mixed fortune. The city survived, although it seems that a new group of the western Mesoamericans took control of it, which is another sign of an upsurge in wars at the period. The natural disasters led to dwindling resources, which prompted much fiercer competition for them, leading to an escalation of war between the Maya states. All these factors combined led not only to cultural hiatus and power shift from south to north but to a major depopulation of the entire Maya region as well, leading to further weakening of the Maya civilization. But no matter how disastrously the Preclassic period of the Maya history ended, it was an important period that established the basics of their civilization, which remained in place until the final demise of the Maya during the Spanish conquest.

Chapter 3 – The Golden age

So-called hiatus of the Maya civilization that occurred in the late Preclassic era, no matter how apocalyptical the accounts of it sound, didn't actually mean the end of the Maya story. That period was more of a pause in development and blossoming of the Maya. The biggest consequence was that the Pacific Coast region lost its place as the most advanced region, leaving that title to the southern Lowlands. That area became the heart of the Classic period, marking the apex of the Maya civilization. Many changes occurred, mostly building on the foundations laid in previous centuries. Rulers weren't only seen as connected to the gods through ceremonies and rituals, but were venerated themselves. And Classic-era rulers were now depicted usually wearing warrior outfits, symbolizing their evolution to warrior-kings. Writing spread, but remained focused on religious and state affairs, while the temples were still the center of public life. Maya art became more colorful and detailed, reaching new levels of finesse. This golden age allowed also the Maya population to rise substantially, yet the political landscape never allowed them to unify into a single empire. This left the civilization split into many states which managed to outshine and dwarf the states of the early Maya civilization.

As almost all aspects of the Maya classic era had their roots in the previous age, so did most cities and states. Tikal, a major power of the middle Maya civilization situated in northern Guatemala, was no exception. It was one of the cities that managed to benefit from the fall of El Mirador which dominated part of the Maya homeland, leading to Tikal becoming an important trading hub that connected east and west Mesoamerica. The political power of this state was apparent, as it managed to take control of surrounding cities, and install allied dynasties in cities that were further away, in present-day Yucatan or Honduras. The city of Tikal itself grew to levels unimaginable to the Maya of the Preclassic era. It covered an area of 60km^2 (23mi^2), but even more impressive is the fact that the city fortifications defended an area of 123km² (48mi²). The population of this huge city is estimated to have been between 60 and 100 thousand people, which is another sign of its power and wealth. By 300 C.E., Tikal grew so powerful that it established not only trade, but diplomatic connections to Central Mexico, making it the mightiest state of the early classic age.

Of course, the Tikal kings, as all previous Maya rulers, wanted to mark their success and power. They did that on monuments, or to be more precise, on stelae. They carved important dates and names on them in celebration of themselves, subsequently leaving behind some of the most important sources historians today have about the era. On one of them, a founding ruler of this city is marked as Yax Ehb Xook, who ruled around the 1st century C.E. Historians are certain he wasn't the first ruler, since the city was founded way before that, so they assume he garnered the title of "founder" for helping to achieve political independence. These monuments demonstrate how Tikal ended the independence of the cities around it, since in conquered cities, there are no traces of stelae dedicated to local rulers. One of the most interesting stories that we can see from these monuments is a dynastic change in Tikal. In 378 C.E. a king named Chak Tok Ich'aak I (Jaguar Paw) died when Siyaj K'ak' (Smoking Frog) arrived in the city. If at first, that seems like a coincidence, the fact that next king, Yax Nuun Ayiin (Curl Nose), was crowned a year later by Siyaj K'ak' clearly shows it wasn't. That takeover wasn't peaceful, as most of the stelae built before 378 were defaced and vandalized. Also, it appears that Yax Nuun Ayiin didn't claim the throne by any signs of legitimacy, as records show he claimed to be a son of a ruler of an unspecified kingdom.

Central Plaza and the temple in Tikal. Source: https://commons.wikimedia.org

Although the exact origin of Curl Nose isn't stated on the monuments, historians narrowed it down to the one, almost certain candidate – the city of Teotihuacan, in Central Mexico, later Aztec region. Evidence for that lies that sources indicate that Smoking Frog and his army came from that direction, but also because Yax Nuun Ayiin is shown adorned as a Teotihuacano. Of course, that proof isn't completely conclusive, but the fact that Teotihuacan was one of the largest and most powerful cities in all of Mesoamerica, dominating from 1st to 6th century C.E., also supports that theory. The might and reach of the city were so big that some historians even argued its rise was one of the disruptive factors in Maya trade that caused the Maya hiatus. But it is important to note that around 400 C.E., the Central American "superpower" Teotihuacan also installed its vassal allies in Kaminaljuyu, which, combined with control of Tikal, meant that Teotihuacan obtained more direct access to prestige resources like jade, obsidian, jaguar pelts, and tropical bird feathers. This interaction between two regions also influenced the Maya culture as well, influencing their art style, architecture, and other aspects of their civilization. Teotihuacano conquerors also brought their more advanced and lethal weapons, which were quickly adopted by the Maya, while this foreign influence also helped the rise of warrior-king symbolism and its cult, which was already established in the Central Mexican region.

The influence of Teotihuacan wasn't limited just to culture; it impacted the economy and politics as well. Being an ally of the most powerful state in the region, and part of its extensive ally network was certainly beneficial to Tikal. Access to much greater resources through Teotihuacan's trade network made Tikal far richer than before, making its economy the strongest in the early Classic period of the Maya civilization. At the same time, an alliance with the Mesoamerican powerhouse raised the political influence of Tikal, making it the mightiest state of the period in the Lowlands, and subsequently the entire Maya homeland. A strong economy coupled with political might, of course, led to military expansion. Some cities, like nearby Uaxactun, Tikal incorporated directly in its kingdom through direct control. Ones that were further away like Copan, located in present-day western Honduras, had their dynasties overthrown and substituted by rulers loyal to Tikal. So, suffering a fate similar to Tikal, those states were also put in a sort of vassal position to their power center. But, by achieving such dominance, Tikal made a lot of enemies, who were likely opposed to both its economic and political supremacy, as well to the foreign factor in their rule and culture. That is why slowly an anti-Tikal alliance, led by the city of Calakmul, was being formed.

Calakmul was a city located in present-day southeastern Mexico, near the border with Guatemala, 38km (24 mi) north of El Mirador. And similarly to Tikal, it controlled part of the trade routes that went through the Lowlands. At its height, the city had an estimated population of 50 to 100 thousand people, living in a 20km^2 (8mi^2) area surrounded by a network of canals and reservoirs which, to a certain extent, served as fortified protection from outside attack. The early history of Calakmul is not known, but some evidence has its origins in the late Preclassic period and connects its first dynastic ruler with El Mirador. But by 500 C.E., it became powerful enough to challenge Tikal's supremacy, and Calakmul rulers started building alliances with states that surrounded their enemy. The biggest diplomatic success was turning Caracol, formerly Tikal's ally, to their side during mid-6th century. This city was founded in the late Preclassic or early Classic period in what is today western Belize. In that earliest period, there are signs of central Mexican influence, making it a part of Teotihuacan's trade network. At the time of confrontation with Tikal, it was a rising city, which at the height of its power had about 100 to 120 thousand people covering over 100km² (38mi²).

The confrontation between Calakmul and Tikal started in the 530s when Tikal's allies managed to defeat Calakmul. But that defeat wasn't total as, by the end of the decade, Calakmul recovered. The major turning point came in 553 C.E. when Lord Water from Caracol switched sides and allied with Calakmul. Though Tikal, under Wak Chan K'awiil, managed to achieve the first victory in 556 C.E., it wasn't enough to end the war. When Sky Witness was crowned as the king of Calakmul around 561, fortunes changed. Historians think that he orchestrated the defeat of Tikal in 562 C.E. by the hands of Lord Water, who in his raid on the enemy also managed to capture Wak Chan K'awiil. The Tikal ruler was sacrificed, but the war lasted with lessened intensity for about another decade, concluding with a complete loss of Tikal. There are many reasons why this powerful state wasn't able to come out of this war was as a victor. For one, during this period Teotihuacan started to decline, partially because of the draughts, but there are signs of a military defeat there as well. Secondly, during its supremacy, Tikal acted in such a way that it alienated most of the other Maya states, so it couldn't count on wide support from its neighbors. And finally, it seems Calakmul was able to impact its trade, weakening its material power so vital in waging war.

In the end, for Tikal, the loss didn't mean just loss of wealth and power. It marked the end of its independence for roughly 130 years. Its rulers were subjugated to the kings of Calakmul, who didn't allow them to build any monuments and stelae. Most of the city's financial gain went to their new master as a tribute and, as a result, the population growth in Tikal stopped. That period of suppression of this former major Maya power is now called Tikal's hiatus, during which there weren't any advances in the city. Of course, this wasn't limited only to Tikal. For example, in Uaxactun, which was under Tikal's control, building completely stopped during this period, and the hiatus spread over many cities that were subjugated by Tikal. Logically the biggest winner of this war was Calakmul, which gained a lot of political power, expanded its area of control, and, without Tikal as trade competition, prospered. Caracol was also boosted by the defeat of its former ally, experiencing tremendous growth in population and size, as well as in economy. But unfortunately for the Maya, this war didn't bring permanent peace to the region.

With Tikal gone from the political scene of the Maya civilization, a great vacuum in power was left which Calakmul wasn't able to fill on its own. Its rulers managed to exploit the victory, and the city gained a lot, but they didn't manage to convert their military alliance in more permanent political domination over other Maya states. Their allies decided to resist Calakmul's authority and maintain their independence. And many cities, including Calakmul's allies, grew during the power vacuum. This led to more Maya states being able to compete against each other in competition for political influence and control of trade. That kind of political landscape brought a long period of wars and fighting among the Maya, which marks the transition from the early Classic to the late Classic period of this civilization. And even though escalation of warfare marked this era, Maya civilization actually prospered. This was a period of cultural growth, with advances in astronomical knowledge and the calendar, art sophistication, and even wider use of texts displaying new levels of scribe skills. The constant war didn't dampen the tremendous growth in the Maya population, which peaked at about 10 million. But, the elite class did use the continuous struggle to expand their power and control over the commoners, while at the same time extending sizes of their states to new levels. And as Teotihuacan fell, the Maya became the most developed civilization of Mesoamerica, spreading its art style and influence across the region.

At the beginning of the late Classic period, in the late 6th and early 7th century, Calakmul and Caracol continued to expand their power, attacking other states, conquering them, or creating vassal states from them. It seemed their supremacy was unquestioned. But almost constant wars took their toll, and their power was no longer unquestionable. As they weakened, kings of Tikal managed to regain part of its vitality. During the 640s C.E., A side branch of Tikal's royal family settled a new city, Dos Pilas, to serve as both a military and trade outpost. It was located 105km (65mi) to the southwest, in the region of Petexbatún Lake. As expected, Calakmul wasn't going to allow this without a fight, and in 659 they attacked Dos Pilas, defeating it most likely without much trouble. The ruler of that city, B'alaj Chan K'awiil, managed to escape execution and became a vassal of Yuknoom the Great, the Calakmul king. Yuknoom, in a rather smart political move, turned his new vassal against its former allies, putting two branches of Tikal royal dynasty into direct conflict. But even though Dos Pilas had a powerful ally, in 672 C.E., Tikal managed to take back the control of its former colony. Calakmul intervened five years later to reinstate B'alaj Chan K'awiil on the throne, driving away the occupying forces. And, as it was obvious to Yuknoom the Great that his ally and vassal wasn't able to fight Tikal on his own, in 679 C.E., he helped him to achieve a decisive victory over his own family. Although texts at Dos Pilas talk about piles of heads and pools of blood, this confrontation between old enemies showed that even though Calakmul was still the most powerful Maya state, it wasn't untouchable.

Another shock to the supremacy of Calakmul was when in the 680's two of its allies, Caracol and Naranjo, started a war between them. Naranjo was a city, also located in northern Guatemala, which suffered a lot from the clashes for supremacy between other larger states. In the beginning, it was an ally of Tikal, then it was taken by Calakmul, and in the early 7th century it switched hands from Caracol and Calakmul. Yet Naranjo somehow managed to gain independence in 680 C.E., and then used the opportunity to settle the ongoing feud it had with Caracol. Yuknoom the Great decided to support Caracol, probably since it was an older ally, and managed to crush Naranjo's resistance. It would be expected of him to incorporate Naranjo back under his direct control, so he married the daughter of the Dos Pilas ruler to a Naranjo noble to restore dynasty in that city. Historians aren't in agreement as to why he did that, but the move actually managed to strengthen Naranjo, and during next couple of years it raided and attacked Caracol's territory. Calakmul's ability to control its allies and vassals was clearly fading, which was only worsened by the death of its eminent and successful king, Yuknoom the Great, in 686. C.E.

Tikal's new king Jasaw Chan K'awiil, who was crowned in 682 C.E., decided to exploit Calakmul's weakness. First, he strengthened his position in his own city, building new temples and stelae, erecting the first monument with the name of the ruler after Tikal's major defeat 6th century. It was him who brought Tikal out of so-called hiatus. With the restored prestige of his dynasty, in 695 C.E., he first attacked Naranjo, and later that same year he fought against Calakmul directly. In both battles he won, managing to capture a lot of prisoners who were later sacrificed. Historians aren't certain what happened the Calakmul's king, as there are some vague and unclear references to him being among the captured, but even if he managed to escape death at the hands of Jasaw Chan K'awiil, he soon vanished from the political stage. On the other hand, Tikal's king ruled for roughly another 40 years, completely renewing the power and status of his state. He managed to retake supremacy over the Maya states from Calakmul, but the rivalry between these two Maya "superpowers" continued for well over 100 years, through the late Classical period.

Even though Calakmul suffered a major defeat, Dos Pilas remained its ally. But it was no longer a subjugated vassal, as its growth in strength secured its independence. Heirs of B'alaj Chan K'awiil, who died soon after Yuknoom the Great, continued to spread their influence and territories through war and marriage. They managed to create what historians today call the Petexbatún Kingdom. In 735 C.E., Dos Pilas rulers managed to conquer Seibal, the largest city in their region, and by 741, the Petexbatún Kingdom had an area of 4000km^2 (1544 mi^2) under its control. With that expansion Dos Pilas also gained control of trade routes that went into the highlands, giving them a significant economic boost. From that quick success, it was likely that this kingdom would grow enough to compete for supremacy with Tikal and Calakmul, but its fortunes quickly changed. The city was attacked by their local enemies, who were fueled with revenge. Rulers of the Petexbatún Kingdom tried to defend their capital by quickly fortifying it, sacrificing their palaces and monuments to build walls, but it was futile, and in 761 C.E., Dos Pilas was ransacked. Petexbatún managed to survive, switching to another capital, and the war raged on with such ferocity that by 800's much of the region was abandoned, as people moved to safer places. By then. through constant warfare and destruction, Petexbatún Kingdom was dissolved.

One of the factors that contributed to the fall of Petexbatún is the fact that during 740s its mighty ally Calakmul suffered yet another defeat by Tikal. The cause for another clash was Calakmul's incentive to the city of Quiriguá to rebel against Copan, an old Tikal's ally. The city of Copan during the 7th century C.E. managed to expand its prestige and power, covering a sizable area in what is today western Honduras. At the height of its power in the early 8th century, one of Copan's kings even proclaimed it was politically equal to both Tikal and Calakmul, as well as Palenque, a city which we'll talk more about later in the chapter. Under control of that mighty Copan state was a much smaller city of Quiriguá, located about 50km (31mi) to the north of the capital. It was an important outpost for Copan as it allowed it to control jade trade as well as fertile valley around it. In 736 C.E. Calakmul's ruler met with his peer in Quiriguá, most likely giving him his support to rebel against Copan, which happened two years later. With new power behind it, Quiriguá managed to win its independence from its former masters and became an independent state, now connected to Calakmul. Copan lost economically important territory, and although it was never subdued by Quiriguá, it started to lose its prestige and might. On the other hand, Quiriguá managed to expand its power and wealth, becoming to some extent more powerful than its southern foe. That kind of meddling in its ally's affairs wasn't something Tikal could allow to go unpunished. So, in retaliation, Tikal attacked and conquered El Perú-Waka in 743 and Naranjo 744 C.E., these settlements being Calakmul's important allies and trade partners. That loss weakened Calakmul even further, and it never managed to regain its former glory. In contrast, Tikal once again gained complete control of east-west trade through the Lowlands, becoming yet again the unquestionable, number-one power of the Maya world.

Putting aside for a moment the struggle between Tikal and Calakmul, which seems to be the central political and economic problem of the late Classic era of the Maya civilization, there is another major city deserving of mention. That is Palenque, located in the western lowlands, the present-day southeastern Mexican state of Chiapas. Being on the edge of the Maya region, surrounded mostly by non-Maya tribes, Palenque managed for most of its history to remain uninvolved in the fight between the two Maya "superpowers." It was founded in the mid-5th century C.E., along a trade route that connected central Mexico and the Maya homeland. As such it was most likely part of Teotihuacan's trade network and at some point, an ally of Tikal. That is the only reason why Calakmul would have attacked a city that is 227km (150mi) away two times. Those demonstrations of Calakmul's power happened in 599 and 611 C.E., during Tikal's hiatus, and were the only extent of Palenque's direct involvement in the Tikal-Calakmul fight. Later, during the 7th century, Palenque flourished and managed to become a respectable and mighty state in the west, attacking and conquering a lot of its neighbors. But at the beginning of the next century its power started to waver, and in 711 and 764 C.E., it suffered two major defeats from an enemy state in their region.

It is clear that Palenque didn't play such a significant role in Maya politics, as it was on the margins of their world, but it is important for the historians. The reason for that is the culture and art that its citizens left behind. Palenque boasted some of the finest architectural work in the middle Maya civilization with elegant temples and, for that time, inventive vaulting techniques. Their artisans were masters of portraiture in stucco and Palenque kings left lengthy texts about their rule. And in those inscriptions, they don't write only about dynastic successions and wars, but also about their mythology. Because of that, they contain most vivid examples of how the Maya kings used legends, history, and religious beliefs to support their status and power. So even though the city of Palenque was smaller, politically weaker and less significant, it was culturally at least equal, if not superior, to both Calakmul and Tikal.

The Palace at Palenque with the aqueduct on the right. Source: https://commons.wikimedia.org

That, of course, doesn't mean that other Maya cities and states were culturally undeveloped. The period between roughly 600 and 800 C.E., was the Maya golden age that gave rise to many technological achievements and artistic accomplishments; many great cities were built, and the population blossomed. And those achievements are evident in all Maya states, especially the wealthiest ones. Yet as the 9th century came to a close, the major polities started to collapse. As we have seen from examples of Palenque and Copan, their previous vassals rebelled against them, challenging their supremacy. The same happened to Tikal and Calakmul as well, and large kingdoms of the Classic Maya started to fragment into smaller polities. It was the first signs that glory days of the Maya were passing. One reason for the decline was that central dynasties were getting weaker, while the local elites were getting stronger, which could have been caused by almost constant wars that lasted for two centuries. The warfare certainly exhausted the wealth and might of the dynasties, making them more and more dependent on their subordinate elites, while the elites themselves at times gained a lot through fighting.

But the fall of the Classic Maya states didn't end with just loss of their territories and former vassals. By the mid-10th century, most of them had collapsed completely, being no longer centers of power. Some of the cities were totally abandoned, while others regressed into small villages with only a small agricultural population. Historians were for a long time uncertain how and why the Classic Maya civilization collapsed, arguing that it could have been brought about by droughts, overpopulation, wars, and uprisings or foreign invasions. Today it seems that the cause was actually all of those together. Political turmoil and fighting undermined trade and dynasties lost their power, while overpopulation of the central region combined with droughts, and overuse of soil led to food shortages. And one by one, southern Lowland cities were abandoned. As mentioned before, the Petexbatún region was abandoned by the 800s, and in other cities, the last inscribed monument is taken as the circa time they fell, since it is a clear sign of their loss of power and wealth. Those monuments are dated to 799 in Palenque, 810 in Calakmul, 820 in Naranjo and in Copan, 822 C.E. Caracol and Tikal lasted a bit longer, as their last monuments are dated to 849 and 869 C.E., respectively. With their fall, the golden age and so-called Late Classic Maya period ended.

Chapter 4 – From the golden age to the age of disaster

The fall of the southern Lowland cities, which were the most advanced in the Maya homeland, would have seemed to indicate that their civilization was also disappearing. Yet that was not the case. Their collapse only meant that the centers of power shifted to northern Lowlands, or to be more precise, to the Yucatan Peninsula. In that area there were many old Maya cities, some even dating back to the late Preclassic era, which profited from the downfall of the southern Lowland trade centers. These cities quickly seized the chance, becoming an important factor in trade connections between central Mexico and Central America. As those cities continued the traditions of the Classical Maya civilization, which clearly was in decline, historians refer to this new period as the Terminal Classic era. Another reason for that name is that during this period, the classical culture of the Maya civilization went through a change, and by the mid-10th century it had evolved into a new, more pan-Mesoamerican culture. The best example of the entire era and the changes that occurred during it is no other than probably the most famous Maya city today, Chichén Itzá.

The city of Chichén Itzá was located in the arid north of the Yucatan Peninsula, near two large limestone sinkholes or cenotes, explaining the translation of its name "the wells of the Itza." Its rise to prominence started during the Late Classic period thanks to trade, as the area wasn't as fertile as the southern Lowlands. Chichén Itzá, like many other Yucatan Maya states, used the maritime type of trade that went around the peninsula as the base of its economy. Of course, that maritime trade existed for a long time before the Terminal Classic period, but with political turmoil and disappearing trade routes in the southern Lowlands, it gained in importance. Another important factor that helped the expanse of this type of trade was a rise of new powers in Central Mexico that had arisen after the fall of Teotihuacan. By the Terminal period, this route connected the Gulf Coast of Mexico, which offered volcanic ash, obsidian, and jade, to Costa Rica and

Panama which were rich with copper, silver, and gold. In between, the northern Maya offered fish, cotton, hemp rope, and honey. But the most important commodity of the Yucatan was high-quality salt, which coincidentally was the main resource traded by Chichén Itzá. This city annually exported 3,000 to 5,000 metric tons of it. But what is more impressive is the fact that Chichén Itzá is far away from the coast. To participate in trade the rulers of this city built and fortified a harbor that is located 120km (74mi) from their capital. And to protect the transportation of goods, they established secondary centers every 20km (12mi) along the route that connected Chichén Itzá to its port.

That ambitious project allowed this city to connect with many non-Maya cities through its trading alliances. Beside material gains, this allowed Chichén Itzá to culturally interact with other Mesoamerican civilizations. From that connection, the northern Maya incorporated some aspects of pan-Mesoamerican symbolism and motifs into their art. They combined it with artistic traditions, architecture, and rituals of the Classical period, which they also exported to other parts of Mesoamerica, mainly to their most important trade partners in central Mexico. From that mixture, a pan-Mesoamerican style evolved that was equally "global" as it was Maya. This cosmopolitan nature of Chichén Itzá certainly made trade and understanding with the foreigners easier, explaining how a city with a population of "only" 50 thousand managed to become a center of a trade network that covered almost entire Mesoamerica. But the change in art styles wasn't the most important change in Maya civilization at the time. The biggest shift was in the ruler's cult, which started to lose its strength. Slowly the scenes on the monuments started to depict groups of people in rituals and processions, instead of the portrayal of a single ruler that was common in the Classical era. New administrative buildings erected in this era could accommodate large groups of people, while the ball game courts became more important, also symbolizing the move to a more pluralistic society. With the culmination of those changes, around 950 C.E., came the end of the Terminal Classical period, and Middle Maya civilization, giving rise to the Postclassic era.

Temple of the Warriors at Chichén Itzá. Source: https://commons.wikimedia.org

Even though the ruler cult was getting weaker, and the economy and trade was the base of Chichén Itzá's power, the state also expanded through war and conquest of its weaker neighbors. Yet unlike the Classic period, those victories were secured by the new flexible political system that arose in the Postclassic era. Evident from the construction of council houses, called Popol Nah in Mayan, used for both commercial and political activities the ruling over the Chichén Itzá state was not solely in hands of the king. It is more likely he shared it with the council of the elite lords, both from the capital and to a certain extent other localities. And it seems that as time passed council's influence grew as the ruler's faded. Though it may seem counterintuitive that the decentralization of power would help the stability of the state, it actually was crucial. First of all, the new system disassociated the rulers of Chichén Itzá with the failed dynasties of the Classical era. Secondly, it lessened the political turmoil that usually came with changes on the throne, while at the same time lessened dependency of the state on the individual capabilities of the king. As the ruler shared the responsibility of decision making with the lords, their collective abilities could "fill in the gaps" that their leader may have. Finally, many of the lords and their families that came from the conquered cities, besides being political advisors, were effectively hostages, preventing their hometowns from revolting too often.

But the stability of the new system of rule wasn't enough to ensure Chichén Itzá's survival for long in the Postclassic era. In the mid-11th century C.E., power and influence of this state started to decline, and around 1100 C.E., it suffered destruction caused by war marking an end of the

Chichén Itzá. The site wasn't completely abandoned, but any kind of political strength was gone. Historians today aren't exactly sure what caused the decline and fall of Chichén Itzá, as the evidence is scant. The military loss was only a part of it, as it was probably caused by an already weakened economy and lessened might of this city. Currently, the most likely theory is that the downfall was triggered by similar causes that led to the fall of Late Classic states, droughts, and the disruption of trade. And like before, it wasn't limited to just one or only a few of the cities, but it was an issue that impacted the entire Maya world as well as other parts of Mesoamerica. The disruption caused by these factors, unlike before, left the Maya civilization without a dominant power for about a century, indicating that the issues were too severe for the Maya to overcome as easily as when they were just exiting their golden age. By the time the new crisis hit the Maya, their might and wealth were considerably lower than in the Late Classic era. Yet this doesn't mean the Maya civilization completely collapsed: it was yet another hiatus.

When the hiatus ended around 1200 C.E., the Maya entered the Late Postclassic era that marked a complete shift from the hallmarks of the Middle Maya civilization. The most notable change was further development of Chichén Itzá's rule system that became known as "multepal;" roughly translated from Yucatec Mayan it means "joint rule." This type of government relied on various elites that weren't part of the royal family to fulfill more active and acknowledged roles in the state, while the ruler cult tradition was almost lost. That change was followed by decentralization of the state seen in the lack of large urban centers. Cities were considerably smaller but much better fortified. And in that period, they were usually built on hilltops instead of the valleys. Another change in society was that the Maya became more oriented towards entrepreneurship and profit instead of displays of royal power. Wealth was now much less invested in major public projects, and it seems that almost all citizens were directly or indirectly involved in the trade. With the much wider spread of profit gained through trade, the social distinction between classes became less prominent.

In the northern Lowlands, on the Yucatan peninsula, the best and probably the only example of this change is the city and state of Mayapan. The city was founded around 1185 C.E., roughly 100km (62mi) west of Chichén Itzá, whose architectural style it tried to mimic, but on a much smaller scale. Covering an area of only about 4.2km^2 (1.6mi^2) and with a population of 15 to 20 thousand, it was considerably smaller than its role model, not to mention that Late Classic centers were 10 to 12 times bigger than it. It clearly shows how drastically the power of the Maya states had decayed. But in contrast to its giant predecessors, Mayapan was much better fortified, with encircling walls and four gateways that were carefully planned to offer best possible protection from enemy attacks. The copying of Chichén Itzá, as well as some other former Maya powers, wasn't only smaller in scale, but buildings were erected with inferior craftsmanship, which also indicated the fall of the Maya civilization, especially considering the fact that the Mayapan was undoubtedly the wealthiest and most powerful city of the Late Postclassic period.

Mayapan's power came from the salt trade, similar to the Chichén Itzá, even though Mayapan was 40km (25mi) away from the coast. Another important resource was the rare clay which when mixed with indigo made the highly desired "Maya blue," which was even exported to the Aztecs in Central Mexico. But the connection with that part of Mesoamerica went beyond just trade. Many lord houses ruled Mayapan in a fully developed multepal system of government in which members of each house took part in both civil and religious offices. One of the houses known as the Cocom originated from Chichén Itzá and used mercenaries from the Aztec region to gain control over the city and the state from the original founder house of Xiu. That shift in the balance of the lord families happened in the last decades of the 13th century C.E. and could explain why later rulers of Mayapan tried to copy the style of Chichén Itzá. The Cocom house didn't stop there and, in a move to secure their supremacy in the state affairs, they expelled large part of the defeated Xiu family around 1400 C.E. That action is what eventually led to the fall of Mayapan state.

The territory of Mayapan was divided into provinces which were organized into a state that was more similar to a confederacy than a true monarchy. Centralization of the Mayapan state was secured with the fact that the leaders of each province actually lived in the capital, making it easier for the rulers to keep a close eye on them, and prevent them from rebelling. But when the Cocom exiled the Xiu instead of weakening them, they just left them largely uncontrolled. Bitter and driven by revenge members of the banished house organized a revolt in 1441 C.E. The city of Mayapan was sacked and destroyed, while almost all members of the Cocom dynasty were brutally killed. Soon afterward the city was abandoned and the last centralized state of the northern Maya had fallen. It territory fragmented into about 16 petty kingdoms, most likely corresponding to some extent to former provinces, ruled by other surviving elite houses. As the rivalry between them continued, they were locked in a cycle of constant infighting. By the mid-15th century C.E. all of the northern Maya economic might and political influence was gone, and the capitals of the petty kingdoms were only a pale comparison even to Mayapan, not to mention the cities of the golden age.

Panoramic view of Myapan. Source: https://commons.wikimedia.org

But unlike during the Classical era when the Lowlands was the only region that was influential, during the Late Postclassic Maya civilization the Highlands managed once again to grow strong enough to compete with their northern brethren. That power came from forming of Quiché (or alternatively known as K'iche) Confederacy, which first became an important factor in late 14th and early 15th century under the rule of king K'ucumatz ("Feathered Serpent") who managed to grasp control of central Guatemalan highlands through series of wars and conquests. His successors continued to expand their kingdom, which spanned from present-day El Salvador to southeastern Mexico, including the Pacific Coast region, which by that time had managed to recover from the volcanic eruption that ended the Preclassic period. It was one of the biggest Maya states in history covering an area of about 67.500km^2 (26.000mi^2) with an estimated population of around one million Maya. That massive kingdom was, like Mayapan, governed by the multepal system, which was one of the reasons why it managed to grow exponentially. But it was probably also the reason why the Quiché state broke up rather quickly, by the end of the 15th-century C.E.

The cause of fragmentation of the Quiché kingdom was a rebellion of one of the elite houses in the state around 1475 C.E. The success of that revolt sparked other allies and lords to rise up as well, and by the beginning of the 16th century, the Highlands were no longer united. By the time the Spaniards came, the Quiché were no longer at their peak, but the Europeans were impressed by the capital of Utatlán. It was a somewhat small urban center located in one of the hilltops of the Guatemalan highlands with a population of about 15 thousand. The heavy fortification of the city, which to a degree resembled the citadels of medieval Europe, was the thing that impressed the Conquistadors the most. From their records, it is clear the Spaniards saw the Quiché capital as a threat because of the fortification, that the only choice they had was to destroy it, which they eventually did. Yet, no matter how impressive the Utatlán stronghold was, for historians today the more important aspect of this settlement was its role in culture and civilization of the Maya, as well as our present understanding of their civilization.

One of the characteristics of the Quiché was that they acted as a cultural center of the Late Postclassic period of the Maya civilization. Their capital, city of Utatlán, was also the main hub for learning, writing religious books, and histories marked with so-called Maya calendar dates. One of those books is the famous Popol Vuh, which is one of the main sources on Maya mythology today. It was written down in the mid-16th century, but it was based on a long oral tradition of the Maya. Unfortunately, other books of the Quiché were mostly destroyed by the Spaniards who saw them as satanic due to the hieroglyphic writing in them. Besides the written records, the cultural strength and development of Utatlán are clearly shown in public works which weren't something that could be commonly seen in the northern Maya cities. The site contains four impressively-decorated temples, a ball court, and even a small pyramid only 18m (60ft) high. One of the more interesting details of these buildings detected by historians today are the clear signs of influence from the Central Mexican art style and the Aztec civilization.

Considering that by the late 15th and early 16th century C.E. the Aztecs were the most powerful and influential nation in Mesoamerica, the Aztec influence on Maya style shouldn't be much of a surprise. Especially considering how weak the Maya civilization had become by that period. Their art style, fashion, and architecture influenced all the Maya, from the Pacific Coast to the Lowlands. They used Aztec style to depict their own traditional Maya themes, while some cities even tried to mimic the architectural features of the Aztec capital. But their influence went even further than that. The Aztec supremacy in both cultural and economic power made Nahuatl, the Aztec language, the lingua franca of the Mesoamerican region. It was surely the main language spoken among the traders and in ports, as witnessed by the Spaniards. But some of the Maya nobles learned Nahuatl, both for prestige but also for use in diplomacy. In certain areas, the Aztec empire wasn't content with simply trading with the locals. For example, in 1500 C.E., they exploited the turmoil in the Quiché kingdom and attacked the cacao-rich western borders. The result of those attacks was the tribute the Quiché started to pay to the mighty Aztec empire. It seems they were also preparing to do something similar on Yucatan as well, but the arrival of Spaniards foiled their plans.

It wasn't long before the Aztecs realized that the Europeans posed a serious threat for entire Mesoamerica, and their famous emperor Montezuma (or Moctezuma) urged the Maya to unite against new conquerors from across the ocean. It seems that the Quiché were ready to follow that advice, but before any definitive steps could be taken the Aztec empire had fallen. With the only political power capable to unite the fragmented Maya states against the Spaniards gone, any chance of united front was gone. The first region that became targeted by Europeans was the Highlands in 1524 C.E. Despite the pleas of the Quiché to other states of the region to unite their forces against the Conquistadors; other Maya states were more interested in defeating traditional enemies that fighting against a new threat. With the help of the local Maya, the Quiché state quickly fell. Soon the other Maya states realized that both the Aztecs and the Quiché were right, Spaniards were the biggest threat to them all. But it was too late and by 1530 C.E., the Highlands and the Pacific Coast were under the Spanish flag.

It is unclear if the Yucatan Maya learned from the mistakes of their Highland brethren, or if it was just common sense, but when the Conquistadors first arrived on their territory in 1527 C.E., they fought more coordinated and united against the invaders, pushing them back despite losing a few battles. The Spaniards came back in 1530, but after initial success, the Maya were again able to organize a unified front against them and in 1535 C.E., Yucatan was once again free of the Europeans. Unfortunately for the Maya, when the Spaniards came back in 1541 C.E., their two biggest royal families, the Xiu and Cocom, were once again at war with each other. Without the ability to act together one more time to thwart yet another invasion of Conquistadors, the Maya were quickly defeated. The last organized attempt of resistance happened in 1546 when the majority of the Yucatan Maya revolted, but in the end, their resistance was futile. The Spaniards almost completely conquered the Maya homeland. Some of the Maya stated to flee from their cities to the more remote areas, creating small enclaves where they continued to live in the traditional way. But even those fell under the colonial rule one by one. With the fall of Tah Itzá (Tayasal), a city located in Northern Guatemala, in 1697 C.E., pre-Columbian Maya civilization was finally brought to an end.

The Spanish conquest of the Maya region was in every way a disastrous event for the Maya. The most tragic outcome of this event was the death of up to 90% of the entire Maya population. This was caused in part by war and enslavement, but most of the Maya fell as victims of diseases brought by Europeans. Historians today see those as one of the major reasons for such an easy defeat of both the Maya and the Aztecs, as illnesses weakened the Mesoamericans. Yet the disaster for the Maya didn't end there. Spanish Catholic missionaries saw the Maya culture and religion as heathen and evil, so they aimed to "save" them by forcing them to convert, burning their books and smashing their monuments. The severe consequences of these actions led to massive cultural dislocation even led to some of the Maya refusing to have children. This brutal, almost apocalyptic end of the Maya civilization caused it to be lost and forgotten for a long time, but in spite of this, the Maya have endured to this day.

Chapter 5 – The Maya government and society

As it was shown in previous chapters, the Maya were never able to unite their entire ethnos into a single unified empire, remaining spread into many larger and smaller states. Yet through ideology and beliefs, religion, and culture, they remained a relatively homogenous group. The closest comparison from the "old world" would be ancient Greeks, who suffered a similar fate. Despite that, the Maya for a long time suffered from closemindedness and prejudice on the part of historians who simply could not believe that "savages," as the Conquistadors saw the Maya, could have created a civilization that could rival, or even be compared to, the "forefathers of the western civilization." For that reason, during much of the 20th-century historians believed that the Maya never even managed to form more complex governments. The dominant theory of that time was that the Maya world remained divided into small chiefdoms, with a simple two-class society. But as the more evidence was gathered, historians realized they were wrong

As the archeologists surveyed more Maya sites they found the public projects, from irrigation canals to grand palaces. Then the more detailed mapping of some larger sites showed the researchers that the site was more densely populated. Finally, when the Maya text was deciphered, showing complex hierarchy between the cities, it became clear beyond a doubt that by the end of the Late Preclassic period the Maya society and politics became so complex that they had developed into preindustrial states. That same evidence also debunked yet another misconception about the Maya sites, which were for a long time seen only as ceremonial and market centers of chiefdoms. Archeologists concluded this as they only understood dates and astronomical information which could be read from the inscriptions, and also because the street grid and population density were not as high as in industrial era cities of Europe. But when they took their focus away from large and mainly intact temples, they found remains of many smaller buildings covered by vegetation. After careful examination, it became clear that more than 80% of those were, in fact, residential buildings. That combined with deciphered texts showing of all the complexity of Maya history made the theory of the ceremonial center discredited. The Maya settlements were in fact cities, in a true sense of the word, with at least 20 of them having a population greater than 50 thousand during the golden age of the Classic era.

But even before the glory days of the late classic period, during the last centuries of the Preclassic era, the Maya managed to evolve from simple chiefdoms into states. The main characteristic of chiefdoms was a simpler division of the population into two classes; elites, and commoners, with a shaman-ruler above all others. Yet as their power expanded, so did the area the chiefdoms ruled, creating a three-tier hierarchy of settlements in those larger polities. With that, the Maya society slowly started to create a new middle class. That combined with the increasing strength of the ruler cult was enough for historians to claim that the Maya polities of the Late Preclassic have evolved into early, archaic states. The rise of the Maya society complexity continued in later periods, reaching its limits in the Late Classic era where states managed to develop a five-tier hierarchy of the settlements. On top was, of course, the capital, followed by secondary centers, then came smaller towns, and final to tiers were villages and hamlets. And some of those smaller sites started to specialize in certain fields like trade, stone quarrying or artisanry. Both of those echoed in the social structure of the Maya society, which by that time had stratified both vertically and horizontally.

Painting of a Maya scribe. Source: https://commons.wikimedia.org

On top of that social structure was undoubtedly the king, but the topic of the ruler cult will come later in this chapter, as it is a complex topic that deserves a lot more than just a few sentences. Below the monarch were the elite, which represented about one-tenth of the entire population. Position in this class was represented by both wealth and lineage, and it wasn't easy for non-nobles to move up the social ladder into this caste. The nobles were sometimes called "itz'at winik," which roughly translates to "wise people," which probably referred to their better education and literacy. Most of this class held important positions in the society as higher priests, overseers of the secondary centers, scribes, and in some cases even artists. Below, the elite was the middle class, which wasn't a tight homogenous group as previously thought. This class had various levels of social importance and wealth. It was constituted of low-level priests and government officials, professional soldiers, merchant, and artisans. But it is rather important to note that the line between these two classes is often blurred. Some of the elites were also merchants and warriors, while in some cases middle-class members managed to become high-level officers. And in some cases, certain members of the middle class were as wealthy as the elite, while there were also examples of impoverished elite members. More than occupation and wealth, the main difference between these classes seems to be family and lineage of the individual, which was important to the Maya.

Below these two subsets were commoners, who unlike two other classes were rarely shown in art and never mentioned in texts. Yet they were the enormous majority which was the base of the entire Maya society. Most of them were farmers, laborers, unskilled craftsmen, and servants. They lived in villages and outskirts of cities, in relative poverty when compared to the higher classes. But when archeologists excavated a village that was covered by a volcanic eruption around 600 C.E., they found out that even the commoners had decent lives. Researchers even noted that living conditions there were even better than those of the 20th-century Salvadoran workers who helped in the excavation of the site. Farmers, which were the backbone of the society, usually worked on their own or their family land, but a number of the landless farmers worked on estates of the nobles, which were inherited with the land. The lowest class of the Maya society were slaves, which actually weren't that numerous. Most of them were commoners captured in war, as the captured nobles were often sacrificed, and the elite used them as a labor force. In some cases, thieves were also enslaved so they could repay what they stole. Interestingly, unlike most other societies in the world, the Maya didn't consider children of the slaves to be slaves as well. Those children were given the chance to live their lives according to their abilities and weren't made to pay the price of their parents "mistakes."

Social structure started to change with the transition from the Late Classic to the Postclassic Maya civilization. With the development of multepal system rulers started to lose power, and nobles were even able in some cases to rival the royal dynasty. The flattening of the vertical social hierarchy went further down, as the goods that were previously available only to the elite class, like shells, obsidian, and ceramics became more widely distributed and attainable even for commoners. Distinction and difference in wealth between these classes were lessened; in some cases, it could be even claimed the middle class had disappeared. This could have happened if the only division between the elite and non-elite was the lineage and knowledge about the religious rituals. But at the same time, it would seem that the horizontal social structure grew. With the rise of multepal system, bureaucratic apparatus grew both in size and complexity, making government officials more numerous than ever before, with more intricate hierarchical ranks. Of course, higher and more important ranks were reserved for members of the elite, and were usually hereditary, while the lower ranks were open to commoners who were appointed only for a period of time.

After it became abundantly clear that the Maya had developed states and that their society was more intricate than was thought before, the next issue of debate between historians was about the nature of those states. One theory is that the Maya polities were, in fact, city-states that only controlled their nearest surrounding areas, up to 20km (12.5 mi) around them. That is based on an approximation of the how far could the Maya travel in one day by foot, limiting the efficient communication, transport, and control of the capital. And according to this theory, no matter how sizeable the capital was, it wouldn't be able to sufficiently rule over area further than that. Contrary to this, there is a theory of the so-called regional state, arguing that the Maya capitals managed to extend their limit of control via secondary centers, which would be close enough to be controlled from the capital. Thus, the secondary centers would in turn extend the reach of the capital by at least another 20km (12.5 mi), or even more if we add to that a secondary center, which would further expand that control to another secondary or tertiary city. This theory fits amazingly well with the distance between secondary centers of Chichén Itzá that guarded the path to its port. Yet when all is considered, both theories aren't exactly in agreement with the current archeological findings.

Furthering the problem is the fact that those two theories are polar opposites. The best illustration of the differences between those two ideas is the issue of Late Classic states, around 790 C.E. 60 sites met the criteria of city-state theory. If the regional states theory is applied, however, there were only eight. The problem is that evidence shows there were significant connections and interaction between the states, supporting the regional state model. But at the same time, warfare, political instability, and clashes between the cities that were supposedly controlled by one of the capitals support the concept of a city-state. So, in an attempt to somehow bridge the gap between two opposing theories, historians created the so-called "superstates" theory. According to this theory, in certain cases, the power of a single Maya state grew so much that it managed to create dominance over a large territory, but instead of ruling it directly, those political formations were more of a vassal confederacy in which smaller autonomous states paid tributes to the capital.

Military conquest or simple threat didn't in all cases force these autonomous vassalages. In some cases, smaller states simply gained prestige by allying to the major power. So, they willingly became part of these superstates. Dynastic marriages and trade networks sometimes reinforced the connections between the states. Of course, in some cases, superpowers conquered weaker states and installed rulers loyal to them. And these confederacy superstates existed as long as the central states were powerful enough to maintain them. At the first sign of weakness, they would start to crumble. But also, as soon as the central states' power was reestablished, the superstate would build up quickly. This theory is still being developed, yet it seems to be the best explanation of the Late Classic politics of Tikal and Calakmul. It can reconcile the fact that influence and control of those Classic Maya superpowers was wide-reaching, while at the same time the Maya homeland seemed to be covered with independent city-states. Another plus for this theory is that it seems to be more of a typical Mesoamerican type of rule since it also resembles the way the Aztec empire functioned. And the only reason why historians haven't yet elevated Calakmul and Tikal to the rank of empires is the fact that their reach never extended outside the Maya region.

Despite the uncertainty about the size and exact nature of the Maya states, historians are sure of one thing. Monarchs ruled the Maya states. That has been the case since the early ages of the Maya civilization when first individual rulers became powerful enough to leave behind monuments and inscriptions. In those early times, those monarchs used the title "ajaw," which we today translate as either king or lord. During the Middle Maya civilization, to emphasize their even greater strength and position in the social hierarchy of the society, Maya rulers started calling themselves "k'uhul ajaw," which is roughly equivalent to as divine or holy lord/king. For some rulers of Tikal that alone wasn't enough, so they also used "kaloomte'", a title that is today translated as supreme king, but this title wasn't as widespread. Interestingly, the rulers who were subjugated to their more powerful neighbors still used the same title, k'uhul ajaw, but they also added they were "yajaw," or vassal lord, of some other king. But no matter what title a ruler used, one thing remained the same through the almost entire history of the Maya civilization. The base of the monarch's control of the subordinated population was rooted in his economic supremacy and religious importance.

Stelae of the 13th Ajaw of the Copán Dynasty. Source: https://commons.wikimedia.org

The religious authority of the Maya rulers has its root in the era of chiefdoms, where chiefs were also shamans, able to communicate with deified ancestors and mediate with the gods. But when the society grew more complex, and the power of the rulers increased, kings started to claim they were direct descendants of the gods, similar to the pharaohs of ancient Egypt. Thus, the rulers' cult was created, in which kings themselves were revered as divine. This was evident from the title of k'uhul ajaw. With religious authority behind them, they became important for carrying out certain religious rituals and ceremonies done for the benefit of the entire state. But theocratic power alone wasn't enough to cement their supremacy in the society. Royal dynasties were also the wealthiest, and their power was based on control of important resources. Sometimes it was water or food, in other cases maybe obsidian or other valuable export goods. Through the control of those resources, rulers gained enough wealth to reward those who were obedient and also to pay for great public works and other exhibitions of power and prosperity. But at the same time, rulers threw state feasts through which they demonstrated their ability to provide for the entire population, not only the Royals. Of course, that kind of spending together with economic supremacy was more easily maintained since almost the entire population, with the possible exception of the highest nobility and members of the royal family, paid tributes to the ruler. Though economic and religious authority created a strong base for absolute rule, it was also a double-edged sword.

If the ruler was capable and had a bit of luck on his side, his authority was unquestionable. But if he lost a battle, if trade routes were cut or even if the harvest wasn't good enough, it was seen as a bad omen. It meant the king had lost the favor of the gods. Both his religious and economic supremacy were shaken. Those kinds of disasters could topple dynasties and crush entire states. When we consider that fact, it becomes clearer why after a single defeat or other sign of weakness many vassals decided to either switch sides or simply declare independence. That is why the Maya often tried to capture and sacrifice the enemy's king. It was the ultimate sign of weakness, which in some cases dealt such a religious and political blow to a state that it could never fully recover. On the other hand, long and successful rules like the one of Yuknoom the Great, meant the king was in the good graces of the gods, attracting more and more allies as time passed. When all that is taken into account, it seems that the authority of the Maya rulers relied only upon individual charisma and capabilities. A ruler had to be a victorious general, successful diplomat, and a fortunate religious leader. But as we have seen, the Maya cared a lot about family and lineage. This was even more important for the ajaws and their dynastic ties.

Dynasties in the Maya world, especially during the Classic period, were extremely important, as they were probably the most important thing that connected the ruler to his divinity. Without a connection to a deified ancestor, kings wouldn't be holy. That is one of the reasons why the Maya kept such close records of their rulers, and always held the founding ruler of the city in special regard. This connection gave legitimacy to the successors. Another dimension to the importance of dynasties in the Maya society comes from their tradition of worshiping their ancestors. And the royal families represented the most powerful and most important ancestors. Going against their heirs might upset the powerful forefathers. Dynastic ties weren't only achievable by birth, however. They were also created through marriage, similar to medieval Europe. A smaller state and dynasty would gain in prestige if a king's bride came from a strong and respected lineage. This helped not only in foreign affairs, but also to strengthen the authority of the ruler in his own state. A good example of that is the already mentioned marriage between a Naranjo noble and Dos Pilas princess. Her bloodline elevated this noble, and their heirs, to a royal family.

Although this shows to a degree how important woman could get into Maya politics, it wasn't their only means of power. The Maya dynasties were patrilineal, but in certain extreme cases when the male line, from father to son, was broken they could become matrilineal as well. That way the state was preserving the royal family and connection to the founding king through the blood of the queen or a princess, which would in that instance become the ruler. So far historians have found only five examples of this, though there could be more. Among the examples we see two different examples of women rulers. One was the example when they briefly ruled as regents to their sons, which was something that was common in dynasties around the world. One of those was the previously mentioned princess that went to Naranjo, Lady Wac-Chanil-Ahau, also known as Lady Six Sky. Although she was probably never crowned, she unquestionably ruled over that city during the end of 7th and at the beginning of the 8th century C.E. Lady Six Sky took on religious roles, got involved in diplomacy, with some monuments even depicting her in warrior-king form, probably due the fact that Naranjo achieved some rather impressive military victors under her rule. But one of the queens, Yohl Ik'nal of Palenque, actually ruled with full titles of the king, as if she was a male heir of the dynasty. Lady Heart of the Wind Place, as she was known, ruled from 583 to 604 C.E. Not much is known about her reign, but she kept the direct blood connection of the future rulers with the founder of the Palenque, as the same royal family stayed in power. This was an important flexibility that provided an extra level of stability on the throne of the Maya states.

Yet no matter how flexible the Maya dynasties were, none of them were really eternal. Some of them died out naturally, other violently. Some were dethroned by outsiders, others by their own nobles. It would then be reasonable to assume with an end of one dynasty, the link with the founding king and the ancestor would be broken, especially if the new monarch came from outside of the community, placed on the throne by a king of another state. But that wasn't the case. All rulers of a single city claimed they were continuing the line from the scared founder. That kind of regal continuum is clearly marked by the fact that the Maya numbered their rulers, starting from the founder. A great example of this is the takeover of Tikal in 378 C.E. When Yax Nuun Ayiin was crowned as a king, he was marked as the fifteenth successor to Yax Ehb Xook, the founder of the city. And he wasn't even trying to present himself as a legitimate pretender for the throne. In that way, the title of k'uhul ajaw could on its own give authority and power to the bearer and his successors, as its connection to the founding father was more symbolic than realistic.

What was certainly real was the power of the king, which at the height of the rulers' cult, was unquestionable. But even the mightiest and most capable monarch couldn't rule the whole state on his own, especially ones as big as Tikal and Calakmul. That is why it comes as no surprise that nobles served the ruler in his higher-ranking administrative offices. Even the title, "sajal," that was awarded to king's official hints at it, as the literal translation is "noble." There was also a position of "baah sajal," or head noble, which probably was in charge of several sajals, reporting directly to the king himself. Of course, there were more titles reserved for the elite, like "ah tz'ihb" or royal scribe. And exact roles in a court of some titles, like "yajaw k'ahk'", or lord of fire, still remain a mystery for the historians. Nonetheless, it clearly shows that the Maya rulers had to rely on the help of their elite to effectively rule their growing states. At the same time, it was another way of binding the nobles to their rule, as those titles were also given to governors of secondary and tertiary sites.

This kind of "buying" and confirming the loyalty of the elite worked as long as the kings were successful. But this political maneuver backfired for the later rulers in the Terminal Classic and Postclassic era, when the royal cult started to die off. Powers given to the nobles became too much to control, and the elite were unhappy with the end result of the monarchs' rule. They eventually started to limit the authority of their rulers. An example of this is seen through the creation of the council house, the Popol Nah. No longer could the Maya kings rule absolutely; they had the noble council to answer to. At the same time, nobles were able to advise their ruler more and steer the state politics more to their liking. An example of this council type of monarchy is seen in 9th century Copan, where archeologists found a Popol Nah decorated with glyphs representing various noble lineages, proving that this building wasn't created solely for the ruler and the royal family. Today historians assume that during the Terminal Classic period there was tension between the royal and noble families, if not more open struggle for powers. But the lack of evidence prevents them from creating a more accurate picture of that.

What is certainly clearer is the fact that, as the ruler cult was more frequently abandoned in the Late Postclassic era, the council system evolved into the multepal system. In theory, it was a system of joint rule by several noble houses, which didn't necessarily need to originate from the state capital. But this oligarchy system actually rarely worked as intended. The flaws are best seen in the example of Mayapan. This state was certainly formed with the multepal system, in which several noble houses ruled together, sharing government offices among them. But after a short time, it became clear that one house, the Cocom, had become stronger than others, since its leader assumed the role of the king. He even kept representatives of other noble families as hostages in the capital. Although his rule wasn't as absolute as the rule of Late Classic kings, it wasn't a true multepal anymore. But the Maya didn't completely abandon the idea of the joint rule. After the Mayapan state collapsed, many smaller states were created. Most of them were ruled by kings, now holding the title of "halach uinic," meaning real/true man, supported by influential councils. The title itself is one more proof of the failing rulers' cult. But more fascinating are several smaller states whose texts don't mention halach uinic at all, only councils. These seem to be an example of a real and functional multepal system. Sadly, any further development of this system and the idea of the shared rule in the Maya civilization was abruptly halted by the conquest of the Spaniards.

So far, the topic of the governmental rule was only examined looking at the highest levels of the state, rulers and noble councils, and focused primarily on the capital. Of course, this is rather reasonable considering these were the most important factors in the government, but also because other lower ranks of the government system weren't mentioned in the Maya texts. This lack of evidence was somewhat lessened with the archeological evidence found at Cerén, a classic period site in western El Salvador. Around 600 C.E., this small village, with a population of about 200 people, was covered by ash during a volcanic eruption. Archeologists have found that the largest building of the site, with the thickest walls, lacked any common household items, but it was fitted with two benches on the sidewalls and a large jar near one of them. The interior walls also have signs of decoration in the form of lines and punctuation. All this led the researchers to conclude that this was a public building, most likely used for local governance and community meetings. Village elders and leaders would gather on the benches, discuss local affairs, make decisions, and settle any disputes in their community. Drink ladled from the large jar was probably used for the ceremonial purpose of sealing the actions of the community council. Furthermore, archeologists think that this "village hall" was used to deliberate on and announce any orders that came from the capital, as well to inform the villagers about their corvée labor duties. Even though most of these are assumptions made by archeologists based on scarce evidence, thanks to the "Pompeii of the Americas," we have at least a vague idea of how the Maya government system functioned on a local level.

Chapter 6 – The Maya warfare

It is evident both from Maya texts and monuments, as well as some other archeological findings, that warfare played an important role in Maya civilization. During most of their history, the fragmented Maya states were locked in the almost perpetual state of war among themselves. Not even the foreign threats, like ones coming from Teotihuacan or the Aztecs, could make the Maya call a truce and unite against the common enemy. When the Spaniards came, the Yucatan Maya recognized how dangerous the Europeans were, but even then, the urge to settle old scores was too great for peace and unity to last longer than a couple of years. It would be expected that something as crucial to the Maya as war would be well-documented, and fully understood by the historians, but that is not the case. Not much is known about logistics, the organization of the military, or their training, as they are not described or even mentioned in texts and carvings. Monuments sometimes contain depictions of battles, but mostly they focus on celebrating victories and mentioning wars waged by the Maya kings. This lack of concrete evidence hasn't discouraged archeologists and historians in their attempts to uncover at least some mysteries of Maya warfare.

One of the certainties of Maya warfare is that the rulers were supreme war captains, as evident from the monuments. In the Preclassic period rulers were depicted, and in some cases even buried, with trophy heads on their belts. Those represented the sacrificed captives. That imagery later disappeared, and rulers were represented standing on their captives. Sometimes even queens would be shown in the same way. Prisoners of war were important to the Maya kings, as it was a way of proving one's worth to both the gods and subordinates. Some documents testify that before a ruler could be crowned he had to capture at least one prisoner for sacrifice. In some scenes, even the royal ancestors, dressed as warriors, are depicted advising the current ruler on the battlefield. The religious importance of sacrifices, especially of the captives, persisted until the time of the Conquistadors, giving one explanation why warfare was important to the Maya and their kings. It also helps illustrate why wars apparently never stopped in the Maya world, and why rulers often took titles like "He of 20 Captives." Despite all the carvings and texts representing victorious rulers, some historians claimed that the Maya rulers weren't really participating in battles; that they were simply commanders-in-chief, not soldiers. They saw depictions as pure propaganda. Disregarding scenes of kings involved in hand-to-hand combat, the fact that many inscriptions mention rulers that were captured in battles and sacrificed later disproves this theory. Even the Spaniards mention that some of the royal families' heads fought against them in direct combat.

It was also the European conquerors who noted some of the organization and hierarchy of the Late Postclassic Maya military. Spaniards mention a nonhereditary military title of "nacom." This rank was not permanent, but held for a short period of time, not longer than the duration of a particular war, similar to the title of the dictator in the ancient Roman republic. Their task was to gather and organize the army, while also performing certain religious rituals that were likely formerly done by the ruler himself. A nacom from the Yucatan did not personally lead the troops into the fight, but only acted as a chief military strategist. But in the Quiché kingdom, nacom also led the troops in battle, supported by four captains under his command. Those captains were likely ranked as "batab," a title that was given to the rulers and governors of dependent towns and sites within the state. The Spaniards recorded that their obligation was to lead their local armies into the battle under the supreme command of their ruler, or in this case an officer representing the ruler. Historians have linked the responsibilities and duties to the Late Classical period title of sahal, also given to the rulers of vassal cities.

Another Classical period military rank that has been deciphered is the title of "bate." Its true nature remains hidden, but it seems it has something to do with war captives and their sacrifice. This title has been held by both the ruler and the elite warriors, but it's been also attributed to some noblewomen. Although there are some mentions of women assisting in war, they were never mentioned as military officers. So, it seems that bate was a more honorific and hereditary title, given to a person or a family that demonstrated worth in combat. The thing that connects all known military officers is that they were all restricted to the members of the elite, whether they were hereditary or not. This was probably due to the fact that only nobles had any possibility to practice the art of war and of strategy. But having nobles serve as military officers was also beneficial to the ruler and the state as they could raise a large number of warriors through their kinship, tribute relations, and direct control of their lands. This can be compared to feudal lords in European medieval kingdoms. A major difference between the Maya noble officers and the European knights is that in the Maya society a commoner could advance through both military and social ranks if he could prove his prowess in warfare.

Historians today can't be sure how common that type of the advancement was, but it is clear that below the officers came the majority of commoner soldiers. The Maya didn't have a standing army, but some sources suggest they had a small group of warriors stationed in larger settlements, always prepared for battle. Whether these were commoners or members of the elite is uncertain. Whatever was the case, Spaniards report that every attempted surprise attack on the ports was met by a group of the Maya prepared to fight. The regular Maya soldiers were actually conscripts, most likely gathered by their local governors or lords. Their military service may also have been part of corvée labor duties. Service of the common folk was especially needed in times of the full-scale wars, when the majority of the adult male population was conscripted to fight for their king and their state. It is likely they brought their own weapons, used in the peacetime for hunting. And it seems that hunting was the only training a commoner got, which was later expanded by his own experience from previous military campaigns he was involved in. During periods of war, another type of soldiers used were mercenaries. Better trained, yet less loyal, they were in some cases a decisive factor in the course of the war. Their payments were given to them by the war captains who bought their services, but the common citizens housed and fed them.

Mercenaries, as well as the officers and common recruits, brought their own weapons on the battlefield. The most commonly depicted weapon on the monuments is probably the "atlatl" or the spear-thrower. This weapon was brought to the Maya world from Central Mexico by Teotihuacanos around the 4t[h] century C.E. It was a major improvement as the javelin or a dart, with its sharpened chert or obsidian tip, could hit a target from a distance of 45m (150 ft), with at least twice as much force and better accuracy than if it was done by simply throwing. It should be noted that some historians think the use of the atlatl was limited, due to its impracticality in the jungle terrain, claiming that its depictions were common only as a symbol of power borrowed from Teotihuacan art. Beside the spear-thrower, the Maya also used blowguns, which were used in both hunting and in war. This weapon was more likely used by the commoners, as it was cheaper to make, and required less training. Bow and arrow were also known as far back as the Classical era, but it was not until the Postclassic times that it became a common weapon on the battlefield. It was also more commonly associated with the non-elite soldiers, who used reed arrows, pointed with flints or sharp fish teeth. Beside those, the Maya used a variety of hand-to-hand weapons.

The Maya soldiers commonly used wooden spears, axes, and clubs, which were all commonly fitted with razor-sharp obsidian spikes or blades. They had knives and daggers, also made from sharpened obsidian or flint. For Europeans the lack of metal weapons was strange, and they considered it rather primitive. But the Maya by the time of the arrival of first Spaniards already used copper blades, albeit on a limited scale. In general, they tended to stick with stone cutting edges since obsidian was more common, cheaper, more durable, and easier to convert into sharp blades. Also, there was nothing primitive about the obsidian blade, for Christopher Columbus himself noted that the Maya weapons cut as well as the Spanish steel. The Maya warriors were often further equipped with shields. The type of shield used depended mainly on the weapon a soldier was carrying. If armed with a spear, a Maya fighter would usually carry a rectangular flexible shield made out of leather and cotton. Their defensive capabilities were limited and these shields were mostly used to protect from projectiles and give more passive protection to the body. It was most likely that the spear provided both attacking strikes and active defensive parrying. And historians think these spearmen were the most common type of Maya warriors utilized in battles, making them the core of the army.

Ax or club-wielding soldiers were less common and were most likely used to complement the spearmen in battle, or perhaps they were given more specialized tasks. They were also more valuable in small raids on lightly-armored enemies. These types of warriors also carried shields. Usually, those were round and more rigid, made out of leather, wood, and in some cases even tortoise shells. As they were smaller and tightly strapped to the arm, their main use was in parrying the blows of the enemy, as the shorter clubs and axes weren't adequate for that purpose. This type of shield eschewed a larger, more protective size in favor of a smaller, but more maneuverable form. This to a degree lessened the amount of protection the shield provided a warrior. Archeologists have also found a third type of shield which was a rigid, large, and rectangular; it was usually made out of wood, leather, or woven reeds. This was a Central Mexican introduction, as it was more common in that area. But historians assume its use was limited, mostly intended as a sign of power and prestige. This theory comes from the shield's impracticality in the thick jungles of the Maya homeland, and also from the fact that the shields were commonly associated with the Mexican-style iconography and gods, giving the shield more value as a status symbol.

A figurine of the Maya spearman. Source: https://commons.wikimedia.org

It seems that helmets were also somewhat symbolic. They were usually worn by higher-ranking officers, and although they probably offered some added protection, their main use was to represent the status of the wearer. In the Postclassic era, those helmets, usually made out of wood, were adorned with various emblems, effigies, and feathers. Ones from the classical period were even less protective, and more aesthetic. Those were more elaborate wooden and cloth headdresses that most likely represented the spirit animal of the warrior. Carrying the symbolism even further were the kings. In some cases, the Maya rulers would dress in ritual war costumes to inspire their troops. This clothing would offer some extra protection but would be too impractical for combat. That is why it wasn't a common practice and was most likely used in cases when the king wasn't directly involved in the actual fighting. In more usual depictions of rulers in battle, they wore more suitable clothing for protection, like quilted cotton vests and jaguar-pelt leggings. They also carried elaborate jaguar headdresses and shields adorned with the symbol of the jaguar sun god, a Maya deity of war and the Underworld.

Despite the fact the kings were sometimes depicted wearing quilted cotton armor, its usage doesn't seem to have been that common. Most of the common warriors are depicted wearing nothing but a loincloth. So, it seems that, at least in the Classical era, cotton armor was reserved for the nobles. This may have changed in the Postclassic era, as there are records that the Spaniards have been dropping their own steel plates to switch to the Maya cotton tunics. This may indicate that more than just a few noblemen wore it. But it also proves how effective it was. It provided more than sufficient protection against obsidian-based arms, though Conquistador sources indicate that it was just a little bit less efficient against steel weapons. But its major advantages were that it was lighter, more suitable for the high temperatures of the region, and that it was more flexible, making soldiers more mobile than if they were wearing steel armor. Alas, that type of protection wasn't available to the commoners. Since they fought bare-chested, they often applied body paint on themselves. Reasons for that can be found in possible religious ceremonies, to differentiate themselves from the enemy, or even as a psychological warfare tactic to frighten the opponents.

The exact tactics used by the Maya generals on the battlefields are unknown to us as there are no records about them. Some historians argue that the lack of banners and standards points to the fact that they fought out of formation. Supporting evidence for this theory is the fact that dense jungles are not suitable terrain for armies to maintain order. What military historians assume, according to the types of weapons and equipment used by the Maya, is that typical battles started with volleys from projectile weapons. These were aimed at weakening the enemy, both physically and mentally. Then the main combatants of the armies would collide in hand-to-hand combat in a simple straightforward clash. Winners of these battles would be the ones with bigger armies, better equipment, and ultimately higher morale and will to fight. Of course, this can't discount the possibility that at least some Maya strategists used more complex tactics, like encirclement or ambushes. Historians simply don't have the evidence to confirm that possibility.

Not all Maya battles were in the wilderness, since an important tactic of Maya warfare was carrying out city raids. In some situations, the cities that were attacked were defenseless. For example, a defending city's main army might have been defeated prior to the urban attack. The attacking army could then just plow through the city, burning, pillaging, and causing destruction. But the cities weren't always left without any protection. In those cases, the broad streets and open plazas most likely turned into a fractioned battlefield. Of course, the fate of the city and its citizens depended on the result of the battle. As these attacks on the urban centers became more frequent, defenders started building various defensive structures which altered the way those cities were attacked. There is no evidence of siege equipment needed to break through the defenses, so it seems the main tactic was a blockade. The attacking army would try to cut off the city's supplies in hope that the defenders would eventually yield. Proficiency of the Maya in the use of this tactic was confirmed by the Spaniards, who were actually defeated by it during their attack on Yucatan in 1533 C.E. Their camp was surrounded, cut off from supplies. Unable to find food or water they were forced to run away during the night in an attempt to save their lives. Other possible siege tactics may have been used, like surprise attacks, catching the defensive forces off guard. Perhaps people in settlements may have been bribed to allow attacking armies entrance. Yet again, these tactics can't be concretely verified by the sources, so they remain the object of speculation.

Replica of a Maya mural depicting a battle. Source: https://commons.wikimedia.org

What is clearly evident are the remains of the fortifications used to defend cities from the attacks. It seems that initially the most common types of defense were ditches and moats created by diverting the agricultural canals. Some historians argue that moats weren't mainly defensive but were only used as water reservoirs for the city. Both theories about the use of moats are plausible. In peacetime people could use them as a water source. But, during an attack, moats would present a major obstacle to invading forces. Walls were also built, and some were up to 11m (36ft) high. There are fewer doubts about their purpose, as they are clearly made to be part of fortifications. Some have argued that the walls were erected to separate the nobility from the commoners, but it doesn't seem likely as it goes against the Maya idea of open public spaces for rituals and ceremonies. One of the best examples of walls being used for defense can be found at Dos Pilas, where they were built in haste from the materials that comprised the religious buildings. Defenders constructed two concentric walls to create a 20- to 30m-wide (66 to 99ft) killing zone. When the attackers breached the gates, they were caught between two walls and became easy targets for the defenders on the inner wall. Archeologists have dug out numerous projectile points at that location, while burials of decapitated adult males were found just outside the walls. This proves just how effective and bloody the Maya defensive tactics and fortifications could be. But as it was already mentioned, in the end they weren't enough to save the city.

Other cities that shared a similar fate with Dos Pilas made crude, rubble barricades in times of urgency. Of course, those types of defensive structures were less efficient. Another type of protective structures were wooden palisades, sometimes reaching to heights of 9m (30ft). If they weren't built in haste because of impending attack, the palisades could have been covered with plaster to prevent them from catching on fire easily. During the Terminal Classic and Postclassic periods, there was another important leap in fortification systems. Walls became fitted with wider ramparts, parapets, and interior walkways. This came about due to the increased usage of archers in wars since they could fire from greater distances. From the tops of the walls, defenders could use the threat of archers to keep attackers further away. During this period, defensive systems became more complex, being created in multiple rings of defense, with the last ring protecting the sacred and most important city center. But besides making defenses go deeper inwards, some of the cities created smaller forts outside the city's limits. Those were used as the first perimeter of defense; to lessen the chance of surprise attacks. Yet no matter how complex and efficient these defenses were, it seems that in the end, nothing could really protect the Maya cities from the troubles of war. All of them eventually suffered defeat.

The Maya continued to try to prevent those fatal outcomes. Yet another way they tried to improve the defensive capabilities of their settlements was by utilizing landscape. This became more common in the Postclassic era, especially in the Highlands. There, many cities and fortifications were erected on hilltops, which made access to them difficult. Sometimes the only way to get near the city was a narrow path, easily controlled by the defenders. Other times, a city was surrounded by a ravine which could be crossed only by a plank bridge that defenders could remove. But fortifications like these became more of a citadel type, used primarily for defenses and not as dwellings. In the Lowlands, the main use of natural defenses were islands on the lakes and coasts, which couldn't be crossed without a canoe or a ship. The Spaniards have also mentioned the use of traps as defensive measures. One example of that was the Maya trying to lure the Conquistadors onto a narrow pathway and then cutting off the exits. The idea was to defeat them in a high space where their horses were unable to maneuver, making them easy targets for both archers and spearmen.

Another important question that needs to be answered is why warfare was so important for the Maya. This is best explained by analyzing the types of wars they waged, or more precisely by determining what the main goal was to be achieved by the attackers. Most commonly, the Maya states went to war in the attempt to expand their territories and influence. This was done to economic gain, mostly through control of trade routes and resources, and additionally to attain political advancement. Wars could be motivated by the desire to defeat an ally or a vassal of an enemy state, by quests to remove a dynasty, by the urge to improve the political strength of one's own state, or even by revenge in some cases. Added benefits of successful wars were the tributes paid by conquered cities. Revenge sometimes gave war other dimensions, transforming a confrontation from a territorial conflict into a mission of destruction. This was less common, as it obviously didn't yield as many benefits as conquering. If it was done, it was usually a culmination of years of animosity and hostility. The best example of this was Dos Pilas, which was destroyed without any signs that the attackers had tried to conquer or subdue it. Another example of a destruction war was when Chichén Itzá annihilated one of its competitors in maritime trade. There was no motivation for revenge but for the simple calculation that a competitor needed to be destroyed without giving any chance of later revival; recovery would have been possible if it was merely turned into a vassal city.

But gains and revenge weren't the only reasons for the Maya to go to war. Another crucial motivation was religion and rituals. As we have learned, it was an important part of the rulers' image to be presented with captives to be used in the ceremonial sacrifices needed to please the gods. Catching those victims was certainly one of the motivators for Maya wars. Though it should be emphasized that unlike previously believed by archeologists, this wasn't the main cause of war. With "common" wars being fought regularly, most states didn't lack the captives for those needs. But in some cases, when Maya kings needed to prove themselves and acquire sacrificial victims, it could lead to conflict, though not likely full-scale war. And though religion wasn't often a cause of war, it certainly was commonly used to justify it. The Maya would often look at the night sky, looking at the movement of Venus, which was associated with war. Wars were typically waged when it was visible in the sky. Indeed, these wars have been marked with a star war glyph on the monuments and in texts. This meant that the war was sanctioned as a divine mission, similarly to the crusades or jihad. It was commonly used as justification for territorial warfare, making so-called "Star Wars" not-uncommon occurrences.

Chapter 7 – Economy of the Maya civilization

So far, in previous chapters, it could be noticed that the economy was one of the important drives of the Maya civilization. It was a base which propelled their polities from chiefdoms to states, it allowed the expansion of culture and great architectural achievements, because of it, wars were started and ended. Even the Maya realized how important the economy was to them, especially in the late Postclassic period when their society turned to rapid commercialization. To fully understand the Maya history, development, and culture, one has to get to know how their economy worked as well. It started from its early tribal backgrounds of hunting and foraging, then switched to farming when the Maya ancestors chose a sedentary way of life. Since then, the foundation of the Maya economy was agriculture. Early on, during the Preclassic age, the Maya figured out that water management was the key for both better and more reliable harvests. That is why they built wells, canals, and in some extreme cases like Kaminaljuyú, created massive irrigation systems. Besides those, it was common to create water reservoirs from natural and manmade subterranean caves, as well as quarry pits that were lined with clay to make them more watertight. In some cases, in Yucatan, the Maya even deepened the natural water-retaining depressions and cultivated water lilies to slow down the water evaporation.

Droughts weren't the only problem the Maya faced in agriculture. Flooding and heavy rains were also troubling, but the canals and other water management systems also drained water. Where there was no need for canals they used the drain and raise technique, where the fields were covered in a network of drainage ditches which took away the excess water, while simultaneously earth dug up from the ditches was piled up on the same fields, elevating them from the floodplain. Another problem faced by the Maya farmers was maintaining the fertility of the soil. They used various techniques for that, from planting complementary species near each other, like beans and maize, to using fertilizer made from household refuse, and crop rotation. The Maya farmers also used swidden agriculture methods, but this was primarily used to create new fields. And although altogether these approaches to preservation of soil show a real understanding of agriculture, it wasn't enough to maintain food supplies when the population grew too much. Thus, many of the fertile fields were overused and depleted by the time the Classic era was coming to an end.

Nonetheless, the Maya agriculture endured, while farmers searched for new fertile soils in which to plant their crops. Those can be divided into two major groups, food crops, and export or cash crops. Major food crops were maize, manioc, squash, sweet potato, papaya, pineapple, avocado, tomatoes, chili peppers, and common beans. Beside those, the Maya also grew some medicinal herbs in smaller house gardens. And although the food was sometimes traded, main trade income would have come from the cash crops. Most important of those was probably cacao, which was highly sought-after by the higher classes for making of chocolate beverages. Cacao was also linked to the gods, and it even served as currency to a certain extent. Another important export crop was cotton which, thanks to the climate, grew well in the Yucatan region. Unlike cacao, cotton was most commonly first turned into a finished textile produce before being exported, and it was important source of income. A third major cash crop was agave plant which was used to produce hemp fibers for inexpensive commoners' clothing and sandals, as well as strong ropes. Additionally, they cultivated tobacco, which was used for both religious rituals and individual pleasure. Despite the development of agriculture, hunting and foraging also remained sources of food and income for the Maya.

Animals that were hunted ranged from large deer, through peccaries and monkeys, to quail and partridge. They also hunted for crocodiles and manatees. For larger game, the Maya hunters used mainly spears and bows, while for monkeys and birds they used blowguns. They also employed traps which were mainly used to catch tapirs and armadillos, as well as turtles and iguanas, who in addition to meat were a source of highly-favored eggs. As with farming, not all animals were hunted for food. Jaguars, macaws, and quetzals were primarily hunted for their feathers, claws, pelts, and teeth, which were in high demand by the nobles for clothing and accessories. That made them valuable trade items. But the jungle was also suitable for foraging, giving the Maya more food like mushrooms, sometimes hallucinogenic, and various berries, as well as greens like tree-spinach and radish-like root plants. Rainforests were also sources of medicinal herbs and spices, like oregano and allspice. They also gathered vanilla pods, both for flavoring and fragrance, sometimes even cultivating vanilla vines deep in the tropical jungle. Of course, the Maya also fished, both on sea coasts, and further inland, and on lakes and rivers. They caught shrimp, lobster, various shellfish, and fish. The ocean-sourced fish were sometimes salted and traded as a delicacy to interior regions.

All of the previously listed economic activities are fairly common around the world, so it's not surprising that the Maya practiced them as well. What can be a bit of a shock is that animal husbandry was never truly developed by the Maya. They only domesticated dogs, for hunting and as pets, while turkeys and Muscovy ducks were only semi-domesticated. In some cases, they would capture and hold a deer for a while before eating it later. But the Maya did practice beekeeping, especially in Yucatan. There they would make hives from the hollowed tree trunks, which they plugged on the end. Honey was important as the only known sweetener to the Maya, which made it both important part of the diet and a valuable trade item. But more important than sweet honey was salt, necessary to maintain life. And although nearly all the Maya that lived on the coast were producing it, Yucatan salt was most valued and produced in much larger quantities. It was sought-after even by the Central Mexican nobility. Another product that was in some cases reserved for the nobility was alcoholic beverages, mostly consumed during feasts and rituals. The most famous examples of Maya alcoholic drinks, and which are still made today, are balché, a mild liquor, and chicha, a maize beer.

The second major branch of the Maya economy was crafting and artisanal work. The range of those products, as well as skills of the makers, went from simple and crude to exquisite artistry. And though most of them were commoners, highly skilled artisans often rose the middle class, while even some of the nobles practiced forms of craftwork. Of all the products those craftsmen made, ceramics were probably the most important for the economy. First of all, ceramics were essential in everyday life; everything from cooking pots to storage jugs. These goods varied in quality, beauty, and shape. But, if they were painted and adorned, they served a more ornamental role, like vases and figurines. Then ceramics became a rather important trade commodity, highly-valued by the nobility. Importance of ceramics in the Maya society can be further demonstrated by the fact that they developed a means of mass producing it. They created molds from which they many copies of the same product, from which even artistic figurines were made. And if needed, the "blank canvas" of those products could be embellished or individualized through painting or adding handmade details. More important is the fact that mass production meant ceramics were getting easier to make, cheaper, and more available. They were useful in trade, for both carrying other goods, and as an item of trade in and of itself.

Those who painted the ceramics, depending on their skill and the quality of their work could in some cases even be considered artistic, while others are more artisans and simple painters. They all used a variety of brushes and tools that resemble the wooden stylus of the ancient Near East. Those, with other tools and weapons, were another important part of the craftsmanship of the Maya pre-industrial workers. The toolmakers' main resources were, as was already mentioned, obsidian and chert. Those tools were part of the ceramics trade, but also necessary as a consumer good. Toolmakers also made wooden weaving battens, handles, and levers, while bones were used for needles and fishing hooks. For heavier work tools, such as chisels, scrapers, grinding stones, and axes they used basalt. Those types of tools were commonly used and are found at all sites. But precise work tools, like micro-drills needed for the finest lapidary work, are found only at the elite quarters of the urban centers. This indicates that those artisans were either of noble descent or were held in high regard by the ruling class. Again, it shows how some parts of the craft industry were appreciated in the Maya society, at least in the Classical period.

By the Postclassic period, around 13th century C.E., toolmakers embraced a new technology and resource for their products. They started using copper to create axes, fishing hooks, and tweezers.

This debunks one of the most common myths that the Maya didn't have any knowledge of metallurgy. The truth is that copper wasn't that much better than the stone tools they created. And, in their region there weren't any copper mines, but obsidian, chert, and basalt were present in abundance. The only metal they had was gold, and it was panned in small quantities in the Highlands. Most of their precious metals were traded from the southern parts of Mesoamerica, and those were usually imported as finished products. While there were some gold and silver artifacts that were most likely created by the Maya craftsmen, it seems that they didn't develop many such skills. They focused on working with precious stones, which were also abundant in the Maya homeland. Jade, serpentine, turquoise, and pyrite were most commonly used. From those, they fashioned jewelry, home decorations, figurines, and other pieces of art. Pyrite was specifically used to create divining mirrors. Of these, jade was both the most precious and also the hardest to work with. Historians today find it remarkable that the Maya artisans were able to work with jade without any metal tools and think that great skill and dedication was needed to produce high quality from that particular stone. The Maya craftsman also used red shells and bones to make jewelry and other artwork. All of these products were highly valued in trade.

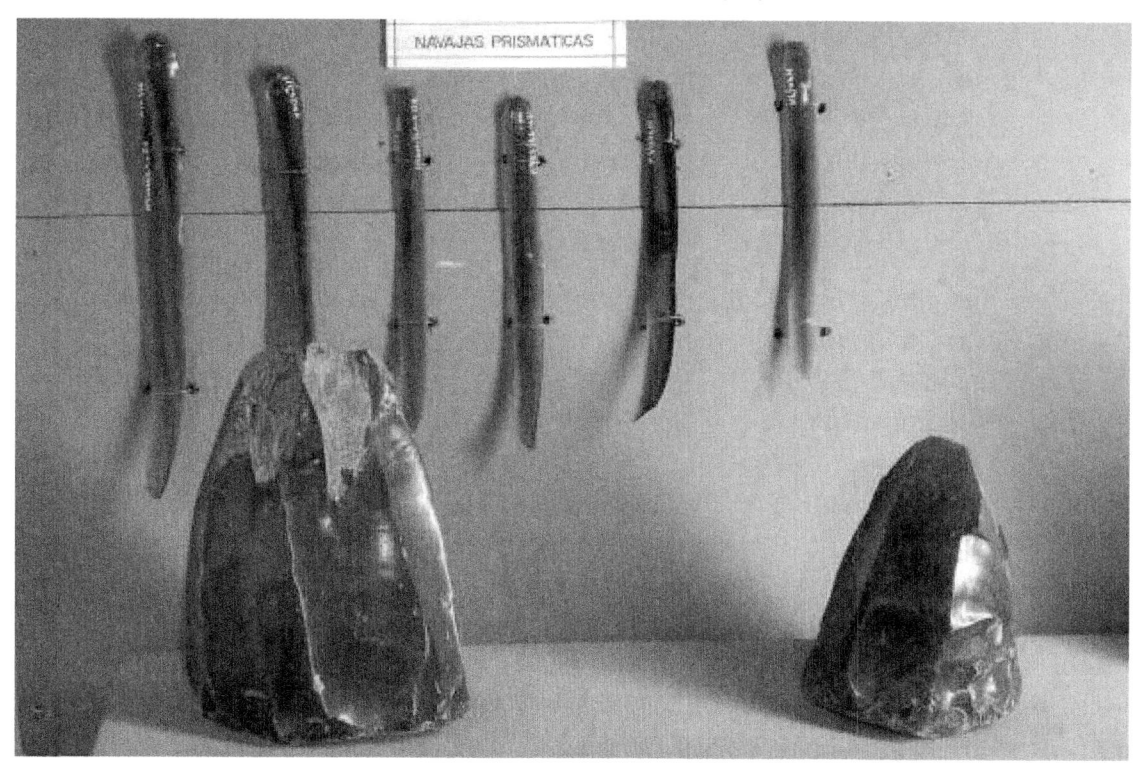

Raw obsidian and obsidian blades crafted by Maya artisans. Source: https://commons.wikimedia.org

Another tradable item was cotton clothing. As mentioned, cotton was grown by the Maya farmers, but expert weavers did the processing. They used a variety of complicated techniques to create pieces of cotton fabric used to make clothing. It was reserved for the nobles, in some cases even used as tributes and gifts to the royalty. They were adorned with various abstract symbols, most often connected with cosmological and religious motifs. In some cases, feathers were also woven into the clothing, which was commonly colorful. They used dyes made from plants, insects, and shells, and the most commonly used colors were dark blue, red, purple, and black-purple. Weavers also produced cotton tapestries and brocades, as decoration and as art. All of this indicates that the textile enterprise was another important part of the Maya economy. Of course, that type of highly-priced cotton textile was reserved for the elite. In some rare cases the Maya commoners had clothing made of lesser quality homespun cotton, but more often they wore simple loincloths made from various hemp fibers. Another type of common attire was pounded bark cloth, which some historians argue was used only for ceremonial occasions.

A more interesting use of pounded bark material was for making a crude version of paper. This Mesoamerican paper, referred to as such because its exact origin is unknown, was made usually from wild fig bark which was boiled in maize water, treated with lime or ash, then peeled in thin leaves. Those leaves were laid crisscross on a wooden board, then beaten with a stone into a single sheet of paper. Finishing with a thin layer of plaster ensured that the final product was smooth enough to write on. The most notable use of this paper was for writing books and codices, which were unfortunately almost all destroyed by the Spaniards. But Mesoamerican paper was also likely used in rituals, and for keeping records of trading, tributes, and other state business. The Maya made other products from plant fibers and vines, most notably mats, baskets, and fans. Mats were connected with the ruler and with authority, making them at least symbolically important. Baskets were in most cases used as an everyday item for carrying various items, but in some situations, they were linked with ceremonies of sacrificial offerings to the gods.

After listing all the important products of two major branches of the Maya economy, it is time to turn our attention to the third branch which created nothing except profit. Of course, this branch is trading. By now it should be clear that a lot of Maya life revolved around trade, and historians think it was the most important "motor" that drove the advance and growth of the Maya civilization. Most of the strongest Maya states drew strength from the control of the trade routes, and they often fought for them. But trade also facilitated connection with both other regions of the Maya homeland, and also with other surrounding nations. As a result, the Maya weren't only exchanging goods, but also ideas, technologies, and beliefs. That is one of the reasons why the historians have been so focused on the long distance, interregional trade, that connected present-day New Mexico with Panama and Columbia. The Maya held the central position of that trade. They exported and imported nearly all the resources and products mentioned in this chapter, except food. They also imported resources not commonly found in their homeland like silver, gold, pearls, copper, rubber, turquoise, etcetera. But the Maya traders also played a role of middle-man in trade between northern and southern Mesoamerica, and in some cases even larger areas.

This is not to say that a single Maya merchant traveled from Panama to New Mexico. Long-distance trading was done in stages, like a relay race, where the goods would be carried by a single trader only for one part of the route. Yet, the Maya merchants did have an enclave in early classic

Teotihuacan, 1600km (1000mi) from their homeland. And this close connection with central Mexico continued when the Aztecs became the major power in the region. Another important factor of interregional trade is that it reinforced the authority and prestige of the ruler, as the royal family most often controlled the vital resources traded by the Maya. So, when the Maya traded for luxury goods, acquired products went to the ruler, and in some cases the highest elite. That way the king and the nobles were the ones profiting the most from this type of trade. Of course, this wasn't the only kind of commerce. There was also a regional trade, between the Maya themselves. As it was already mentioned, not all regions of the Maya homeland were suitable for producing everything or had access to the same raw resources. That is why there was a need for cities to complement each other with various products. Best example would be that the exchange of obsidian products for salt between the Highlands and Yucatan states. These trade connections were obviously strong and so frequent that they kept the Maya tightly connected in one rather homogenous civilization.

This was facilitated by the rulers, who of course benefited from trade. They sponsored and organized markets in their city centers, trying to attract more people to trade on their land. Although archeologists aren't completely sure, it is likely that the large and permanent Maya markets were under strict government control. Its officials enforced rules, settled disputes, and of course collected taxes. Naturally, these central markets were also used by the local population to acquire the goods they needed, and it is also likely that smaller and less permanent local markets existed which were used for local trade. This third type of trading was used between neighbors, trading among themselves for produce they lacked. All the families were focused and specialized on one type of production, so they created surpluses which they traded for items that they were missing. This type of trade wasn't that profitable and wasn't done by the professional merchants. It was the common people who bartered among each other. It is also likely that it wasn't as regulated as the higher levels of trade. Yet it was important for the survival of the local communities and the common citizens.

By getting familiar with all three levels or types of trading, as well as the reach of the merchants, it is possible to make a general idea of how the Maya trade network looked. But there is another important issue regarding this network yet to be discussed: the transport of goods. The first method to develop, and more commonly employed in the local and partially in regional trade, was overland transport. Without any animals to facilitate land transport, it was all done by human porters. In some cases, they carried the goods on their back, in other two or more of them would carry a litter. These were also used to transport richer travelers. These carriers used trails and sacbeob when they existed on their routes. Relay teams were used to make the transport faster and easier, especially if the cargo was heavy or if the final destination was further away. But in any case, this type of transportation was rather hard, slow and in essence inefficient. That is why the Maya used waterborne transport whenever they could. It was first done using rivers, connecting the inland cities. But as shipbuilding technology improved, and the Maya commerce began to expand further and further away, they also started to use the sea for transport.

Maya depiction of a man in a canoe. Source: https://commons.wikimedia.org

For that, they used canoes, which by the beginning of the 16th century were about 2.5m (8ft) wide and as long as galleys, according to the accounts of Columbus' son. Their vessels were fitted with palm canopies to protect passengers and goods. And in the same description, it was stated that the Maya canoes could carry up to 25 people on board, which means they carried substantial amounts of cargo as well. That fact also pushed the expansion of the sea trade, which led to the rise of up to 150 ports on the Yucatan coast in the Post-Classic period. This, of course, caused a lot of the Classical era Lowlands trade centers to lose their power and importance. But throughout the periods some aspects of trade didn't change much. One of those was a payment system. It seems that the most common "currency" was cacao beans. They were deemed valuable, and there were some reports of counterfeiting them by filling an empty cacao shell with dirt. Yet exactly how the Maya governments controlled its value and protected the cacao as a type of money remains an enigma for historians. Besides paying with cacao, it seems some other luxury items were also used for payments, also with what seem to have been fixed market values. These were jade beads and oyster shells. Later on, with the introduction of metals, the Maya merchants also started using gold and copper. Of course, barter was also a common form of payment, especially in local markets.

To ensure the trade deals would go through without problems the Maya merchants even created contracts, especially for larger or more valuable exchanges. These contracts might have been only oral, since they were sealed by public drinking. This may have given a rise to a culture of traders' integrity, as the Spaniards have observed that the Maya merchants were rather honorable. They also noted that usury didn't exist among them. All these factors combined demonstrate that the Maya trade was quite complex and very organized, not at all primitive as was once thought. That, combined with developed agricultural and craft production makes it apparent that the Maya had a robust and diverse economy. It shows yet another part of the Maya civilization that was thriving, pushing it to new greatness.

Chapter 8 – The Maya achievements in arts and culture

The highly developed and rather complex Maya civilization managed to create stunning pieces of art, bearing witness to the level of sophistication that the Maya culture achieved. Their creations ranged from monumental and breathtaking architecture and monuments, through beautiful and finely made figurines, paintings and books, to the less tangible and equally amazing intellectual achievements. With those, the Maya left a clear mark on both Mesoamerican and global culture, giving yet another reason for present-day researchers and historians to focus on uncovering their stories and achievements. The first thing that caught their attention, of course, were grand buildings and ruins that were left, lost to the wild jungles. The question of who built those big structures was the mystery that initially attracted the historians to the Maya civilization. And it was a first step in dismantling the old prejudices of the natives being only barbaric primitive tribes. From the first glance, it was clear that no backward society could have ever built something like the Maya pyramids and temples. And the somewhat interesting fact is that the biggest examples of those structures actually comes from the Preclassic era, not the golden age. But though smaller in size, those buildings, maintaining their basic form and look, were built until the arrival of Spaniards.

Also, common types of structures were palaces, ceremonial platforms usually up to 4m (6.5ft) high, council houses, ball courts, tombs and acropolises, observatories, sweat baths, and ceremonial stairways. These were generally public buildings, except palaces, which were usually placed around a central city plaza. They played an important role in the religious and political life of every urban center, and those were adorned with various carvings and other types of decorations. And as they were built to last, those buildings were usually built out of limestone, but also other types of stone like marble, sandstone, and trachyte, depending on local availability. In areas where the stone wasn't as common, those buildings were built out of adobe clay, which was more typically used for the homes of commoners. For mortar they used limestone cement, while plaster was used to seal the exterior walls as it was easier to decorate. The Maya masons also mastered the technique of corbelled arches to create tall yet narrow doorways and domes. The reverse "V" shape of these arches, or vaults as they are also called, is one of the architectural hallmarks of the Maya, as almost none of the other civilization of Mesoamerica built them. Structures with these arches resembled their original thatched huts but were also better cooled which is an important advantage in the tropical climate. Also, the vaults made the buildings look more impressive from the outside, which was always an important factor for the Maya.

All these features are common among the Maya cities, distinguishing them from the rest of Mesoamerica. But some local differentiation in style existed, as well as certain evolution and development as time passed. Those were both caused by the availability of resources and different foreign influence, but also by the individual tastes of particular rulers. But no matter the fine details, there is no doubt that the Maya, in general, were capable and skilled masons, as their structures still stand tall and proud. Yet the details that are commonly considered to be their most beautiful feature were not done by them. There were specialized stone carvers which were tasked with creating those artistic masterpieces. They were usually carved in stucco, with scenes that were either taken from mythology or which celebrated the ruler. Often those two were interconnected, as the rulers were shown performing various rituals. But the Maya sculptors didn't only decorate the walls. They also used their skill to adorn lintels, altars, thrones, and most notably, stelae. And today historians praise their work not only for the sculpting skills of the Maya but also because those carvings are one of the major sources of information about the civilization's past.

Similarly, the murals and wall painting, usually done on the interior walls, also became important evidence of the Maya history. Though not many are saved, ones that are preserved today show us glimpses of the court life, ritual ceremonies, wars, and battles. Those scenes are painted with vivid and bright colors, which are a clear reminder that the Maya cities were rather colorful places. It the Classical era it was common for the wall paintings to have hieroglyphic text accompanying them, giving more detailed context to the scenes. And the skill level of the Maya painters is no lesser than that of the carvers. Besides sharing the similar, if not the same, imagery, they also share the same stylistic characteristics. Most notable of these is the naturalistic and rather realistic representation of places and humans. Yet in most of the artwork people, even the rulers, lack the individual traits that would distinguish their facial characteristics. Another fact that binds them is the fact that their main purpose was to celebrate and promote the rulers and their cults, which suggests that they were mostly commissioned by the royal families. Only in the Postclassic period, when the ruler cult was dying out, did the scenes focus more on religious and mythological topics, as well as on the noble lineages. But the fact remains that these artists worked only for the members of the elite, and most likely worked in patronage systems.

Not everything the artists created was as large as the wall decorations. Both painters and sculptors also worked on smaller items. Sculptors created many decorative masks, celts (axe heads), pendants, and figurines out of precious stones, most notably jade. Depending on their purpose, their themes changed. In some cases, they were made to represent a certain deity or mythological creature, while some of the celts were fitted with the representation of kings. And most famous masks were usually death masks, without any specific facial features. As creations made of such expensive materials wouldn't have been as available to the less fortunate, the Maya sculptors also carved smaller wooden figurines and effigies. Again, main themes were the rulers, and even more often they are the representation of gods. On the other hand, the Maya painters worked on adorning various pottery products, but most notably vases and bowls. Their artwork was rather similar in every aspect to the murals, except in size. Themes remained connected to religion, rulers and court, done in a colorful pallet. And both paintings and sculptures retained naturalistic form and a sense of realism.

Copy of a Maya mural with restored colors. Source: https://commons.wikimedia.org

Unlike other Maya artists, pottery makers weren't only focused on making objects of stunning beauty. They also had to focus on practicality and usefulness. Based on that idea, it is possible to separate the types of Maya pottery into two main groups. The first one would be ceremonial, made for the elite and for religious needs. That type of pottery was often polychrome, with a mixture of more than one mineral slip, and was often decorated with paintings. These vessels were also more elaborate in shape and form, adding a base flange, knobs in shape of animal or human heads, and mammiform- or leg-shaped supports. Some of the vessels were shaped and decorated as human or animal heads. The Maya potters also made naturalistic figurines representing people doing various types of mundane activates. These were mostly painted, probably made for nobles, as they were likely to be costly. Utilitarian pottery was more commonly used by the lower classes, as they were cheaper and less finely-made. In contrast to ceramics made for the elites, these were monochrome, simple in shape and form, and without many decorations, if they had any at all. The main focus of pottery makers, in this case, was to make them useful in everyday life, while not being too concerned with beauty. And the already mentioned mass-produced pottery, by using a mold, was usually created for commoners, not the elite. For one, it was cheaper and more available, but also the nobles liked their possessions to be more unique, representing their position in the society.

The same role of social status symbols was assigned to clothing and jewelry, which also represented the skillful artwork of the Maya artisans. But these will be discussed in a later chapter about the daily life of the Maya, as those art forms are better suited for describing their lifestyle than artistic and cultural achievements. On the other hand, books and writing could be seen as the pinnacle of the Maya cultural achievements. As was mentioned before, the books were written on crude bark paper, covered with a thin layer of plaster. There were probably thousands and thousands of Maya codices, as their books are more commonly called, written during their long history, yet today only four remain, since the Spaniards burned them as blasphemous and evil. All four books are linked to rituals, religion, mythology, astronomy, and astrology. But it's not unlikely that among many others that were burned were books about their history and past, about their scientific and philosophical findings, poetry, and stories. Alas, we will never know for sure. What is striking is the beauty of the books, in which illustrations complemented texts. Those drawings, in similar style to the paintings, are colorful and naturalistic. In the four remaining codices, they represented gods and mythological heroes, which isn't surprising considering their theme. Hieroglyphic writing is done in one color, mostly red or black. Even those glyphs can on their own be seen as art motifs, as they are no less stunning or interesting than the illustrations. And similar to modern books, the pages of the Maya codices were protected with covers made out of tree bark or pelts, in some cases even jaguar skin. In that aspect, every book represents a singular artistic creation worthy of any great civilization.

But books and other Maya texts for that matter represent more than just art. They convey a message that can transcend both time and space. And developing a writing system is a step of utmost importance in creating a developed civilization. Unfortunately for historians, not only did the Spaniards destroy the books, but they also destroyed the Maya literacy, at least when it comes to their own hieroglyphs. That is one of the reasons why for a long time historians and archeologists debated about Maya script, with skeptics claiming that it's not really a writing system, but rather religious illustrations or symbols, similar to Christian icons. Of course, through long and hard work by many generations of linguists and Mayanists, there is no longer any doubt that the Maya have indeed had a fully developed writing system, one which could transcribe everything they spoke. According to some researchers, the Maya are the only civilization in pre-

Columbian Mesoamerica that developed a fully functional script, yet this claim is uncertain and could be disproven if any other Mesoamerican script is deciphered.

The origin of the Maya writing system isn't exactly clear. Some historians believed that the Maya adopted their script from the Olmecs. The Olmecs, mentioned earlier as one of the oldest civilizations in Mesoamerica, had a writing system that is currently being studied by researchers. However, that system does not show signs of the full development evident in Maya hieroglyphs. One reason this theoretical connection between Olmec and Maya script is the similarity in the glyphs and the style of writing. Others think the Maya developed their writing system on their own. One of the reasons for that is that the first signs of Maya proto-writing date to around 400 B.C.E., a time when the Olmec's civilization was near its end. And, the first recognizable scripts date to around 50 B.C.E., when the Olmecs were long gone. Yet, even if the latter theory is right, it is likely that the Olmecs at least slightly influenced the Maya script. Whatever is the truth, today we can say with certainty that the Maya writing system was a mixture of a phonetic and logographic script. This means that certain glyphs represent syllables consisting of a consonant and vowel, which combined together could spell out any word. While other glyphs represented on their own the whole word. Today most of these glyphs have been translated, with new discoveries being made constantly. Thanks to this important work, historians can now decipher and translate almost all Maya texts.

Pages from one of the Maya codices. Source: https://commons.wikimedia.org

Text wasn't written only in books, but on just about anything; from walls and monuments to a variety of pottery, celts, and stone tools. On bigger objects and walls, they told a story, conveyed a complex message about achievements of the king or details of a certain ritual. On smaller objects, like jars or vases they were simple tags, marking either their maker or their owner. They were even found in permanent markets, marking areas or stands with the type of products that were being sold there. This widespread use of writing, especially on objects not related to the royalty and the elite, brought up a question of general literacy among the pre-conquest Maya. Of course, there is no way to be exactly sure, but some historians argue that literacy, at least a basic one, was rather widespread among all the people. Otherwise, there wouldn't be any point in writing on common objects and places. Full literacy, however, was limited to the higher classes with their specially trained scribes, given that there were about 800 glyphs, of which about 500 were commonly used. But, as the Spaniards fought their cultural war against the Maya, they found one way to save at least part of their legacy, mythology, and traditions. This was for the Maya to learn to use the Latin alphabet and then transcribe some of their original works. Those kinds of books were not always seen as evil by the Spanish clergy, and some managed to survive, though it is reasonable to assume that the Europeans discouraged the Maya from their preservation efforts. The most famous example of Maya literature transcribed into Latin is the Popol Vuh, which was most likely written in the second half of the 16th century.

Maya intellectual and cultural achievements didn't end with writing. They were also superb astronomers, who probably started to gaze at the stars so they could praise their gods. It's precisely because of this that some of the commonly-found buildings in all major Maya cities were observatories. After a while, the Maya observers started noting certain patterns, noting them with tremendous accuracy. With nothing more than their naked eyes, strings, and sticks they calculated that the revolution of Venus around the Sun took 584 days. Today's astronomers measured it to be exactly 583.92 days, making the Maya margin of error about 0.01%. Of course, they also tracked movements of other celestial bodies, which was used to align important buildings, like temples or palaces, with the position of the Sun on the horizon at the solstices and equinoxes, as well as with the zenith passages. But more commonly, those movements and positions of celestial bodies were used for divination and fortunetelling. So, in a way, the Maya sky observers were a mix of astrologers and astronomers. One example of this is looking at the position of Venus before going to war, as it was considered that fighting without that planet in the night sky would anger the gods and bring bad luck. Going further, they also created their own zodiac, dividing the sky into sections and constellations. It is likely they used it like all ancient societies, and like it is still used today, to predict fortunes and future events. Yet exact details on the number and positioning of the Maya constellations, their celestial signs, and their position in the night sky are unknown, and under constant debate among the experts.

From their ability to track the cycles of the night skies, as well as other observations in nature, the Maya were able to become excellent timekeepers. For that purpose, they used an intricate system which combined three different calendars. But this system shouldn't be seen as a pure creation of the Maya. Almost all Mesoamerican nations used it, and it likely originated from the Olmecs, though that has not been conclusively proven. Thus, phrases like "the Maya calendar" aren't correct, and they should be substituted by "the Mesoamerican calendar." The shortest of the three calendars the Maya used was called the Tzolk'in, and it was 260 days long, divided into 13 "months" which numbered 20 days. Researchers were unable to find any astronomical significance for this period of time, but it has been suggested it was linked with the period of human pregnancy, which usually lasts for about 266 days. This connection is still used by the present-day Maya women. Another possible link is maize cultivation, giving an approximate time when to plant and harvest this important crop. But, its main use seems to be for divination and fortune-telling. There is evidence for this in the Maya codices, which contain Tzolk'in almanacs. Those were used by the diviners to guide the rulers before making any important decisions. Today the Maya still use it to pick a date for a wedding or a business trip, so it is not unlikely that the commoners in the past did the same.

Less religious, but more practical, would be the second calendar the Maya used called the Haab'. This calendar was 365 days long, coinciding with a solar year. It was divided into 18 months of 20 days, with an extra five days added at the end. Because of its structure, the scholars today call it the vague year calendar. The main use of Haab' was for agriculture, as the name of the months suggests a seasonal division of the calendar. Water and dry months were grouped together, as well as the earth months and the maize months. The 5 days added at the end of every year were called Wayeb' and were considered very unlucky throughout Mesoamerica. It was believed that during these five days, connections between the underworld and the mortal realms were heightened. Nothing was preventing the gods or other creatures from coming into the world and causing death and destruction. This is why during these days, the Maya performed various rituals to prevent the destruction of their world and to ensure coming of the new year.

Using two rather different calendars could have confused the Maya, and so they found a way to avoid this. They created the so-called calendar round date, by combining both the Tzolk'in and Haab' dates. That date would repeat itself after 52 Haab' or 72 Tzolk'in years, making a single calendar round. But there was still one more problem left with those two calendars, and that is measuring the long periods of time, since it became possible to confuse specific dates within different calendar rounds. This can be compared with the form in which we sometimes write our dates, e.g. "5.3.18." When writing the date in this way, we could be referring to May 3, 2018, or to May 3, 1918. To avoid that confusion, the Maya used the cyclical Mesoamerican long count calendar, which is often wrongly named the Maya calendar. The base of this calendar was Haab', with cycles starting from one day (k'in), growing to one month (winal) of 20 days, to one year (tun) made of 18 winals. A tun was 360 days and did not include the unlucky 5 Wayeb', which weren't counted as a true part of the year. The cycles continue, with the k'atun cycle being 20 tun, or years, long, following with b'ak'tun cycle lasting 20 k'atuns, or about 394 years. The scale continues, with every new cycle lasting 20 times more than the last. The last, 9th cycle called alautun lasts a little bit over 63 thousand years. The Maya themselves usually stopped at b'ak'tun when they inscribed their dates. That is why their Long Count dates are marked by series of 9 numbers, with first one representing b'ak'tun and last one representing k'in. Modern scholars note these dates in the same way, for example, January 22nd, 771 C.E., would be written down 9.17.0.0.0, with every number representing a single cycle.

Those cycles are being counted from the Maya mythological creation of the world which, transcribed to the Gregorian calendar, is dated to August 11th, 3114 B.C.E. And, similarly to the end of the Haab' cycle, the Maya revered every other important cycle. Misinterpretation of the nature of Maya traditions and nature of the Long Count calendar led to now infamous 2012 "end of the world" media frenzy. According to some Maya text, the world we're currently living is actually the fourth iteration, with the previous three ending after 13 b'ak'tuns. And on December 21th of 2012 C.E., the 13th b'ak'tun from 3114 B.C.E., was coming to an end. This led some people to interpret this as the Maya prophecy of the world ending on that date, though this was not explicitly mentioned. It is possible that the Ancient Maya would have seen this date as religiously important, but there are no clear signs that would see it necessarily as a beginning of the apocalypse. It is more likely that for them that date was just another end of a cycle in their calendar. They would likely have performed a ritual or a ceremony to pray to the gods for good fortune in the new cycle. The cyclical nature of their calendars influenced the way the Maya thought about history and nature around them. Everything had its beginning and an end; nothing was permanent. And everything was repeating.

One of the significant concept in all three calendars that Maya used was the use of the number 20, with months lasting 20 days, and in the Long Count calendar cycles also being based on 20, with the exception to this rule being a tun made of 18 winals. This may seem strange to most of the people today as our numerical system is the positional decimal numeral system, meaning it is based on number 10. But the Maya, as well as most Mesoamericans, used the vigesimal positional numeral system, based on the number 20. The Maya had only three numeric symbols. Dot represented number 1, the horizontal bar was 5, and shell glyph represented a 0. With those three they would write out any number from 0 to 19. For example, 16 would be three stacked bars on top of each other with a single dot above them all. And if the Maya wanted to go above that, they added another line above, which would mean that numbers in that line would be multiplied by 20. For example, 55 would be written with two dots in the upper line, representing 2x20, and in the bottom line would be three bars, which would be 15. And the Maya could add lines as much as they wanted, with every line being multiplied once again by 20. Thus, the third line would be multiplied by 400 and fourth by 8000.

Though this base 20 system is interesting, more important is the Maya use of zero. Similar to both the calendar and numerical system, the shell glyph 0 was also used in all of Mesoamerica, and the exact origins of the glyph remain a mystery. Some think it was created by the Olmecs, while others attribute it to the Maya, but it may also be from some other Mesoamerican civilization thriving in last millennia B.C.E. The shell glyph was first detected in the Long Count dates from the 1st century B.C.E., where it was a placeholder that represented the absence of particular calendrical count, but it is likely that it was created before that. By 4th century C.E., it had evolved into a proper numeral that was used to perform calculations. And it was used for writing numbers; for example, 40 would be two dots on the second line, and a shell glyph on the bottom. Today this system sounds confusing and it seems that it requires a lot of math to use, but in reality, it was rather practical. Sources tell us that the Maya merchants, using easily transportable beans or kernels as placeholders, could write and calculate large quantities, making their system rather efficient. This seems especially so when compared to the alphabetical systems of ancient Greeks and Romans. And it is yet another sign of how advanced and capable the Maya civilization was, despite being thought of as barbaric for a long time.

Chapter 9 – Religion and rituals in the Maya society

Religion played an important part in almost all ancient societies; the Maya were no exception. It permeated every part of life, from the everyday troubles and hopes of the commoners, to matters of trade, agriculture, and economy, and to the state matters of wars and the cult of the rulers. Everything was guided and influenced by the omens and foretelling of both the future and the past, rooted in the religious beliefs of the Maya. That is why men of faith were an important part of their society. The first type of these holy men to appear in the Maya society were the shamans. Their origins can be traced to pre-civilized society of the Maya ancestors. They played a crucial role in establishing the basics of the calendars and the world order through their tracking of nature and the stars. They used that kind of knowledge to predict rains, a proper time for planning the crops, cure illnesses with herbs and, of course, perform divination rituals. Also, shamans in those early days represented the link with the ancestors, as well as the gods. They held a decent amount of power and prestige at the time. But with rising complexity of the forming Maya civilization most of those early shamans started to transform into the elite class of religious full-time specialists we now call priests. Yet the role of shamans was not entirely extinct, since many commoners took on that call in their local communities. They performed similar roles as before, but their reach was only on a local level, tending to the need of their fellow men.

In contrast to the shamans, priests, now members of the nobility, were responsible for the religious well-being of the entire state. They managed the calendars, divination for more important state affairs, books about both the past and the future, and public rituals and ceremonies. All those activities and responsibilities were linked with the prosperity and success of both the ruler and entire state. With that kind of power and importance, priests gained substantial political and social power. And as the number of political and government offices was limited, many of the younger elite and royal children saw those functions as a way to stay close to the status they were born into. But being of noble descent wasn't enough to become a priest, as all new acolytes had to pass a period of learning and training to become fully pledged priests. Then they would put on their elaborate and stunning robes and, through the many public rituals they conducted, they inspired awe, admiration, and ultimately obedience of the masses to both the state and even more so to the king. At the same time, they advised their rulers, helping them choose a path and lead their polities into the future.

Yet the importance of the priests in religious matters was overshadowed by none other than the king they advised. The ruler was also the chief priest, not only tasked with protecting his subjects from harm in the material world, but also from the suffering caused by the spirit realm. He would also perform various rituals and acts of divination, in an attempt to appease the gods, secure the success of his state, and ultimately to maintain order in the universe. As it was stated in previous chapters, this conjecture of religious and political power led to the forming of the ruler's cult, leading many to refer to the Maya rulers as the shaman kings. To emphasize this religious aspect of the royal rule, rulers wore robes with symbols of various deities, carried scepters and wore headdresses that were linked with some of the gods. Going even further, they claimed to be divine, either as the direct descendant of gods, or at least their voice on earth. Rulers also represented themselves as being in the center of the universe, connecting all the worldly plains, in an attempt to balance their forces. Ultimately, it is through the ruler and the rituals he performed that the supernatural powers merged with the activities and the lives of the humans, while at the same time binding religion and politics with an unbreakable bond.

Figurine of a Maya priest. Source: https://commons.wikimedia.org

For the Maya, the bond of supernatural plains and the material world also existed in nature. Most potent of those were mountains and caves, as they contained magical portals to otherworldly places. Mountains were usually connected to gods and the sky realm, they represented good, potency and were considered the origin of maize. On the other hand, caves had a more dual role in religion. Since they led into the interior of the sacred mountains, they were also seen as places of possible potent fertility. At the same time, they were portals to the underworld, making them rather dangerous places. In Yucatan, cenotes played the similar role as the caves and they were considered as sacred, with the various offering being dropped into them. To harvest the supernatural powers of the places and transport them into their cities the Maya built pyramid temples, now one of the most famous aspects of their civilization. Of course, the pyramid represented the mountain. But in some cases, there were certain chambers inside the pyramids representing the caves. In one of the pyramids that chamber was an actual cave on top of which the temple was built. And on top of the pyramid, the Maya built what is the actual temple, the house of the god, as they called it. It was there that the kings and priests connected as directly as possible with the gods and their realm. Of course, not all temples were built on top of the pyramids, especially in smaller cities and villages. There they were more similar to the houses, representing more the connection with the ancestors. And they were seen as less supernaturally potent. The Maya also built small shrines, sometimes even on the very mountains they praised.

Of course, as the pyramid temples represented the most potent place for establishing connections with the gods, they were used for central public ceremonies. Those could be single-day events, or large celebrations that would last several nights and days. In those types of ceremonies, there would be several hundred or even thousands of people involved, most likely in the open plazas that were built in front of the temples. The ceremonies were led by the kings and priests, dressed to represent the gods, possibly even assuming their identities in the state of religious ecstasy. They would perform rituals leading the ceremony, in an attempt to connect with the supernatural forces, while the common people played music, danced, feasted, and drank. But not all ceremonies were state affairs. There was a whole range of ceremonies that involved commoners and local villages. Yet all of these ceremonies, in spite of being small, followed a similar pattern. The community would gather, eat and drink together, and dance while the shaman, dressed in symbols of the gods, tried to communicate with the gods and ancestors.

But no matter on what level those ceremonies were held, they had to be carried out in the correct way. First, the proper date had to be found through divination methods, then the ones who led the ceremonies, if not everyone involved, endured several days of abstinence and fasting, symbolizing spiritual purification. And most of the ceremonies included similar rituals, most commonly some form of divination, expelling the evil forces, dancing and music, and offerings to gods in various forms of sacrifices, bloodletting, food, or precious materials. All those rituals were usually accompanied by the burning of incense, whose smoke was supposed to more directly convey the message or the plea to the gods in the sky. It was also common for both shamans, as well as priest and kings, to consume various hallucinogenic substances to induce a trance-like state. Commoner population and local shamans for that purpose usually used strong alcoholic beverages and wild tobacco, which was more potent than the tobacco smoked today, while the "professional" high-ranking priests consumed various mushrooms, which were stronger hallucinogens and contained more psychoactive substances. All of the hallucinations and other types of experiences that the men of faith perceived during those altered states were conceived as communication with the gods. Those supernatural messages were either foretellings of the future or possible solutions and answers to the questions and problems that the gods were asked to help with.

In certain cases, it was required that clothing and objects used in a ceremony were new and unused. For those particular ceremonies, all of the items were made specially. Also important was the water, which was commonly used in many rituals. But for rituals that allowed the use of already used objects, clothing, and other equipment, the items still had to be purified with the smoke of burning incense. If the ceremony was of great importance, the Maya holy men would collect fresh "virgin" water from the caves to be used. Another important part of all major ceremonies was the music. From the archeological findings, it is obvious that percussion instruments were most common with various wooden drums, turtle shell drums, gourd rattles, and bone rasps. There were also flutes made from wood or clay, ocarinas, shell trumpets, and whistles. Music was vital for the opening procession of priests that usually started the ceremonies, but also for punctuating important parts and steps in the ritual. It is likely that the Maya felt that the music pleased the gods, facilitating the success of the ceremony. And of course, music was crucial for accompanying the ritual dances performed during the ceremony.

Undoubtedly for the Maya, those dances weren't entertainment, but rather serious religious practice. Dancers were dressed as the gods they tried to connect with, reenacting important scenes from their mythology. They felt they were almost becoming the deity in question, as well as gathering the life force that was in the nature around them, which was needed for interaction between the realms. Besides the clothing embedded with religious symbols, dancers also commonly carried scepters, banners, staffs, spears, rattles, and even live serpents. Maya art shows that the ritual dancers were among others kings, priests, nobles, and even warriors. But it is also likely that the local shamans danced during their rituals while trying to connect with the supernatural forces. Of course, dances differed, being specifically tailored for a certain ceremony and achieving a certain goal. Also, some of those dances were performed before the battles, praying for good fortune and victory. Dances were usually performed with more than one dancer. In some cases, one person was leading the dance or played a central role. Also, in some carvings, there are female dancers depicted, but it seems they weren't as common as males. But rituals, no matter how intricate and well thought out, weren't going to please the gods without the addition of offerings.

A mural of Maya musicians during a ceremony. Source: https://commons.wikimedia.org

Ritual offerings to the gods varied according to the importance and urgency of the ritual. For less important, more common ceremonies and prayers, less precious and symbolic items would be enough, as evident from the offerings found in the sacred cenote of Chichén Itzá. But the Maya believed that what the gods actually craved was more of the life force. Thus, more often they offered food. The lowest on that scale were plant offerings, as it was considered that plant "blood" was potent. And as importance grew, so did the power and size of the being that was sacrificed, and whose blood was to be offered. For example, in a local village ceremony done by a common shaman, an offering of a bird or a small monkey would suffice. For a larger state ceremony led by a priest it is more likely they sacrificed a deer, or even several. Yet, no matter how big and powerful the animal was, human blood was seen as the most potent offering that could be made. This was done by the Maya of all classes, but again, when the members of the elite did it, it was most commonly done for the wellbeing of the entire state and its population. Most common source of the blood was the hand, but there are depictions of other body parts serving as the source, like the tongue or a cheek. There is also evidence that in some rituals kings drew blood from their penises, most likely in an attempt to pray for increased fertility. Blood, no matter of what origin, was most commonly soaked up with bark paper and burned or smeared onto the idols representing the gods.

But no matter how potent the blood of the self-inflicted bloodletting, it wasn't always enough. That is why the Maya practiced human sacrifice, which became one of the most notorious and well-known facts about their civilization and religion, and yet another reason why they were seen as savages for a long time. But for the Maya, it was a logical extension of offering to the gods, as there was nothing more powerful than an entire human life. It was the ultimate sacrifice. In no way was this an everyday event; it was used only for special occasions like crowning a new king, to bless his rule and connect him with the gods, or when a newly built temple needed to be dedicated. Human sacrifices were also used in times of great peril and trouble, be it drought, famine, disease outbreak, or a great and dangerous war. The most common victims were members of the enemy elite captured during the wars, as capturing prisoners was one of the major goals of the Maya warfare. Less often the sacrificed captives were from the lower classes, and even rarer was an enemy king. But in some dire cases there weren't any prisoners to be sacrificed, so the local population was used, though most likely starting from the commoners, then possibly working the way up to the elites if nothing else helped. And in these cases, it becomes unclear if the victims would volunteer themselves or if they were forcibly picked, or if it was a mix of both. And as most victims were war captives, men were more commonly sacrificed, but there is some evidence of both women and children being offered to the gods as well.

Though probably the earliest and most common way to execute the victim was a simple beheading, later the Maya sacrifices became more gruesome and bloody. They tied the captives to the poles and disemboweled them or executed them with a volley of arrows. In later periods, through influence from central Mexico, they started cutting out still beating hearts of the victims, offering the very core of human life to the gods. In Chichén Itzá, during the Postclassic era, they started performing sacrifices in which the prisoners were thrown into their sacred cenote. Victims were either killed by the 20m (65ft) drop or from drowning, perhaps weighed down by stones. Also, during those later periods, another practice was imported from the Central Mexican region. The Maya began painting their victim with blue sacrificial color. Finally, the famous Mesoamerican ball game, played on specially designed courts, was also used to perform human sacrifices. Exact details of the game, its purpose and use are under constant debate by historians, but it is clear that at least part of it was tied to the religion. Some think that teams who played against each other, in a game where the goal was to push the ball through a ring without using legs and arms, actually reenacted famous battles from both history and mythology. It is also suggested that the movements in the game represented the movements of the sun and the moon, while the court itself was seen as the representation of the Underworld or even the gateway to it.

A Maya vase depicting human sacrifice. Source: https://commons.wikimedia.org

It is suggested that the losing team, or at least its captain, was sacrificed to the gods when the game ended. That led researchers to conclude that the players were most likely, as were other victims, captives. Yet some evidence, mostly the depicted gear in some carvings, suggest that this may not always be the case. It is also possible that free people would volunteer for the game, knowing that they may end up being sacrificed, either because of their religious beliefs or more simply in an attempt to prove themselves and rise on the social ladder. But it should be pointed out that the ball game wasn't a purely religious event. It also contains certain elements of entertainment and competition. Some historians also suggested it could have been used to settle disputes between various communities that were part of the same polity. Whatever may be the truth, one thing was certain, sacrifice or not, everyone eventually dies, and death was an important part of the Maya religion. That is why the burial rituals have been seen as rather important. Common practice, no matter the social class, was to put maize or a jade bead into the mouths of the deceased, representing life itself. Alongside the body, various effigies were put, as well as an item that represented that person's life, for example, a book for a priest. Of course, if the deceased was more important and wealthier, he was also buried with various other treasures, even some sacrificed men, possibly to act as servants in the afterlife.

Another common practice was to wait a couple of days before burial, so the soul would have a chance to leave the body and continue its journey. Actual places where the dead were laid to rest differed both from the time period, and of course, from the class the deceased came from. Commoners were either buried on their own estates, in family graves or were left in caves. Some evidence also leads to a conclusion that certain "cemeteries" or burial grounds existed on the outskirts of larger cities, where the commoners were buried. Members of the elite and the royal families were buried in more elaborate tombs, with some of the significant rulers being buried in temples, in the city centers, so they could be revered as powerful ancestors. Even the commoner's graves were visited by their descendants on certain dates, who then burned incense and prayed to them in hope of guidance. This is yet another example of the Maya admiration of their ancestors, which was an important part of their religion. And from this chapter, it is obvious that the Maya religion was actually a complex system of rituals, ceremonies, and beliefs that guided their lives on an everyday basis. That intricate matrix of religious ideas, no matter how bloody or barbaric it may seem from our modern point of view, is yet another example of the complexity and advancement of the Maya civilization.

Chapter 10 – Myths, legends and the gods of the Maya

The Maya religion was polytheistic with an intricate and rich folklore of various myths, legends, and stories. Considering how important and complex their religious practices and rituals were, this shouldn't be much of a surprise. The Maya used these myths to explain and describe the world around them, to set certain guidelines in life, to give their universe some meaning. And to be able to understand both their religion and their society, one should first understand how their universe was divided. Vertically it was split into three realms. First was the Upperworld (Kan), the sky realm where the many of the gods lived and where most of their actions played out. According to some evidence, this realm was further divided into 13 ascending levels, and also it may have had a role similar to the Paradise of Christianity, into which warriors who fell in battle and women who died during childbirth were admitted directly. The second realm was the Underworld (Xibalba), which was an underground place that was also filled with gods and other supernatural creatures. It was imagined as a watery place, which was both the frightful realm of illness and decay, as well as source of great generative powers and fertility. It was divided into 9 layers, and here people who died a peaceful death were sent.

In between those two realms was Earth (Kab), the material world in which the Maya lived. It seems that they believed that the Middleworld, as it is also called, was the back of some kind of a reptile, either turtle or a caiman, that swam in the primordial sea, explaining the watery nature of the Underworld. This realm was divided horizontally into 5 directions of the world. East was the direction where the Sun was reborn, and its color was red. West was where the Sun died, and as such was the direction of the Underworld, or rather its entrance, represented with black. North was representing the noon and the sky, a place of the ancestors, and its color was white. South was the direction where the Sun wasn't visible as there, probably in the Underworld itself, it was fighting lords of Xibalba to be able to be born again. The color of the south was yellow. And the center was considered the fifth "direction", as it was the central axis of the universe, where the sacred World Tree connected all three realms, sharing their spiritual energy and allowing the transport of the souls and gods between them. It was symbolized by the cross. And when the rulers wanted to represent themselves as the center of the universe, they would adorn themselves with symbols of the World Tree, emphasizing their role as the connectors of the realms, directly linked to the gods.

But the question of gods in the Maya pantheon is rather complicated. So far, the researchers have singled out about 250 names of Maya deities, yet they don't think that all 250 of them were separate, distinct gods. Unlike most of the western pantheons, where gods are rather distinct and singular, the Maya deities were much more fluid. One Maya god could manifest different aspects of his power and nature, and for every manifestation, he would be named and represented differently. Some of the gods existed in quadripartite form, with every manifestation corresponding with four world directions and colors. Others existed in dual forms that represented opposites like good and bad, or young and old. Yet in the core of both cases, it would still be a single deity. On the other hand, many of the gods, in those manifestations, overlapped with each other. Their identities, roles, and functions could be mashed up together. This is why most researchers tend to think of the Maya pantheon being made out of clusters of gods, not individual deities. The fact that the Maya also believed that some gods were zoomorphic, capable to turn into animals, or combining human and animal elements also adds another layer of complexity to the pantheon. But some major deities have been identified and more clearly separated from each other.

The Maya god Itzamná. Source: https://commons.wikimedia.org

Among the most important of the major deities was Itzamná, who came the closest to being a supreme deity of the Maya. He was depicted as a wise old man, often as a scribe, sometimes with black obsidian mirrors used to read the past and the future. He was fundamentally a god of creation, playing an important role in creation. Itzamná was also attributed with the invention of books, thus the scribe depictions. As the Lord of the Gods, he presided over the heavens, both during the night and during the day. As such, representing an aspect of his fluidity, he has also been manifested as the principal bird deity called Itzam-Ye or Vuqub Caquix. Itzamná's importance is further underlined with the fact that he was the patron of the day Ahaw, which was the day of the king in the ritual Tzolk'in calendar. He has also manifested powers of healing illnesses, giving him the attributes of a medicine deity. He's married to one of the moon goddesses. Next in line of importance and power was the youthful god of the sun, K'inich Ahaw (the sun-faced lord). In some cases, he and Itzamná shared a duality of old and young, as K'inich Ahaw sometimes looks like a younger version of the creator god. As the sun god, he represented the day cycle and the solar energy that was vital for all natural life, which is why he was rather important to the farmers. But when the Sun went down to the Underworld he would transform into the Jaguar god, who through his battle for rebirth became the patron of war as well. As such the Maya kings often connected themselves with him.

Another god that was important to the farmers was the rain and storm god named Chaac. He was represented with various reptilian features and it was said that he dwelled in moist and wet places like caves. In his benevolent form, he was associated with giving life and creation, as the agriculture and all life depended on seasonal rains. Because of his importance, he was also important for the Maya kings who used his symbols to emphasize their authority. The god of lighting, K'awiil, was also important for the rulers' cult, and his symbols were engraved on the royal scepters. And, as maize was quintessential for the Maya survival, they also had a deity for that. In Popol Vuh he's known as Hun Hunahpu. He had two manifestations, as both an old and young maize god, and in essence, he was a benevolent god that represented abundance, prosperity and ultimately life. He's also notable as a god that died and was reborn, and as the father of the Hero Twins. Their names were Hunahpu and Xbanalque, and they played a crucial role in the creation of the present world.

In a shortened and simplified version of the creation myth, the gods created three worlds prior to the perfect and current version, which was among other things filled with humans made out of the maize dough. To make humans, first they needed to free maize to grow in the Middleworld, which was not possible as their father, the Maize God had been killed in the Underworld. The Hero Twins were invited to Xibalba to take part in series of tasks and a ball game created by the gods of death. One of the important tasks was sacrificing themselves and being revived, making self-sacrifice heroic act, which was important for the Maya rituals. In the end, they manage to beat the death gods and revive their father who then grows out of a turtle shell into the Middleworld. As he was reborn, maize was again available on the Kab, and from Kab the gods finally created humans. This fact is another religious explanation for sacrifices in the Maya world. If humans grow and eat maize, then it is normal that sustenance of gods would be humans, which they created. And as a reward for their feats, the Hero Twins ascend to the heaven.

Despite their triumph, at least one god of death prevailed. His name is Kimi, and he's usually shown either as a skeletal figure or as a bloated corpse. In addition to death, he's also related to war and all the consequences of war, including human sacrifice. Owls are also seen as the representation of death, as vicious night predators, and in some myths, they are even messengers of Kimi. Among many deities were two merchant gods, though two of them may be related, or be part of the same "deity complex". Both of them are shown carrying merchant packages, indicating trade and wealth. One of them known as Ek Chuaj is also a patron of cacao, an important trade resource and a form of currency. The other merchant god, whose name yet hasn't been decoded, is shown with a cigar in his mouth, depicting his connection to shamans, and he is considered to be one of the oldest gods. Interestingly both of them, besides wealth and trade, show signs of war and danger. The older merchant god is shown with attributes of an owl and a jaguar, both related to war and death. On the other hand, Ek Chuaj's connection is clearer, as he's shown carrying a spear. Through these symbols, the Maya represented the dangers that followed a life of merchants, who often had to defend themselves.

Fulfilling the role that, unlike the merchant gods, was more of cosmological importance was a god named Pawahtun. He was one of the gods that had quadripartite form, and each of his manifestations was tasked with holding one of the corners of the world. But despite his serious task as a world-bearer, he was often pictured drunk and in the company of young women. Even more important was a pair of so-called Paddler gods, which are depicted as rowers in a canoe. As they sit in the opposite sides of the canoe, they represent day and night, as they travel across the sky. Modern researchers named them Old Jaguar Paddler and Old Stingray Paddler, as they are represented by those animals. They are sometimes depicted traveling across the Underworld waters, which may indicate they had some connection with the transportation of the deceased to the afterlife. It was also suggested that the Paddler gods also played a role in the creation of the universe, but more common was their connection with ritual bloodletting and sacrifice. They are depicted in scenes of those rituals, while one of the more constant parts of the Paddler gods' imagery were some of the tools used in bloodletting ceremonies.

Not all Maya deities were male. An important role in their pantheon was played by two Moon goddesses, one young and one old, again representing duality in the Maya beliefs. The younger goddess, sometimes represented by a crescent moon and a rabbit, had her powers and godly duties overlapping with the Maize god, in form of fertility and abundance. This is probably connected to the lunar cycle, which was important for determining when to plant crops. That is why some scholars linked her, or at least one of her manifestations, with the Hun Hunahpu's wife. Other think she was paired with the Sun god, as the portrait of a ruler's mother was sometimes depicted within her symbol, while the solar sign was used for the father. Older Moon goddess, Ix Chel, served also as a rainbow deity, which was seen as the mark of the demons, leading to the

Underworld. Due to that fact, she had a certain duality of good and evil within her. When connected with rainbow she was connected to storms, floods, disease, and ultimately destruction of the world. But when she was linked with the moon, she was associated with water as a source of life. She was then linked with creation, being the patron deity of medicine and childbirth, as well as divination and weaving. As such, she was married to Itzamná.

The Maya goddess Ix Chel. Source: https://commons.wikimedia.org

There is another important deity, which has to be mentioned to emphasize the fact that religion, as all other aspects of the Maya culture, was also influenced by contacts with other Mesoamerican civilizations. It is K'uk'ulcan, or as the Aztecs would call him, Quetzalcoatl. This deity, a famous Feathered Serpent of Mesoamerican religions, existed since the early days of the Maya. And, it may have been originally the product of Olmec influence. In those early days, K'uk'ulcan was more connected with war and conquest. But with the later contact with central Mexico, he became more connected with learning and merchants, while he was also a patron deity of rulers. He also served as a god of wind. K'uk'ulcan came to prominence only in the terminal Classic and Postclassic periods, becoming one of the central deities in Chichén Itzá and Mayapan. It is today considered that this shared reverence of the Feathered Serpent among all Mesoamericans helped to facilitate trade among people of different ethnic and social origins. But despite the origins of the people, Maya believed every living human possessed several souls. This is yet another example of the plurality in the Maya religion, to which exact details of number and nature are blurry.

It was believed that souls are eternal and that morality resided in them. It was considered that loss of a certain amount of souls led to sickness, and the shamans were tasked to cure patients by returning the souls to normal. Souls played an important part of shamanism in other forms. For example, it was believed that some of the souls were actually linked to the animal companion spirits, which was crucial for shamans and their connection to nature. Death arrived only when all souls had left the body. Some of the souls died along with the body, others traveled to the afterlife. It was also considered possible for certain types of souls to be reborn in a new person, possibly a future descendant, creating yet another link with of the Maya and their ancestors. With complicated and numerous souls, it is rather difficult to exactly specify in what kind of afterlife the Maya believed. There are certain ideas of an afterlife, with possible rewards and punishments similar to Christian heaven and hell. At the same time, the idea of reincarnation also existed. For kings, deification was also a possibility. The concept of an afterlife may have varied across different regions of the Maya world, as well as all other parts of the Maya religion, which is one reason why researchers find it difficult to puzzle out the complete picture about it. The truth is that both through time and across space, the Maya beliefs changed and had their own unique features, with certain central themes remaining the same. Yet there is no denying it was another part of the Maya civilization which showcased how elaborate and developed the Maya were.

Chapter 11 – The Maya everyday life

It is common in all civilizations of the world that artists and writers often focus their attention on the higher classes: their lives, rituals, and obligations. And historians, due to the more substantial evidence, also tend to give more time and effort in learning about them. It is pretty much the same with the Maya, and so far in this book, the main focus has been on the upper castes of the society. Yet the commoners constituted about 90% of the Maya population, and as such are at least equally important in the story of the Maya civilization. This chapter will be focused as much as possible on their lives, with only occasional throwbacks to the elite, mostly by way of comparison. One of the first important questions regarding the commoners was what their trades were. Today, estimates state that about 75% of the Maya population were involved in some type of food production. Men were mostly tasked with farming and hunting, while the women maintained kitchen gardens, foraged, and prepared food. It is likely that in some cases women helped their husbands in the field. Yet the food was produced year-round, and during the breaks, the Maya weaved, worked on constructions, made tools, or even served as warriors. The other 25%, including the elites, were professionals in different crafts. They were potters, artists, painters, sculptors, merchants, soldiers, priests, stonecutters, jewelers, artisan toolmakers, government officials, and others. Almost half of these non-farmers were members of the noble classes, and they held more socially-desired jobs of priests, soldiers, and even artists and jewelers.

One of the things that was common to all the classes was the importance of families. This was notably demonstrated by nobility, yet the commoners also paid a lot of attention to lineage. Most marriages seem to have been arranged by a third party, and it was forbidden to marry someone who had the same surname, to prevent mixing within the same family. Yet it was socially desirable that both newlyweds were from the same town and class. After the marriage, the husband and wife kept surnames of both their mother and father, to keep track of their lineage. In the first couple of years, the couple lived with the wife's family, where the husband worked to "pay off" the price for her hand. Then they moved to the husband's family where they built their own house and home. It should be noted that most of the Maya were monogamous, especially the commoners, and divorce was possible and seemingly easy to perform. Married couples started having children as soon as possible, with women praying to Ix Chel for fertility and easy childbirth. Babies, when born, were nursed as long as possible, even up to the age of five in some cases. It is at that age that they went through a ceremony in which they were clothed for the first time and became a more functional part of the family. As they grew older, passing through puberty, they would go through a public ritual signifying they became adults. After that, they usually waited for a marriage to be arranged for them. During this waiting period, it was expected of young women to behave chastely and modestly. On the other hand, men were freer, and some evidence points out they may have enjoyed the company of prostitutes. After they were married, both partners were expected to remain faithful.

Formal education didn't exist, and the family was supposed to teach its own children. Parents were in charge of teaching them traditional household tasks, farming techniques, and basics of tradition and religion. In cases of more specialized skills and trades, like pottery making or stonecutting, they learned and apprenticed with extended family members. In cases of the elites, there was some sort of formal education and training for trades that required more esoteric knowledge of rituals, astronomy, medicine, and of course literacy. A sort of school may have existed for scribes, though this may also have been more of an apprenticeship. Parents were also tasked with morally upbringing their offspring to become functional parts of the Maya society. This was important, as the punishment for crimes could be severe. Perpetrators of violent crimes as murder, arson, and rape were usually sentenced to death by sacrifice, stoning, or even dismembering. Though in case of murder, the victim's family may ask for material retribution instead. This was a norm for property crime like theft, where the offender either paid back what he took or was enslaved until he worked off his debt. Adultery was also a serious crime, but mostly for men, who often suffered death penalties, while it was considered that public humiliation was sufficient for women. And this inequality under the law was common in social status as well. A thief of noble descent had his entire face tattooed as a symbol of his disgrace, while the killing of a slave wasn't seen as a serious offense. It is also likely that some laws prohibited commoners to adorn themselves with items connected with nobility, like exotic feathers, pelts, and jewelry. High-ranking town officials, often from noble descent, acted as judges, and though it would be likely they would be partial in some cases, most sources tell us that they acted impartially.

And as the family was the core of the Maya society, their households played an important part in their everyday life. Those were usually composed of several buildings, used for both accommodation and storage, centered around a patio or a courtyard. And it was common for several generations to live in the same household. This pattern was followed no matter the class or wealth of the family, going from the simple clay and thatch cottages of the commoners to the stone palaces of the royal family. The buildings also served as work areas for making homemade pottery, tools, baskets, clothing, and cooking. The food of the commoners varied, but on most days, they ate simple dishes made from squash, beans, and of course maize. Those were complimented with herbs, other vegetables, fruit, and meat. They also made various drinks, most notably a warm maize gruel called atole, and a fermented drink chicha. Nobles also drank a chocolate drink for which it seems a Central Mexican name, xocoatl was used. It is also interesting that famous Mexican tortillas weren't that common among the Maya. According to the remains found, even Maya commoners were well fed and healthy.

Besides good nutrition, an important part of maintaining health was cleanliness. The Maya cleaned their homes, washed their hands and mouth after eating, and occasionally took steam baths. These baths may have been part of certain religious rituals. The Maya shamans also performed curing rituals, likely connected to the idea of the missing souls previously explained. But those were also paired with various herbal cures and ointments. And though some were rather efficient and potent, even relieving some heart conditions, other were completely counterproductive. For example, the Maya believed that smoking tobacco would cure asthma. Besides health and hygiene, they also cared a lot about their looks. And while for us today their ideas of beauty seem unimaginable, they put a lot of effort into it. Most notable was the ideal of elongated and back-sloped foreheads. This was achieved by flattening the still-soft foreheads of babies with two pieces of wood tightly bound on the back and the front of the head. In earlier research, it was assumed this was done only by nobles, as a sign of their stature. But recent surveys show it was actually done by most of the Maya, probably in the attempt to resemble the maize cob.

Another, by today's standards, strange ideal of beauty in the Maya society were slightly crossed eyes. This was also achieved at a very young age, by tying tiny strand balls in front of the baby's eyes, making them focus on it. More relatable to modern fashion were practices of tattoos and piercings. Tattoos were done in a very painful way, by scarring the painted skin, infusing the pigment in the scars. Because of that, as well as the fact it could easily cause infections, tattoos weren't that common and were mostly done to prove and showcase personal bravery. On the other hand, piercings were more common, with ear, lip and nose plugs, which were often adorned by wealthy nobles with precious stones and colorful shells. Both of these practices were done by men and women, though in slightly different fashion and measure. Interestingly, men had not only more tattoos but also more piercings, which was also used to indicate someone's position in the society. A tradition which didn't leave permanent marks was body painting. Warriors used red and black paint to look fiercer and more dangerous. Priests were sometimes painted in blue, for their religious rituals, while women used various colors to emphasize their beauty, almost like makeup. Black paint was also used by people involved in cleansing and other rituals, as well as for ceremonial fasting.

The hairstyle was also an important factor in the Maya style and beauty. It seems that both men and women wore long hair. Male hairstyles were simpler; sides were cut short, while the back was kept long. They usually kept it in ponytails, but sometimes the long tresses were braided with feathers or ribbons. Women had their long hair arranged into elegant and adorned braids and headdresses, more commonly adorned with feathers, ribbons, and other types of accessories. It is also possible that the front of their heads was shaved, to emphasize their elongated foreheads, but this may only be an artistic representation that heightened the desired look. In reality, it is rather difficult to pinpoint the exact look of Maya hairstyles as they are often depicted wearing elaborate headdresses and hats used in various rituals and ceremonies. Men usually avoided beards, and though some of the rulers were depicted with them this was possibly fake, and something worn only for ceremonial purposes. And, as the Maya lived in hot and tropical climates, they used perfume and ointments to lessen their body odors. There were made with various herbs and fruits, though it seems vanilla perfume was the most common.

A figurine of a Maya female. Source: https://commons.wikimedia.org

And although most of the ideals of beauty and fashion were rather similar for both sexes, clothing was somewhat different. Women wore skirts, blouses, and used scarf-like jackets and sarongs around their torsos. Not all women covered their breasts. Beneath their skirts women wore breechcloths. Men wore long capes and only breechcloths, though sometimes they are depicted wearing something looking like a male skirt or a kilt. Complicated robes and jackets were worn mostly by nobles performing rituals. The more formal clothing was often adorned with embroidered feathers, pelts, and symbols of the gods. Regular clothing, especially items worn by the commoners, were less ornate, yet possibly brightly colored. To emphasize their looks, the Maya also had non-piercing jewelry like necklaces, collars, pendants, belts, and bracelets. Again, men wore them more than women, as they were an important indicator of the social status. The material used to make those varied both through time and between the classes. While nobles used various precious stones, most notably jade, as well as precious shells, and later gold, commoners used more often wood and bone, sometimes colored to make it more special.

But good looks and trinkets weren't the only vital part of the Maya everyday life, nor did they provide fun and excitement. For that, they had various entertainment. Most important were, of course, great religious ceremonies, that lasted for days, with music, dancing, and feasts. But these weren't meant for everyday amusement. For that they played a variety of board games, they gambled, and played less brutal types of ball games, played on simple dirt fields, without any religious meaning behind them. They also sang and danced, again without many ritual connotations, and some researchers believe that certain types of codices were written for public readings and performances, resembling a theatrical show. Nobles also had banquets and private feasts, with a lot of food, drinking, and various entertainment like musicians and jesters. Also, an important part of the Maya society were more private family celebrations for events like weddings and ancestor anniversaries, which also provided some leisure time. But all this entertainment was probably less common than we would consider normal today since most of the Maya, especially the commoners, had to work hard throughout the day, and didn't have too much leisure time. But despite that it seems that in most cases, everyday life of the Maya wasn't all that bad, leaving most of them healthy, happy, and well fed.

Chapter 12 – From colonial times to today, the Maya persist

Many books about Maya history and civilization end with the arrival of the Spanish conquistadors. After a brief description of how they were overpowered by technologically superior Europeans, aided by diseases, the Maya story ends. It almost looks like a conscious decision made by the historians to alienate the present-day Maya from the greatness of their ancestors and their culture. And it also sends a message to the world that Maya civilization died under the colonial rule. Though it is true that it was severely altered and influenced by the Spaniards, mostly in religious matters, it would be wrong to think all of their traditions were abandoned, in spite of the Spanish colonial government doing all it could to make the Maya forget about their past. With about 90% of the Maya population ravaged by diseases, the colonial government was instructed to gather up what remained of the Maya and concentrate them in villages and towns built to resemble Spanish settlements in Europe. There it would be easier for them to control and convert the indigenous population. And though some of the Maya resisted until the end of 17th century, eventually pretty much all of them were relegated to the settlements.

In centers of all new settlements were two main buildings, a church and a seat of the civil government. With furious zeal the new masters worked on converting the Maya, pressuring them to forget their gods, mythology, ceremonies, and rituals, to burn their books and erase their traditional writing system. Instead, they offered them their one god, the savior Jesus, The Bible, and the Latin alphabet. Ritual human sacrifices further fueled the religious fervor of Christian priests in converting newly conquered population. They deemed it as satanic, evil, and completely immoral. Yet they found that the burning of infidels at the stakes, torturing them in various cruel manners, and all other practices associated with the Spanish Inquisition, were completely fine, moral, and in accordance with "civilized" nations. At the same time, colonial masters also imposed new civil and government systems. For one, the Maya lost their independence and their voice, while at the same time being used almost as a slave workforce and forced to pay taxes and tributes. Spaniards also changed the economy of the region, introducing steel tools, domestic animals, and ultimately shutting down local trade as every valuable resource from the Maya homeland was shipped to Europe.

But despite all the degradation of everything Maya under the Spanish rule, the Maya culture and civilization managed to survive. Though their religion was ultimately lost, certain aspects managed to fuse with Christianity and survive. One of those was respect for their ancestors, while in some cases Christian rituals were updated with local practices. In some cases, even the sacrifices continued, though they were performed on animals, mostly chickens. And some of the more educated Maya used the newly adopted Latin alphabet to transcribe at least some of their traditional books, like Popol Vuh, saving certain elements of their culture in them. Among other aspects of the culture they preserved were symbols and patterns they used on their clothes, though these were also mixed with Christian symbolism and done on European-styled clothing. But most importantly the Maya preserved their own Mayan language. But thanks to the separation of different groups of the Maya, their language, as well as other traditions, grew apart during the colonial rule. With that the colonial and postcolonial Maya population and their civilization, was fractured and separated, again lacking the unity to fight for its own needs.

But it should be noted that the conquest of the Maya heartland wasn't completely successful. Despite trying to "civilize" the Maya, the Spanish lords and the Ladinos, non-elite Spaniards and Hispanicized people, lived separately from them. And as they were outnumbered, they lived in confined communities. Around and in between them was the local Maya population, which was more than aware of the differences between them. Essentially, attempts of the colonial government to assimilate and incorporate the local population into their own civilization were thwarted by their own disdain towards the Maya. They were treated as lower-class citizens, basically without any rights. And for a very long time, the Maya had to put up with that because they had no power to fight back. But in the 19th century, the Spanish Colonial Empire crumbled and new Mesoamerican states sprouted up. In spite of certain expectations that with the colonial system gone the locals, including the Maya, would live better, basically nothing changed. Descendants of Ladinos continued to rule the countries, oppressing the Maya the same as before. And finally, that led the Maya to rebel.

The Yucatec Maya took up guns and in 1847 started the war against the Mexican central government. For the white elite that exploited them, this became known as the "War of the Castes," which is yet another confirmation that they saw the Maya as the lowest class of people. During this rebellion, it seems that ancient warrior spirits woke up among the Maya fighters as they managed to take over control of almost all of Yucatan. Mexican government troops were confined into a few cities on the coast. For a short period of time, it seemed like the conquest was reversed and that they gained back their freedom. But as the planting season came, the Maya army just like in the pre-Columbian times returned to their homes to work on their fields. However, this wasn't the end of this uprising. The skirmishes and localized fighting continued, but in 1850 a new upsurge in fighting spirit happened within the Maya. They were inspired by the manifestation of so-called "Talking Cross," through which they thought God communicated to them, telling them to continue their struggle. Once again, religion was infused with warfare, and with newfound power, the Maya of the southeast Yucatan managed to fight off the government troops and establish their semi-independent state. It is often called Chan Santa Cruz, named by its capital just like in the heyday of the Maya civilization.

The question of independence of this Maya state is rather complicated. The Mexican central government didn't have any control over that territory, the Maya were factually free. But except Britain, no other country recognized its separation from Mexico City. And the only reason why Britain did so was because of the trade between British Belize and Chan Santa Cruz. There are also some suggestions that some of the weapons used in the rebellion came from Belize. Other smaller groups of the Maya also declared their own independent path, but they were less successful. Some of those groups even opposed the Chan Santa Cruz as they saw worshiping of the Talking Cross as swerving from the path of true Christianity. And of course, the central Mexican government didn't remain passive , it attacked the Chan Santa Cruz, even arriving close to the capital on a few occasions. Fighting continued for the next 50 years, with the major turning point happening in 1893 when Britain signed a treaty with Mexico, in which among other things it was recognized that Chan Santa Cruz was under Mexican sovereignty. This was a major setback for the Maya because they couldn't resupply their weapons and ammunition from Belize. And in 1901 they were finally defeated by the government troops. It is estimated that during this war between 40 and 50 thousand people died, mostly Maya.

Oil painting of Caste War, c1850. Source: https://commons.wikimedia.org

Despite losing the war and their freedom, there were some positive consequences of this Maya uprising. Around 1915, the central government implemented certain reforms. Among these were agrarian reforms that abolished colonial labor system, and that solved some of the problems that caused the revolt. But, of course, the Maya were still treated as second-class citizens, and their position, in general, didn't improve much. And as the Maya themselves didn't care much about integration into the Mexican society, they remained relatively separated both politically and economically, living mostly as poor farmers. But the policy of Mexico City changed in the 1950s and 60s. Through many initiatives they tried to modernize and incorporate the Maya into the Mexican community, creating a migration of the Maya by offering them unused lands, as well as parts of the jungle they could clear, so they could create new farms. These initiatives were of very limited success, and the biggest consequence was rising anger of the non-indigenous Mexicans who felt their land was given to the Maya. That is why by the 1970s these initiatives were stopped. But at approximately the same time, the Maya of Guatemala went through the darkest period since the arrival of the Spanish conquistadors.

During that period Central American countries were sucked into the whirlwind of the Cold War, where the leftist rebels, backed by some socialist countries and some of the indigenous population hoping for more equal society, clashed with the right-wing military dictatorship supported by the

United States. As part of this wider political problem the Civil War in Guatemala started in 1960, and from the beginning one of the major targets of the right-winged government were the Maya. Though their limited support to the rebels played a part in this decision, more often it was caused because of racism and intolerance of the Ladino government towards the Maya, whom they often saw as impure and unworthy. Ultimately for them, the Maya were the hated lower race. The terror towards the indigenous population escalated from 1975 to 1985, during which period the Guatemalan army carried out more than 600 massacres and destroyed more than 400 Maya villages. Somewhere between 150 and 200 thousand people were killed, more than 40 thousand "disappeared," and around 100 thousand women were raped. Besides those, there were about half a million refugees that sought security in surrounding countries and in the US. The vast majority of these victims were the Maya, with estimates varying from 80 to 90%. Some other smaller indigenous groups were targeted as well. The Civil War lasted until the mid-1990's, but its consequences are still felt today.

After the civil war ended, this terror was internationally recognized as a genocide, usually called the Guatemalan genocide or the Maya genocide. Another, though a less used name was Silent Holocaust, partially because it seemed that no one cared about the Maya victims as the genocide occurred. They were silenced and ignored by the majority of the world who was much more interested in the Cold War aspect of the Civil War. A United Nations commission even concluded that part of the responsibility for the massacres should be laid on America's training of the Guatemalan officers in the counterinsurgency techniques, though this brought no consequences for the United States. And, as the Guatemalan Maya finally found some peace in the 90's, things once again turned for worse for the Mexican Maya. The main issue was that, in order to join the North American Free Trade Agreement (NAFTA) with the US and Canada, Mexico had to modify certain articles in its constitution, among others one that protected the communal indigenous land. That land was the main source of food and income for many Maya, as well as some other native groups. With redaction of that article, the central government could privatize and sell those lands. Furthermore, the local population that depended on those communal farms became illegal land-squatters, and their communities became informal settlements.

Once again, the central government was deaf to the Maya complaints and it amended the Mexican constitution. This caused an armed revolt of the Maya in January of 1994, which this time occurred in the Mexican state of Chiapas instead of Yucatan. The Zapatista Army of National Liberation led the insurgency, with demands for cultural, political, social, and land rights for all the Maya in Mexico, as well as for all other indigenous population in the country. The Mexican army quickly responded and after only 12 days the ceasefire was announced. Yet this event shocked the Mexican government. Politicians in Mexico City weren't used to the idea of indigenous people revolting so openly. But more worrying for them was the support the movement gained across Mexico and across the world. The Maya achieved that through excellent use of media, especially the internet, which was still a new technology at the time. Under pressure, the government agreed to negotiate with the Maya and promised that the native population of Mexico would be protected. Yet as soon as the dust settled they continued with their own plans, the same way as before. And to this day the Maya protest, trying to get their voices heard, while the Mexican politicians are more and more trying to avoid them, ignoring them. In those tense situations, some local fight and skirmishes do occur, but mostly between civil populations, and there are no signs of improvement.

Today Maya of all countries live in relative peace, although their lives are far from ideal. Rainforests are being destroyed, their traditional farms are taken from them, substituted with cattle ranches; the army is a looming threat. Yet they are still fighting for their political rights, and in recent years the Maya leaders are slowly realizing the only possible solution for their salvation is connecting all the various Maya groups living in all Mesoamerican states. Despite their linguistic differences, working together is the only way to preserve their culture, tradition, and history. Yet the last couple of decades another change has occurred. With extra attention, both from science circles and from media made their civilization better known to the world. With interesting culture, breathtaking remains and colorful nature around them the Maya became rather popular in tourist circles. More and more visitors arrive in their communities, owing to the greatness of the Maya past. And this is a double-edged sword. On one side, no country would dare to commit atrocities as before, both because of the negative media image but also because of the economic impact of tourism. Of course, economic gains are also beneficial to the Maya, who are now able to earn more money and are less dependent on farming. Also, their culture is now much harder to destroy, as it has become more recognizable and popular.

A Maya woman making souvenirs. Source: https://commons.wikimedia.org

And that is where the blade strikes back on the Maya. Most tourists come to the Maya with certain expectation what they should and want to see. And in those expectations are many common misconceptions and half-truths, to which some of the Maya pander. They don't want to lose the customers that bring in much-needed income. And under that pressure, tourists at the same time save and change the Maya culture. Also, in a way, tourism degrades their rich culture and traditions into something trivial. Their craftwork and art are reduced to a trifle bought in the flea market as a keepsake from the trip. For them, there is no deeper meaning to it. But for now, there is no alternative for most of the Maya people. And considering both political situations and tourism begs the question of the Maya future. While there is great danger lurking for them, there is no doubt they will prevail. As so many times in the past, they will adapt and overcome obstacles, trying to maintain their traditions and civilization.

Conclusion

Hopefully, through this guide, you have gained the basic understanding of who the Maya are, what their culture and civilization represent. You now see how complex and intricate their history was, with their political struggles, alliances, and wars between their ancient states and developed societies. And, you have learned how crucial their role was in the Mesoamerican region, connecting it through trade, sharing ideas, culture, and mythology with civilizations around them. More importantly, it should be obvious that the Maya weren't some backward savages that lived in the jungles before the Europeans came to show them what true civilization means. They created stunning art, grand architectural marvels comparable with the ancient wonders of the world and tracked the stars and planets with unbelievable precision. And although their view of the world was rather different from how we perceive it today, it was no less elaborate and well-thought through. Their religion, despite the controversial sacrifices, was a complicated system of beliefs, myths, moral guidelines, and rituals. And in no way should it be considered primitive or less worthy than any other ancient religions. Also, seeing some aspects of their everyday life should bring them closer to us, with the understanding that they too lived their lives filled with hopes and fears, worries and celebrations. This makes them feel less like relics of the past and more like humans that are still around.

Ultimately this guide should have explained why the Maya civilization should be respected and equally praised, along with many other ancient civilizations. At the same time, it stands as a reminder that the Maya, unlike most other praised civilizations of the past, never disappeared. Not only are they still around, but they are trying to preserve their heritage and traditions, fighting for survival. And that fact should be a constant reminder that history isn't always something that happened long ago in a distant land, but something that is still present, echoing in the world of today. The story of the Maya struggle in the recent times should also stand as inspiration that no matter how dark things look, as long as there are people willing to fight, there is still hope. Because of that, respect of the Maya civilization should be extended to the people keeping it alive today, the Maya people of our times. Understanding all that should, in the end, show why it is important for world cultural heritage that the story of the Maya isn't forgotten, and why it should be kept for future generations as well.

Of course, this is a task that goes beyond what this single book can do. So, in the end, this guide, educational and informative, as well as fun and interesting, was supposed to serve only as an introduction to the Maya world, both past, and present. It builds a solid foundation upon which further knowledge should be built. And hopefully, it will light a spark of interest, amazement, and intrigue about the Maya civilization, as there is so much more about it to be told. It is exactly through that spark, that thirst for more knowledge and a deeper understanding of the Maya that this book serves the higher goal. Through that, we make our own contribution, no matter how small, to the preservation of the beautiful, intriguing, and unique Maya civilization.

If you enjoyed this individual book on the Maya civilization, can you please leave a review for it?

Thanks for your support!

Part 4: Aztec History

A Captivating Guide to the Aztec Empire, Mythology, and Civilization

Introduction

For many years, the Aztecs have captured our imaginations. Stories from the original European invaders combined with unique, awe-inspiring ruins and legends that speak of palaces of gold create an image of Aztec society defined by grandeur, wealth, and splendor. But who exactly were the Aztecs? Where did they come from? How did they rise to control such a wide expanse of land? And if they were so powerful, how was it possible for them to fall from power and dominance just three years after contact was first made with the Spaniards?

Luckily for us, we can answer most of these questions. Detailed historical accounts from Spanish conquistadors, Aztec documents such as the Codex Mendoza (a detailed account of Aztec rulers, the tribute system and daily life in the empire created in the mid-15th century after Spanish conquest,, and a wealth of archaeological sites make it possible to uncover some of the secrets of this ancient civilization.

In truth, the daily life of an Aztec commoner was not all that different from the life of today's common folk. Sure, technology was far more primitive, and there was a constant looming threat of complete and total destruction at the hands of one of the many Aztec gods. But apart from this, the average Aztec citizen was responsible for working their land, paying taxes, and providing for their families. When they weren't doing this, they were either off fulfilling their obligatory military service or perhaps enjoying a relaxing game of *patolli* with their friends.

While the life of a commoner in the Aztec empire seems okay, it was one full of hard work and uncertainty about the future. Few Aztec commoners were able to enjoy goods or services beyond the basic necessities for life and worship. Aztec leaders, on the other hand, lived a life of luxury. Servants, concubines, and laborers were bound to the nobility, and this life of luxury helped employ the ever-growing Aztec population.

Overall, the Aztec Empire, or the empire of the Triple Alliance, would grow in both size and population to be one of the largest in the ancient world. It was the second largest empire in all of America in the 16th century; only the Incas occupied more territory. At its peak, the Aztec Empire included some 50 or more city-states and upwards of 3 million people. However, this would nearly all disappear with the arrival of the Spanish. Superior weapons and devastating disease laid waste to much of what the Aztecs had built over the previous centuries.

Many of the secrets of the Aztec Empire have been uncovered. Yet many more still remain. Historians and archaeologists are constantly learning more about the way the Aztecs lived, how they organized themselves politically, and how they interpreted their position in the world and the cosmos.

This guide will review some of the major parts of Aztec history, including a detailed account of who the Aztecs were, how they expanded, how they lived, how they worshiped, how they played, and finally, how they died. By taking the time to remember the Aztecs and their accomplishments, we can all play a part in making sure one of the world's greatest civilizations lives on forever.

Chapter 1 – Where Did the Aztecs Live?

To understand Aztec civilization, it's important to grasp the diverse geographical landscape in which their empire thrived. The Aztecs are considered a Mesoamerican civilization, with Mesoamerica being the term to describe the area extending from North-Central Mexico to the Pacific Coast of Costa Rica.

As you would expect from an area so large, the defining characteristic of Mesoamerican geography is diversity. Coastal lowlands differ greatly from central highlands in all aspects, from climate, soil conditions, and availability of crops. It's important to note that what is traditionally considered the Aztec Empire, the area surrounding Tenochtitlán (present-day Mexico City) in the Valley of Mexico, differed greatly from its surrounding territories and relied on them for a number of different essential and luxury resources.

In general, Mesoamerica can be divided into three major environmental zones. The tropical lowlands refer to the lands lying below 1,000 meters (~3280 ft). These parts of Mesoamerica are referred to as *tierra caliente* (hot lands). All of Mesoamerica lies in a tropical climate, but higher elevations bring temperatures down. Near the coasts, however, this does not happen. Temperatures are hot, the air is humid, and rainfall is heavy. The principal landscapes in this zone are heavy-vegetation forests or savanna grasslands. The Aztecs relied on these territories for such goods as colorful feathers from parrots and quetzals (used for rituals and art), jaguar skins, tobacco, and jade.

As one moves inland, they enter the Mesoamerican Highlands. The highlands refer to areas that are between 1,000-2,000 m (~3280-6560 ft.) and are often referred to as *tierra templada* (temperate country). Temperatures hover around 70°F (21°C), and with distinct dry (January to May) and rainy (June to October) seasons, rainfall is sufficient in most parts of the Mesoamerican Highlands for people to successfully grow crops year-round.

While this territory is mountainous, human civilization has flourished in river valleys and other expanses with relatively flat land. Many other Mesoamerican civilizations found their home here, including the Mixtecs, Zapotecs, Tarascans, and highland Maya. The southern part of the heart of the Aztec Empire falls in this territory.

If you continue climbing up the mountains and towards the center of present-day Mexico, you enter the Central Mexican Plateau. Everywhere you go is at least 2,000 m (~6560 ft.) above sea level, which brings tropical temperatures way down and gives the plateau the name *tierra fria* (cold lands). The heart of the Aztec civilization was in the center of this plateau, the Valley of Mexico. But additional large valleys lie to the north, west, and east. Rainfall varies widely across this part of Mesoamerica, and cooler temperatures make frost a challenge for farmers, shortening the growing season and the overall availability of crops.

In the heart of the Valley of Mexico is Tenochtitlán, the Aztec capital. Built essentially on Lake Texcoco, Tenochtitlán was founded in 1325 and would grow to be a powerful city, the largest in Mesoamerica. Agreements with nearby city-states greatly expanded their capacity to grow and expand in both territorial and cultural influence.

Surrounding the Valley of Mexico, the elevation drops rapidly, and cultural diversity expands. To the north, Otomi-speakers dominated and remained relatively outside Aztec influence. To the west is the Toluca Valley, where Aztec-Nahuatl speakers shared territory with many different language groups. And to the east is the Puebla Valley, where several cities in the northern part of this territory resisted Aztec conquest and remained independent until the Spaniards arrived in 1519.

It's important to grasp the environment in which the Aztec Empire developed. Challenging terrain and cultural diversity made for a state of constant jockeying for power and influence. Establishing dominance in this area required a wise and efficient use of resources, along with a good deal of force and cunning, and the making of enemies along the way. This would be the eventual demise of the Aztec Empire, but it first facilitated a civilization that is responsible for much of Mesoamerican history.

Chapter 2 – Who Were the Aztecs?

The first thing to remember is that the Aztecs are the Aztecs only to us. This is the name historians use to describe the empire formed by the Nahuatl-speaking peoples who referred to themselves as the Mexica. The name Aztec is said to derive from the word Atzlan, which describes a place in Northern Mexico where it's believed the semi-nomadic Mexica originated. The exact location of Aztlan is unknown, though it is generally agreed to be in the north of modern Mexico. Many Nahuatl-speaking tribes claim their origin to be from Atzlan, but even the Aztecs we know did not have a clear idea of where it is. Montezuma I famously sent out a band of warriors and explorers to find it, but they were unsuccessful. The word Aztec comes from *Aztecah,* which means "people from Aztlan." However, this name was not used by the Aztecs to describe themselves. It became the accepted term over time. In general, it's unclear if the Aztecs move to the Valley of Mexico was by design or rather as part of a much larger southern migration carried out by the people of Northern Mexico.

The Aztecs were likely related in some form or another to the Toltecs, a civilization that grew to prominence in Northern Mexico in the 11th and 12th centuries. It was very important for early Aztec rulers to establish some sort of lineage with the Toltecs, as they felt this provided them with legitimacy. Additionally, the Aztecs would adopt and adapt many of the religious and spiritual practices of the Toltecs. For example, the Aztec god Quetzalcóatl, who is considered to be one of the most important gods in the Aztec religion, was the priest-king of Tula, the Toltec capital.

However, despite efforts by Aztec rulers to make direct connections to the Toltecs, it's far more likely that the people we now refer to as Aztecs were actually a combination of different hunter-gatherer tribes. It's unclear why, by early Aztec sovereigns found it necessary to legitimize their rule by claiming lineage with the Toltecs. As the empire grew and consolidated, this became less important. Yet some of the cultural and religious similarities are hard to ignore. However, in the end, it was the Nahuatl language that brought distinct cultural groups together to form what we now know as the Aztecs.

The Aztec Empire typically refers to what is known as the Triple Alliance. This was an alliance between the three cities in the Valley of Mexico, Tenochtitlán, Texcoco, and Tlacopan. The capital was to be Tenochtitlán, and it would grow to be the center of Aztec influence in the region.

The story, or stories, of the founding of Tenochtitlán sheds some light into Aztec values and worldviews that can be seen throughout the empire's history. The first story speaks to the power of religion and myth. After having been forced to settle elsewhere, the god Uitzilopochtli came to the priest Quauhcoatl and told him they should build their city where they find a *tenochtli* cactus with an eagle sitting on top. Legend has it the men with whom Quahcoatl was traveling found this cactus shortly thereafter and chose to settle there.

Another story explains why the Mexica were looking for a new place to settle. They were semi-nomadic, meaning they changed lands according to agricultural or pastoral needs. Forced to the south, they found most of the Valley of Mexico already occupied by other tribes and linguistic groups.

The first Mexica settlement, Chapultepec, was on a hill on the western shore of Lake Texcoco. Founded in roughly 1250, Chapultepec would not last long. By the end of the 13th century, the Tepanecs of Azcapotzalco, the tribe that had established dominance in the area surrounding Chapultepec, had driven the Mexica from Chapultepec and gave them permission to live on the barren lands surrounding the city-state of Tizapan, also in the area surrounding Lake Texcoco.

In 1323 though, the Mexica played a cruel trick on their new ruler. After asking for his daughter's hand in marriage, they promptly sacrificed her and flayed her skin. A priest then presented himself to the king wearing his daughter's skin. Horrified, this caused the Mexica to be expelled from Tizapan. They were once again forced to find a new place to live.

It's impossible to know if the Aztecs chose Tenochtitlán because of divine intervention or out of necessity. Forced to evacuate two prior settlements, the Mexica could no longer be too picky. Tenochtitlán is essentially a swamp, and its growth was due in large part to the tremendous effort of adding dirt and mud to build solid ground upon which a city could be built.

No matter the reason, Tenochtitlán was the center of what we now refer to as the Aztec Empire. Its symbol is, fittingly, an eagle perched upon a cactus. This image appears in the center of modern-Mexico's flag, indicating the role this ancient civilization plays in the collective psyche of one of the world's largest modern nations.

It's becoming increasingly common to refer to Tenochtitlán by its full name: Mexico-Tenochtitlán. The exact meaning of the name is not fully understood. Tenochtitlán clearly draws its moniker from the Nahuatl word for prickly pear, *tenochtli*, but the origin of the word *Mexico* is more difficult to uncover. Most scholars now agree it means "in the center of the moon," with the moon referring in this context to Lake Texcoco. This deduction is confirmed when looking at the how the name Mexico-Tenochtitlán is translated into the nearby Otomi language, where the Mexican capital is referred to as "anbondo amedetzana." Bondo is known to mean prickly pear, and amedetzana means "in the middle of the moon." Many sources and historical documents will refer to the city as simply Tenochtitlán, but those living during the height of the Aztec empire would have used its full name.

These origin stories of Mexico-Tenochtitlán reflect how we would eventually come to perceive this ancient civilization and culture. Aztec mythology and religion has been heavily studied, and most modern depictions of Aztec life include at least some reference to the brutality of human sacrifice. Images of priests ripping out the beating hearts of citizens are aplenty. And while this did occur, Aztec culture was, as you would expect, decidedly diverse and dynamic, especially for a civilization of this size.

Estimates indicate more than 1 million people were living in the Valley of Mexico when Cortés came onto the scene in 1519. And there were likely another two or three million in the highlands surrounding it. These figures make the Aztec civilization the largest in the Americas at the time of European arrival.

It's also important to remember that when we talk about the Aztec Empire, we are in many ways talking about the period of time after the formation of the Triple Alliance. This was an agreement to unite the three major city-states surrounding Lake Texcoco, specifically Mexico-Tenochtitlán, Texcoco, and Tlacopan, and to place Mexico-Tenochtitlán at the center as the capital. The three cities would share bounties from trade and tribute, allowing them to orchestrate their expansion into the surrounding valley.

Chapter 3 – Government, City-States, and Expansion

Aztec civilization can be divided into two main periods: the Early Aztec period and the Late Aztec period. Many of the city-states that would become a part of the Aztec Empire were founded at the beginning of the 12th century. Most would persist and grow throughout the coming centuries, and many would become important city-states in the empire. However, as these towns grew into cities and eventually city-states, much of what had been constructed in the Early Aztec period was destroyed, leaving little archaeological evidence of these settlements.

The beginning of the Late Aztec period is usually associated with the founding of Mexico-Tenochtitlán in 1325. When the Mexica arrived, there was very little land that had not already been settled. Different tribes and ethnic groups occupied the territory, but over time, many of them would assimilate into Aztec culture. The only ethnic group able to maintain its own independent identity was the Otomi, who maintained their own linguistic and cultural traditions despite constant pressure from their Nahuatl-speaking neighbors.

The political system of the Aztecs was despotism. Kings and quasi-kings ruled over city-states and they interacted with other city-states in various ways. Sometimes they cooperated with each other, typically through trade and military alliances, but they also fought each other constantly. As such, relationships between city-states were ever-changing and unpredictable.

Nevertheless, the Aztec Empire is really best understood as a political alliance between some fifty or more city-states that occupied the Valley of Mexico. The only real political institution that bound them together was the system of taxes and tributes that was designed to help raise the status of sovereigns and the nobility and also to suppress and subdue the commoners. As the empire expanded, this tribute system became more demanding. And in cases where city-states fell under the control of the Aztecs because of military conquest, tributes were even harsher.

The golden age of the Aztec Empire began in 1428 with the formation of the Triple Alliance between Mexico-Tenochtitlán, Texcoco, and Tlacopan. This represents the most robust form of political cooperation between any of the city-states in the Valley of Mexico, and it was due to the economic and military might of these city-states that the Aztecs were able to eventually gain control over nearly all of the settlements in the Valley of Mexico and beyond.

This alliance, however, was born from war. Hostilities between the Mexica, or Aztecs, and the Tepanecs, a city-state that also had considerable influence in the Valley of Mexico, intensified around the year 1426. The Tepanecs tried to blockade Tenochtitlán in an effort to extract higher taxes and tributes. While attempting to intimidate the Mexica in Tenochtitlán, the Tepanecs, led by Maxtla, were also harassing the Acolhua in Texcoco. When they forced Netzahualcoyotl, the sovereign of Texcoco, to flee, the Mexica found an ally in their struggle against the Tepanecs. Furthermore, Motecuhzoma, the leader of Tenochtitlán at the time, was attempting to rally support for a rebellion in the Valley of Mexico by pandering to citizens of Tlacopan who were fed up with Tepanec rule and were looking for a change.

Total war broke out in 1428, and with the forces of Texcoco, Tlacopan, Tenochtitlán, and Huexotzinco combined, the Tepanecs were defeated, leaving the Mexica as the primary power in the Valley of Mexico. Being the largest and richest of the three city-states, and also having the largest military, Tenochtitlán was the natural choice for the center of this newly formed imperial alliance. The Huexotzinco, living on the other side of the mountains, were merely interested in removing the Tepanecs, but did not have any further ambitions in the Valley of Mexico. After the war's conclusion, they returned to their home and the remaining three city-states formed what we now call the Triple Alliance.

This collaboration was as much a military alliance as it was an economic cooperation. The first tenet was to agree not to wage war against each other and to support each other in wars of conquest and expansion. Taxes from these conquests would be shared, with two-fifths going to both Texcoco and Tenochtitlán and one-fifth to Tlacopan. The capital was to be in Tenochtitlán, meaning the leader of this city-state was the de facto emperor, yet this leader would be chosen somewhat democratically. An electoral college made up of nobles and dignitaries from all three city-states in the Alliance was responsible for choosing the leader of the pact. Itzcoatl was named the first emperor of the new Aztec Empire, even though Motecuhzoma had been the leader of Tenochtitlán. Motecuhzoma would have to wait his turn to assume the position of emperor.

After joining forces, the new Aztec Empire quickly set its sights on gaining control over the entire Valley of Mexico. Campaigns throughout the 1430s brought the cities of Chalco, Xochomilco, Cuitalhuac, and Coyocan under the influence of the Triple Alliance. After completing these conquests, the Aztecs looked further south, moving into the modern-day state of Morelos. Here they would conquer Cuauhnahuac (the modern-day city of Cuenravaca) and Huaxtepec. Located in lower elevations, the climates in these cities were much more favorable. Intensive agriculture produced impressive yields that the Aztecs desired so as to feed their people and enrich their empire.

In 1440, Itzcoatl died and Motecuhzoma I was chosen as the next emperor. The reign of Motecuhzoma I was an important part of Aztec history. He began construction on some of the more important Aztec temples, including the great temple of Tenochtitlán. But perhaps more importantly, Motecuhzoma I was responsible for consolidating political power into the hands of the Mexica.

As new city-states fell under the control of the Aztecs, Motecuhzoma I would install his own people as tax collectors to bypass the dynasties that had previously existed, centralizing power into the hands of Tenochtitlán and taking it away from competing tribes. Motecuhzoma I also established a new legal code that served to further distinguish the nobility from the common folk.

However, he was also interested in quelling rebellions and keeping city-states that had been conquered under his control. One thing he did to try and do was to create a new title, the quahpilli (eagle lord). Anyone could occupy this position and it was typically given to warriors who had been exceptionally successful in battle.

Motecuhzoma I also presided over one of the darker periods of the Aztec Empire. Severe drought hit the region in 1450, and this led to significant famines over the next four years. Thousands of Aztecs would die of hunger during this period. After the famines ended, there was a significant uptick in the amount of human sacrifices throughout the empire as it was widely believed that this drought and famine was the result of insufficient sacrifices in the years before 1450.

Motecuhzoma I and Nezahualcoyotl of Texcoco began a series of military campaigns in 1458 that would dramatically expand the sphere of Aztec influence in the region. They were able to extend their control well beyond the Valley of Mexico, establishing dominance throughout the majority of the modern-day states of Morelos and Oaxaca.

When Motecuhzoma I died in 1468, Axayacatl, the grandson of both Motecuhzoma I and Itzcoatl, took over the throne. Most of his 13-year rule was spent consolidating or reconquering some of the territories already seized by previous rulers. Axayacatl was succeeded by his brother Tizoc in 1481. However, he was a weak ruler and a poor military leader. He died in 1486 and was replaced by another one of his brothers, Ahuitzotl. Some evidence suggests Tizoc may have been assassinated as those in the center of the empire saw Tizoc as a liability.

When Ahuitzotl took the throne, he began another period of military conquest that would significantly expand Aztec-controlled territory. Specifically, he conquered much of the Valley of Oaxaca and the Soconusco Coast of Southern Mexico. Although they were the farthest from the imperial center, these areas were significant as they were important source of goods such as cacao and feathers, both of which were used by the nobility as means of expressing their wealth and higher social standing.

The reign of Ahuitzotl represents the most prosperous period of the Aztec Empire. Not only did it expand considerably in terms of the territory it controlled, but Ahuitzotl was also able to consolidate power within the Triple Alliance. He replaced the title *tlataoni,* which means "one who speaks," and was the Aztec word for sovereign, with *huehuetlatoani,* which means "supreme king." The other city-states were consulted less about imperial matters who seemed to have little desire in trying to regain control from the leaders of Tenochtitlán. The city's great temple was completed during the time of Ahuitzotl, indicating that his rule also presided over a period of significant economic prosperity.

When Ahuitzotl died in 1502, he was replaced by Motecuhzoma Xocoyotzin, who is often referred to in the history books as Montezuma, or Montezuma II who is not to be confused with Motecuhzoma I.. Following the footsteps of previous emperors that assumed power after a period of significant imperial expansion, Montezuma's reign was largely defined by his attempts to consolidate power. But this time, there seemed to be a more pointed effort to consolidate power not only into the hands of the Triple Alliance, but also into the hands of Montezuma's family. He essentially abolished the status of many nobles, replacing them with people closer to his immediate circle. In court, Montezuma ruled with terror, leading some scholars to indicate that Montezuma may have been taking steps towards creating an absolute monarchy in the Aztec Empire.

The Aztec Empire was at its peak during the reign of Montezuma. It had political, economic, social, and militaristic control over a vast expanse of land that was populated by some 3-4 million people. However, one particular failure of the previous rulers was their inability to successfully conquer the Tlaxcallans, a Nahuatl-speaking group that had made their home near the Valley of Mexico but who had resisted Aztec control.

The Aztec inability to conquer the Tlaxcallans proved to have disastrous consequences, as the Spanish were able to formed an alliance with them.

In fact, it was not hard at all for the Spanish to find support for their cause. To understand why this was the case, it's important to remember why the Aztecs were so concerned with expansion. They were looking for new city-states to subject to their tax and tribute system, and they were also looking to find new victims that could be sacrificed to the gods.

Furthermore, they were interested in expanding the empire's resource pool. A growing population meant increased demand for food. City-states at lower elevations were far more agriculturally productive, so conquest of these settlements made it easier for the Aztecs to feed their population, and it also represented an opportunity to enrich the Aztec elite through the collection of taxes and tributes. This strategy proved to be effective as the Aztec Empire grew in wealth and population considerably after the formation of the Triple Alliance, but it also had the effect of creating lots of animosity towards Tenochtitlán and the Aztec empire, something that would put the Aztecs at a significant disadvantage against the Spaniards. There were plenty of people willing to sign up with the Spanish to help conquer the mighty Aztecs.

Throughout the 100 or so years of the Triple Alliance, the Aztecs took their civilization from a loose collection of semi-aligned but often warring city-states and turned it into the second largest empire in the New World (only the Incas controlled a wider expanse of territory) and the largest empire to ever have existed in Mesoamerica. Their system of expansion and consolidation was steady and directed. Emperors who succeeded in expanding territory were followed by leaders who managed to consolidate and organize the newly acquired lands and cities. Many setbacks occurred along the way—several cities were conquered, lost, and reconquered, for example—but in the grand scheme of things, the empire was growing in both size and influence at the time of Spanish arrival. However, contact with the Spanish would lead to the quick decline of what had become one of the most powerful empires of the ancient world.

Chapter 4 – The Arrival of the Spanish and the Decline of the Empire

With the landing of Christopher Columbus in the West Indies in 1492, the Spaniards were officially the first Europeans in the New World. Eager to explore, they set up a base in Cuba and began sending expeditions out to different parts of North, Central, and South America. One such expedition was that of Hernán Cortés. The Spaniards had heard about a great power in Central Mexico. Rumors of great riches combined with a desire to expand Spanish influence in the new world led Cortés to set his sights on the Valley of Mexico and the Aztec empire.

Cortés' expedition was initially sanctioned and half-funded by the Spanish crown, with Cortés himself putting up the rest of the money needed for the mission to take place. However, shortly before he set sail for Mexico, the Spanish crown rescinded its support, but Cortés sailed anyway. Several expeditions would be sent after Cortés in an effort to arrest him and bring him into custody.

In 1519, Cortés arrived on the coast of Mexico near the modern-day city of Veracruz with about 500 soldiers. They were greeted by messengers from Montezuma, who had heard of these strange men exploring the coast. Montezuma was cautious of them and also thought they might be gods. The Aztecs who greeted Cortés offered him gifts both as a way of forging peaceful relations, but also to confirm whether or not these people were in fact divine. When given the gold, the

Spaniards reportedly went crazy, and this display of greed and lust convinced the Aztecs that the newcomers were in fact not descendants from the heavens.

Cortés began his march inland, making allies along the way. He had heard rumors that the Aztec armies could number in the thousands, and even though the Spaniards had better weapons, Cortés knew he would need more troops if he hoped to be successful in his conquest. Moving inland, Cortés first allied with the Totonacs. Then, they made their way towards Tlaxcalla, the powerful city-state that had resisted the control of the Triple Alliance. After an initial conflict, Cortés was able to convince the Tlaxcallans to join him on his journey inland towards Tenochtitlán. When Cortés finally made his way into Central Mexico, he had several thousand troops under his command.

Their first stop was in the holy city of Cholula. They were welcomed at first, but Cortés feared an ambush and massacred thousands of unarmed civilians. Hearing of this, Montezuma became increasingly suspicious of the Spaniards. Fearing Spanish intentions and the size of their force, he continued to send gifts as a way of trying to win Spanish friendship and discourage hostility, but all this did was increase the desire Cortés and his men had of reaching and conquering the Aztecs. Montezuma kept sending gold, and it was gold that the Spaniards wanted.

When the Spaniards arrived, Montezuma welcomed them by putting them up in what was the equivalent of a royal palace. Cortés responded by taking Montezuma prisoner. He then began to rule Tenochtitlán, pretending that he was acting under the guidance of the Aztec emperor. In 1520, Cortés received word from his scouts that an expedition had been sent to Mexico to arrest him, so he left Tenochtitlán with half of his forces to fight this expedition. He was successful and then returned to Tenochtitlán to finish the job of bringing the Aztecs under Spanish control.

Upon returning to the Aztec capital, Cortés found that tensions had arisen which put the Spaniards in great danger. They made plans to flee the city and regroup, but when trying to escape in the middle of the night, they suffered heavy casualties. Many Spaniards had loaded themselves with gold, which slowed them down and made them easier targets. Eventually, the Spanish succeeded in escaping Tenochtitlán. They retreated to Tlaxcala in the mountains.

In the coming months, Cortés was able to regroup considerably. He marched again on Tenochtitlán with some 700 Spanish soldiers and around 70,000 native troops. They would then lay siege to the city for months. Diseases such as smallpox wreaked havoc on the city, decimating its population, and the Spanish cut off all sources of fresh water and stopped all shipments of food. Eventually, on August 13, 1521, Cuauhtemoc, who had replaced Montezuma as emperor, was captured, and the Spaniards claimed victory. A once great civilization would enter a dark period. The Spaniards, eager to exploit the people and the land for all they could, killed thousands of Aztecs and enslaved many more. The Aztec Empire, after nearly a hundred years of glory in the Valley of Mexico, was finished.

Many people unfamiliar with the way in which the Aztec Empire fell express surprise that such a small party of Spanish soldiers was able to topple such an immensely powerful empire. But this represents a severe misunderstanding of how Cortés was eventually able to conquer the Aztecs. First, his force was much larger than just a few hundred people. Long-standing rivalries combined with resentment towards the taxes and tributes imposed by the Aztecs meant it was very easy for Cortés to recruit allies in the fight to take down Tenochtitlán.

But the Spaniards had another weapon at their disposal, disease. Illnesses such as smallpox had never before been seen in Mesoamerica. While Europeans had been exposed to it for centuries and had developed immunities, the Aztecs had not. Hundreds of thousands would die of smallpox, the measles, the mumps, influenza, and many other diseases. This silent weapon proved to be one of the biggest reasons why the Spaniards were able to seize control over such a powerful empire in such a short period of time.

The story of the Aztec fall from dominance does not do justice to the impressive nature of their empire. They established one of the largest empires not only in the Americas but in the entirety of the ancient world. However, in the end, they were no match for European disease and firepower, and their dominance over the Valley of Mexico came to a screeching halt just a few short years after Cortés and the Spaniards landed on the Mexican peninsula.

Chapter 5 – A Day in the Life of an Aztec Citizen

Social classes and hierarchy dramatically influenced the life of the Aztec citizen. Rights, duties, and privileges were all determined as a result of one's social standing. Nobles, possessing more resources and ability to mobilize them, had the greatest amount of agency and autonomy. However, when taking a closer look at the lives of the most distinct classes, it is clear that upward mobility was indeed possible. Not even a slave was destined to be a slave for his or her entire life, and achieving freedom was not all too difficult, especially when compared to the slavery that would emerge in the European colonies.

Nonetheless, analyzing daily life in Aztec society according to class paints a useful picture as to how people viewed their lives and how they decided to live them. Nobles were largely responsible for tasks such as running the government, owning land, and commanding the army. Commoners were far more numerous than nobles, and they were relied upon to support the nobility with food and other goods. The success of Aztec expansion is due in large part to this balance. A productive and content working class supported a nobility that recognized its power depended upon being attentive to the needs of the commoners.

The Sovereign, the Dignitaries, and the Nobles

The ruling classes of Aztec society can be crudely stratified into three groups. At the top was the sovereign, given the title of *tlatoani* Each city-state had its own *tlatoani* With the formation of the Triple Alliance, the title huehuetlatoani was introduced to refer to the leader of the pact. The term *tlatoani* can be used to describe the head of a city-state, and also the head of the Aztec empire, depending on the context in which it is written.

Below the sovereign were the dignitaries, usually close relatives or friends of the sovereign. And underneath the dignitaries were the nobility, or the *pilli*. These three groups were responsible for the administrative, bureaucratic, and gubernatorial duties of the empire. In the early days of Aztec civilization, this group was small, but it would grow considerably over the centuries, expanding its influence over the affairs of the empire.

The Sovereign

The title *tlataoni* translates into "the one who speaks," and it can be understood to mean emperor. Although the first *tlatoanis* attempted to establish lineage with the Toltecs and the gods, most emperors were elected. While *Ttlataoni* was the title given to the sovereign of the Aztec Empire, it was also the name for high-ranked dignitaries who ruled a city-state and its surrounding area.

It's important to remember that the Aztec Empire wasn't an empire in the traditional sense. It did not have one designated leader who passed power down through his lineage. Instead, the Aztec power was derived from the Triple Alliance. As a result, it's possible to find the word *tlataoni* in reference to the leaders of one specific city-state and also to the heads of Mexico-Tenochtitlán, who, since they resided in the empire's capital, are considered to be the heads of the larger Aztec "nation."

Each city-state had its own set of rules for the succession of leaders. Some followed strict ancestral lines, being careful to emphasize their relation from one particular tribe or another in an attempt to attribute their claim to rule to the gods. However, many city-states chose new leaders by voting after the previous *tlataoni* had died. This is a tradition that traces its roots back to the early days of Aztec life in the Valley of Mexico. The *tlataoni* that was chosen to rule Mexico-Tenochtitlán and the Aztec Empire as a whole was always elected, although as the empire expanded, the group of people responsible for this vote would shrink significantly.

In the beginning, when the Aztecs first settled in the Valley of Mexico, voting took place across the city, with most adult males having the chance to cast their vote for who the leader should be. However, as the empire expanded and it became impossible to gather everyone for a vote, an electoral college comprised of dignitaries emerged to elect the emperor. So, as the empire expanded, the power to elect the next *tlataoni* drifted further and further from the people. In fact, by the time the Spanish arrived at the beginning of the 16th century, the group of people responsible for choosing the empire's leader was around 100. Considering the population of the Aztec Empire at the time of Spanish arrival was in the millions, it's clear that power and government in Aztec slowly consolidated into the hands of a small oligarchy that came from the upper echelons of society.

After taking command, the sovereign had three main roles: commander in chief, representative of the ruling class and enforcer of the rule of law, and protector of the common people. In our traditional understanding of government structures, the Aztec Empire was a monarchy. However, as mentioned earlier, it combined some aspects of democracy, namely the election of the head of state as well as the individual right to vote. The slow degradation of these characteristics over time eroded the Aztec claim to democracy, but it's still important to recognize its presence.

The name *tlatoani* was no mistake. "The one who speaks" fits the Aztec emperor because of the expectation that this individual would be able to command authority in council through long, eloquent speeches designed to sway the opinions and perspectives of the cabinet members. It was in these sessions that the emperor and his council would debate the future of the Aztecs.

The other title of the emperor, *tlacatecuhtli*, is directly derived from the emperor's responsibility as commander in chief of the military. *Tlacatecuhtli* literally translates into "chief of the warriors." A good deal of the emperor's time was spent conducting various military campaigns. Since the three cities of the Triple Alliance were all powerful city-states in their own right, the Aztec sovereign had a considerable force at his disposal to command as he saw fit.

The last major responsibility of the Aztec sovereign was to the people. While Aztec leaders did not formally proclaim a divine right to rule, the voting process, combined with the coronation ceremonies, instilled the idea that the sovereign had been chosen not by the people or the nobility but rather by the gods, specifically Tezcatlipoca, who is known for having great wisdom due to a magic mirror that allows him to see all at all times.

Defending the temple of Uitzilopochtli was one of the primary responsibilities of any Aztec sovereign, in addition to ensuring all the gods received their due worship. After tending to their duties to the gods, Aztec rulers were then responsible to the people.

The Aztec sovereign is traditionally seen as both the "father and mother of Mexico." He is responsible for caring for the people, for helping fend off famine, and for warding off drunkenness and other unwanted behaviors in the cities and towns.

Most scholars of Aztec documents indicate that rulers took this responsibility seriously. There appears to have been a real affinity between the rulers and the ruled. Despite attributing their ascension to the throne to divine intervention, all records point to the fact that rulers still did not consider themselves to be above or higher than their subjects. And there are lots of examples of rulers acting in a truly benevolent manner. For example, Motecuhzoma I is famous for having doled out some 200,000 loads of clothes and maize to people from Auitzol so that they could recover from a great flood.

As with most things in the Aztec Empire, it's important to remember the depiction of the sovereign changes as you move throughout the territory. This close bond between ruler and ruled was one felt mostly in the center of the empire, mainly in Mexico-Tenochtitlán and the surrounding Valley of Mexico. This connection between sovereign and subject was much weaker in provincial territories. Tributes and taxes were felt more harshly and the benefits of these were distributed more narrowly, leaving provincial settlements with a much different understanding of their sovereign than their metropolitan counterparts.

The Dignitaries

Directly below the sovereign in the Aztec social hierarchy are the dignitaries. These individuals were typically the close relatives or friends of the *tlataoni*, and they were responsible for carrying out many of the decisions of the sovereign.

The exact title for each dignitary and their corresponding duties varied greatly from city-state to city-state and from *tlataoni* to *tlataoni*. Each position was filled according to the needs of that particular city. Or, positions were created to give titles and status to the people in the *tlataoni's* inner circle. who were considered significant enough to deserve a position in the court.

The duties of these individuals ranged anywhere from the protection of a temple to the management of granaries and other facilities where taxes and tributes were stored. The diverse names for all the different titles are too great to possibly list. From these dignitaries, the *tlataoni* would choose his council. This small group was responsible for advising the *tlataoni* on all important issues regarding the administration of the state. They were to be consulted before each and every military campaign and their blessing was needed before beginning something new.

Additionally, these individuals often made up part if not all of the electoral college that would be responsible for choosing the next emperor. This represents a stark change from the way leaders were chosen when the Aztecs first settled in the Valley of Mexico. By the time the Spanish arrived, the Aztec state was no longer a democracy but instead an oligarchy protected by a powerful emperor. The main effect of this was to further stratify society. While upwards mobility was possible—a member of the working class could be recruited into the nobles if it proved favorable for the nobility to do so— it was not common.

Somewhere around the time of Motecuhzoma I (early 15th century), the title of *Ciuacoatl* enters into the records of Aztec history. Curiously translated to "woman-serpent," the *Ciuacoatl* was essentially the vice-emperor. He was responsible for carrying out the rule of law, primarily by being the supreme judge in martial and criminal law. He would hear cases and make judgments on appeals, decide which warriors would be rewarded, organize military campaigns, manage imperial finances, organize the electoral college after the emperor's death, and serve as head of state while the election process took place. This individual wielded great responsibility in Aztec administration. Being chosen for this position was considered one of the highest honors a *tlataoni* could bestow upon an individual.

Nobles

The next layer of the ruling class is the nobility, or the *pipiltin* or *pilli* (sing.). Together with the sovereign and the dignitary, the nobility comprised only about 5 percent of the total Aztec population, but they were the ones in charge. The *pipiltin* were not as involved in the running of the entire empire as the dignitaries and the sovereign were. Instead, their responsibility was in managing the territory that had been given to them and in maintaining their palace.

It's clear that the *pipiltin* saw working-class commoners as their subjects, and they considered the primary purpose of the commoner's life to be service to the nobility. There was no uniform level of treatment, though, among the nobility. Depending on the individual in charge and the circumstances of their position, living conditions of the commoners could range from barely burdensome to borderline slavery.

Regardless of the way the *pili* treated his subjects, the common folk were bound to their local lord, and they were responsible for furnishing certain goods for him and also for working his land. Furthermore, since the Aztecs had no standing army, each commoner, specifically the men, was expected and required to serve when a military campaign was launched. Unfortunately, there exists little in the form of numerical or anecdotal data to help uncover the full extent of the duties required of commoners to their respective lords.

One of the defining characteristics of the nobility was their palaces. It was very important that the *pipiltin* found ways to distinguish themselves from the commoners and one of the ways to do this was to build a large, luxurious home, typically on some of the best farmland in the region. Even in small, provincial towns, the local noble would build a large home using the finest materials available. Since many nobles were polygamists, they would often build homes with separate apartments inside for each one of their families.

However, it should never be forgotten that the nobility relied on the commoners to maintain their position of privilege. Each commoner was expected to pay taxes or duties to their respective noble, and the nobles relied upon the commoners to work their land and help produce goods that they could sell and use to maintain their position of prestige in society.

When looking at the way the nobility interacted with the commoners, it's easy to see how Aztec society was rather unequal. The nobility was aware of this, and since maintaining their elevated social position was one of their primary goals, they undertook a series of activities that helped to fortify themselves as the protectors of society who deserved the special treatment they received.

The first way in which the nobility kept people satisfied with the stratified nature of Aztec society was through ideas. By influencing what was spoken about at the temples and by controlling the rhetoric among the people, Aztec nobility was able to entrench in people ideas such as "everyone has duties to perform," "suffering and hard work is the natural state of human existence," and "human fate is in the hands of the gods." These messages helped quell any movements from below to challenge the authority of the nobility.

However, they needed something else to stand behind these words and ideas to make them more powerful and influential. Coercion defined much of the interaction between the nobility and the commoners. Many commoners would come under the rule of a noble as a result of conquest. The punishment for not paying tribute/taxes or for not working the noble's land was a return to conflict. And since the Aztecs had already proved their dominance, this particular path did not offer much promise to the conquered people. As such, it was a far better alternative to simply submit to the new political order than to bother trying to do anything to change it.

The third way in which the nobility separated themselves from the commoners and thus maintained their superior position was material consumption. Nobles were known for wearing the most expensive clothing, eating the most exotic foods, and living in the most elaborate houses. Special rules were also set up to help maintain this segregation. Nobility was only allowed to marry within the nobility, and they were expected to support each other in times of crises.

There was of course a need to ensure that commoners had enough food to eat and shelters to live in. But beyond that, and particularly as one travels further and further from the large city-states in the Valley of Mexico, there was little effort made by the nobility to improve the lives of the commoner. The commoners were the subjects, and they were expected to serve in whichever way made the most sense for the lord and the empire.

Commoners

The life of a commoner in Aztec civilization was dedicated nearly entirely to work. From the moment of birth, gender roles were ascribed to a child; men were expected to grow up to be warriors and to work in the same occupation as their father, and girls were to tend to the household by cooking, cleaning, weaving, and having children.

Because an Aztec commoner was expected to work, they are introduced to this way of life from a young age. Evidence from the Codex Mendoza, one of the most significant primary sources from the time, indicates that by the age of five boys were already carrying firewood and other goods to the nearby marketplaces and girls had already been taught to hold a spindle and spin. At the age of seven, boys were catching fish and girls were spinning cotton.

These demands were enforced on children through a system of threats and punishment. Aztec children were instructed by their parents to not be idle, as this would bring about bad behavior. To give an example, 8-year-old children who were caught being deceitful to their father would be pierced in the body with spikes. Older children were beaten with sticks if they were rebellious. Until the age of 15, children were taught primarily in the home by their parents; after this age they would head off to school for further training according to their gender and the relevant roles they would need to fill.

As with nearly everything in ancient Aztec society, school was divided by class. The school for commoners, known as the *telpochalli*, were established to teach children singing, dancing, and musical instruments (for use in rituals). Most boys would also receive military training. Service was mandatory for all men, so upon completing their training, most men would enter the army and be sent off to support the empire's expansionist strategy. The nobility were educated in the calmecac, where they were taught more advanced subjects such as religion, writing, mathematics, etc.

Marriage was also a critical part of growing up. Typically, pairs were made by parents or other elders, and by the age of 12, most Aztecs were married. From then on, gender roles became even more pronounced. Men were expected to work outside the home, typically in farming. When the seasons changed and agricultural activity slowed down, most Aztec men would be sent away from home. Military service was obligatory as was labor. If men weren't sent away to war, they were sent elsewhere to farm, likely to the land of a noble, as these people were exempt from both military and labor service.

Aztec women spent most of their time in the home cooking and preparing food. She was also responsible for cleaning the home, something considered to be more of a ritual than a chore, and also for burning incense and maintaining the home's altar. As such, women played a more significant role than men inside the home.

While duties and obligations occupied most of the time of an Aztec commoner, this did not entirely predestine their life. There were ample opportunities for a commoner to advance themselves and even possibly join the nobility. Aztec society was set up to receive this kind of movement between classes. One of the primary reasons for this was the way in which land ownership was structured in Aztec society.

Technically speaking, land could not be owned individually. Instead, it was collectively owned under the management of the *calpulli*, the chief. Each man was given individual rights to work a piece of land. They were free to work it as they pleased, but they were required to pay taxes and tribute on the bounty they received from the land. In exchange they were allowed a vote for the *calpulli* and could benefit from public services offered by the *calpull,* such as nicer temples, access to fresh water from aqueducts, and security.

Arable land in the Valley of Mexico, however, was scarce. Most of the best land was that which had a shoreline with Lake Texcoco, and because of this, the vast majority of Aztec citizens lived an urban life, depending on the provinces to supply the cities with goods. This in turn created another distinction in Aztec society: provincial/urban. Both paid taxes, yet the urban Aztec stood in a much better position to benefit from these taxes, as most improvements were centered on urban areas.

While land use was a right of commoners, it did come with certain privileges and benefits, but these rights were not for free. The right to use land was accompanied by the expectation that it would be used. If more than two years passed and the land remained idle, the one granted rights to work it would be subjected to severe admonishment from the *calpulli* and the wider community. After several more years of inactivity, these land rights could be stripped away, dropping that man and his family into the landless class, which enjoyed fewer rights and privileges.

While this was a possibility, it rarely occurred. The commitment to production and the commoner's relative autonomy contributed to the growth of the Aztecs in Central Mexico, and they are a big reason why they became the dominant force of the region. However, as the Aztecs advanced, more and more, exceptions were made to the labor requirement. Less land and more workers meant not every person was needed to effectively work the land. It also helped generate wealth, which expanded the nobility, diversified urban Aztec life, and created further economic and social inequalities.

This stratification occurred largely through changes in the traditional understandings of land ownership and use. The idea of common ownership eroded over time, and nobility were known to take land and assume control over it, limiting the commoner's ability to amass wealth by themselves. This situation was intensified as a result of the tax and tribute system. The whole population of a city paid taxes to the empire, and since there was no money, this duty was paid in goods. The tribute demanded of each city or provincial area was determined by the needs of the nobility at the time as well as the availability of resources. Tribute ranged from cloth, cloaks, corn, and oils to parrot feathers and precious gems.

Although tribute was varied, it's clear it brought a great deal of wealth into Mexico-Tenochitlan, further strengthening the Aztec Empire. A good measure for wealth at the time is the *quatchtli*, which was the equivalent of 20 loads of cloth. One *quatchtli* was considered the equivalent of a year's worth of living. At the peak of tribute gathering in Mexico, some 100,000 *quatchili* were being brought into Mexico from city-states subjected to the Aztez tribute systems, meaning 100,000 yearly livings were accounted for in the capital through cloth tribute alone.

Part of the reason these tribute bounties grew so large is that they were established under hostile circumstances. Conquest was a major part of Aztec expansion, and upon establishing military dominance over a particular region, negotiations would commence between the victorious Aztecs and the conquered. Since the threat of renewed conflict always loomed large, the Aztecs usually found themselves in an advantageous position at the negotiating table, allowing them to place extravagant demands on newly-occupied territories and its citizens.

Military strength and a productive tribute system are the reasons the Aztec Empire was able to grow in both size and influence to become the dominant player in the region. But in many respects, it was one of the reasons why it would eventually fall. The gradual transition from a society where each individual was granted the rights to work a piece of land to one that was expected to produce large tributes for the central empire caused a great deal of resentment towards Mexico-Tenochtitlán and the Triple Alliance.

The mediocrity of daily life in tribal Mexico was slowly replaced. In its place came a life where most of a city or town's efforts were directed at satisfying the needs of dignitaries and the imperial elite. A longing for a return to the way things were led many provincial populations to support Cortés and the Spanish in their attempt to destroy the Aztec Empire, something that would play a pivotal role in the eventual European triumph.

As the empire expanded, however, a new class begin to emerge that would rest in between the nobility and the commoners: the merchants. As cities and towns became more connected, the demand for goods from afar, both for personal use and to meet tribute, expanded. Commoners who were able to successfully trade goods among towns became quite wealthy.

However, the irony of this is that this wealth remained largely undistributed. Unlike the nobility, sovereigns, and dignitaries who were expected to spend lavishly to uphold their social position, merchants were under no such pressure. They were free to save or spend their earnings in any way they saw fit. They certainly lived in much greater comfort and luxury than a commoner, but they were by no means as openly extravagant as those in the ruling class.

This merchant class would grow considerably in wealth, power, and influence as Aztec civilization advanced, but they would never pose any serious threat to the upper classes. And because the wealth accumulated by merchants was hardly distributed throughout the rest of the commoner class, they remained a relatively small group within Aztec society.

While it's true a commoner in 14th, 15th, and 16th century Mexico with their ability to freely work their own land had some degree of upward mobility, the more accurate reality is that the average person dedicated most of their life to labor and military service. Men would spend long periods of time away from home, and women were restricted to the household. This status quo was acceptable for some time, but as inequalities were created and deepened, resentment towards Mexico-Tenochtitlán and the Triple Alliance intensified, resulting in the breakdown of one of the largest civilizations not only in Mesoamerica but on all of the American continents.

Landless Peasants

In between the commoners and the lowest rank in Aztec society, the slaves, was yet another social class worth mentioning: the landless peasants. How one became landless is hard to discern, especially since it was part of Aztec custom that each person be granted a tract of land to work so that they could pay the necessary taxes and tributes required by the local lord. However, with warfare a near constant threat and with people being displaced as their towns and cities were conquered, this landless class did indeed grow as the empire advanced.

These individuals were essentially destined to a nomadic lifestyle; that is until they could find a noble willing to take them in. Nobles were nearly always looking for extra hands to work their often highly-productive land. A noble could take in a landless peasant and allow them to work in exchange for a rent, which was usually a portion of the goods they produced, or additional labor.

It is, however, important to note that being taken in by a noble did not bestow upon a landless peasant the same rights that others in the tribe had. For example, they were not allowed to vote in any of the town's elections. But there was some justice in this arrangement. Although he couldn't vote, the landless owed nothing to the town. He paid no taxes and was exempt from service and military obligations. Essentially, he was beholden only to the noble who had taken him in and given him a place to live and work.

Slaves

The lowest social class in Aztec society was, as is the case in nearly every civilization, the slaves. While the life of the slave was by no means comfortable and luxurious, it was far better than the forms of slavery that would come to the Americas with the formation of European colonies. In fact, accounts from the Spanish explorers and conquerors show the newcomers' surprise as to the rather benevolent treatment of slaves.

On the surface, Aztec slavery is very similar to other forms of slavery present throughout history. A slave belonged to one man and was obligated to complete the work given to him by that man. In exchange, he was clothed, housed, and fed. Men worked as farm-laborers or as servants, whereas women spun or wove clothing. Many female slaves also served as concubines to their masters.

However, beyond this, Aztec slavery begins to differ greatly from the version of slavery that would emerge after the Spanish arrived and conquered the Aztecs, which would be much harsher and much more punishing than anything that existed during Aztec times. One of the most shocking differences is that Aztec slaves were allowed to own goods, save money, buy land, and could even buy other slaves to help them work this land if they had the money to do so. A slave was also allowed to marry a free woman. It was a relatively common practice for a widow to marry one of her slaves, making this slave the head of the household. Any children they had would be born free, as would the children of two slaves. One could not be born into bondage.

And unlike what is often seen in other societies, the children of slaves were not ostracized from society. In fact, there was little to no stigma attached to being born from slave parents. Itzcoatl, one of the greatest emperors in Aztec history, was the son of a slave woman. This status in no way affected his ability to rise up the social ladder to assume a position of great status and responsibility.

Furthermore, slavery was not a perpetual state. There were several very realistic paths a slave could take to earn his or her freedom. For example, slaves were freed when their master died. They could not be passed onto another owner as part of an inheritance.

Slaves could be sold, but there existed a way for them to gain their freedom before being transferred to another owner. At the auction, they were free to run. No one except the master and the master's son could chase them. Should someone else chase after them, the punishment was enslavement. If the slave could escape and make it to the nearby palace or royal enclave, then they would be immediately granted their freedom. Emperors also had the chance to free slaves. Montezuma II, for example, was famous for emancipating large amounts of slaves while in power.

Slaves also had the opportunity to buy their own freedom. They could do this by returning to their master with the price he paid for them. Or, in some cases, they could earn their freedom by finding someone to take their place for them. Brothers and sisters were permitted to serve under the same master, and families were infrequently split. Often one of the harshest images of European slavery is of families being torn apart to be sold to different masters.

Of course, slavery is slavery, but in the Aztec Empire, it was a decidedly milder version of bondage that what is seen elsewhere throughout history, especially compared to what would come to the Valley of Mexico after the Spanish invasion, conquest, and colonization.

In Aztec society, a person could become a slave in a variety of different ways. Prisoners of war were typically sacrificed, but those who were not were usually sold into bondage. Some city-states required slaves as tribute and the towns paying such tribute would usually search outside the empire for people to turn over to the nobility.

Slavery was also a punishment for some crimes. The Aztec justice system did not deal with long punishments, choosing more immediate and often harsher punishments for certain crimes. For example, if a man was caught stealing, he would be forced to work as a slave to the institution or person he stole from for a period of time agreed to be equivalent to the value of whatever had been stolen. The only way he could avoid this forced labor would be to pay the noble or temple the full value of what it was he had stolen. Since few could do this, most thieves ended up in slavery at some point or another.

However, far and away the most significant reason a person would end up a slave in Aztec society was through personal choice. Drunks who could not maintain their land (or who were poised to have it taken from them as a result of it lying idle for too long), addicts of the game *patolli*, whores who no longer wished to remain in the profession, and debtors who could not pay up, among others, would routinely sacrifice their freedom as a way to ensure they could fill their stomachs and have a roof over their head.

It became common practice throughout the Aztec Empire for families to give up one of their sons as a slave as payment for a debt. When this son came of age and was able to be married off, the family would replace him with another son. This arrangement would continue until it was agreed that the debt had been paid. If the slave happened to die before the payment was completed, then the debt would be canceled. Slaves that were payment for debts were therefore often treated exceptionally well.

Another major difference between Aztec slavery and European slavery was that the selling of slaves was not common and was even tightly regulated. If a master was no longer capable of paying for all his slaves, then he could trade them. Oftentimes this would involve the slave himself going out and trying to find the best arrangement for his master, meaning it would not be uncommon to find slaves traveling independently through the countryside, something that is unheard of in other colonial slavery institutions. Slaves could also be sold when they were deemed to be idle or vicious. If the master could prove that he had given the slave three warnings to change his ways and if the slave still refused to work, then the master was allowed to put him in a wooden collar and bring him to the market to be sold. This was very uncommon, though, and only happened in the rarest of circumstances.

Furthermore, slaves were exempt from paying taxes or serving in the military. Their only duty was to their master, and if a slave was able to earn their freedom, then they were only beholden to themselves.

The nature of Aztec slavery speaks to the fluidity of Aztec society. While it's true that social classes stratified people into different groups according to wealth, power, and privilege, there was nothing really standing in the way of someone going from a slave all the way to the nobility. One could earn his or her freedom, associate with a town, work, and amass the wealth and influence needed to achieve a higher position in the empire. This, like all social mobility, was really the exception instead of the norm. And unsurprisingly, slavery became more prominent in the later periods of the Aztec Empire. As military conquest became more and more important, and as more and more tribes were forced under Aztec rule, the number of people put into bondage expanded. This type of social stratification, while useful in helping the empire grow, would eventually be one of the downfalls of the empire and is one of the reasons it was so vulnerable when Cortés and his expedition arrived at the Valley of Mexico in 1519.

Chapter 6 – Agriculture and Diet

To support the size and expanse of the Aztec Empire, which at the time of Spanish invasion totaled somewhere between 3-4 million people, agriculture needed to develop to be able to provide enough food for all these people.

As is the case in most Mesoamerican cultures, the Aztecs could not have risen to their eventual position of dominance =without *maize*, or corn. Maize is special for a variety of reasons. First, it can grow in a wide range of soil and climate conditions. Several varieties are known to have arisen throughout Mesoamerica that adapted specifically to the conditions of that region. Additionally, maize can be stored. In years of surplus, kennels can be left out to dry. Then, when they are needed, they can be soaked and consumed.

The next staple below maize in the Aztec diet was beans. Meat was not common in Mesoamerica, which has led some to question the nutritional health of the Aztecs. But a diet full of corn and beans can in fact supply the body with all 11 amino acids. This designation as a "complete protein" is what makes meat so important in the diet. But there are other ways of acquiring these nutrients, which the Aztecs seem to have been capable of doing on a large scale.

The essential food in Aztec culture, and in much of Mesoamerica today, is the tortilla. These are made by first soaking maize in an alkaline solution, usually water mixed with limestone. While this is done for flavor, it turns out this process is also helpful in releasing additional amino acids found inside corn that the body cannot get to on its own. After the corn has been soaked, it's then ground into a dough, formed into flat tortillas, and cooked in a clay oven. They can be consumed on the spot or later. This made tortillas an excellent option for men who needed to travel far for work or to fulfill their service to the nobility.

While maize and beans represent the bulk of the diet—they were eaten at nearly every meal—the Aztec diet was supplemented by fruits and vegetables, such as avocado, tomato, and nopal, the prickly pear cactus fruit. Chili peppers are frequently found in traditional Aztec foods, and they helped infuse Aztec people with vitamins A and C, as well as riboflavin and niacin.

Insects and worms were also important sources of protein. Other sources of protein came from plants. For example, when the Spanish arrived, they noted that Aztec women would collect spirulina algae from the lake and form it into cakes and breads. The foreigners looked down upon this food, but the Aztecs prized it for its protein content and also for its medicinal properties. Dogs, turkeys, and ducks were the only domesticated animals in the Aztec world, but they were infrequently used for meat. The flesh of larger animals such as cows or pigs was virtually nonexistent in the Aztec diet.

For these staple crops, fruits, and vegetables to be widely available throughout the empire, it was important that Aztec agriculture adapt to be able to meet the increased demand. In general, there are two different types of agriculture: extensive and intensive. Extensive agriculture is passive. Watering is done with nothing more than rain, little to no fertilizer is used, and farmers spend very little time weeding their plot. The advantage to extensive agriculture is that it requires very little human labor. But the main disadvantage is that it produces small yields. In the early Aztec era, extensive agriculture was sufficient, but as the population expanded, it became necessary to adopt more intensive forms of agriculture.

Intensive agriculture gets its name because it's the practice of intensively working a piece of land to be able to maximize its yield. The four main types of Aztec intensive agriculture were: irrigation, terracing, raised fields, and house-lot gardens.

Irrigation is the process of redirecting fresh water towards a field to help steady the flow of water and give the crops the chance to grow faster. In Central Mexico, where rainfall comes only during the rainy season, irrigation allowed the Aztecs to be able to extend the season and also to begin watering crops before the rains came in. This gave them a head start and allowed them to grow for longer, creating larger yields that could feed larger populations.

Irrigation was used wherever possible in Central Mexico. However, it was seen to a far greater degree in the area that occupies the present state of Morelos. This is significant because many of the cities in this area were the most advanced of the empire. Most scholars agree that widespread use of irrigation comes when there is a central authority capable of organizing labor and managing resources. By the time the Spanish arrived in the Valley of Mexico, the Aztecs had tapped into nearly every available fresh water source. Further intensification would have required additional coordination of both labor and resources from a central authority, which can help explain why the irrigated fields were consolidated in the more prosperous and bureaucratic parts of the empire.

Terracing was another important aspect of Aztec agriculture. Since the Valley of Mexico is a hilly, mountainous region, the places where land can be irrigated and cultivated intensively is rather limited. Terracing allowed cities and towns to make the most of their land by turning hills and mountains into arable lands. Most terracing was done with stone, but in some areas where slopes were less dramatic, Aztec farmers were able to use plants mashed together to form a mud-like solid.

Another hallmark of Aztec agriculture was raised fields. Many of the city-states that would come to be associated with the Aztecs lived in areas where swamps and marsh dominated the landscape. To make the most of this land, Aztec workers would dig a ditch near the swamp to drain the water. Then, they would carry in mud and muck from the swamp and fill it into the areas where the water had drained. This created a patch of solid land that could be farmed.

These fields are known as *chinampas*, and they are known for being quite productive. The mud and muck used to create the ground was organic material rich in all the nutrients needed to grow crops. And since these fields were built on top of a swamp, there was a constant supply of water. Furthermore, most of the swamps and marshes were in the southern part of the Valley of Mexico, which is warmer and at less risk for frost than many other parts of the valley. These three factors meant that *chinampas* became highly-productive components of the Aztec agricultural system. They also allowed for the diversification of crops since in most *chinampas* several crops could be planted each year.

The last type of intensive agriculture used in the Aztec era was house-lot gardening. This was the process of using the land on which a family lived to produce food and other goods. Most evidence from the period suggests this was a common practice for a typical Aztec citizen. Crops would be fertilized with organic material from the home, and family members would share the duties of weeding and harvesting. The productivity of these plots varied greatly depending on the size of the lot and the number of family members that were available to work it.

None of these methods of intensive agriculture were new to Mesoamerica. They had been used in some form or another for hundreds of years before the Aztecs. However, what was unique to the Aztecs was the extent to which these methods were used. The vast majority of the Valley of Mexico has been either irrigated or terraced at some point in time, and if one travels to the modern state of Morelos, there are still *chinampas* in use or on display for tourism.

In general, the Aztecs were successful in expanding agriculture to meet the needs of a population that exceeded three million, but had the Spanish not arrived; it's worth wondering how much longer they would have lasted. Arable land was scarce, and most of the fresh water was already in use. It's impossible to know "what if," but it's clear the Aztecs had all but tapped the capacity of the land they occupied.

Chapter 7 – Religion

Religion played a central role in the lives of Aztec leaders and citizens. Comprising a list of all the different ideologies and deities within Aztec religion, however, is essentially impossible. This is largely because there is no one Aztec religion. Instead, Aztecs combined a wide range of beliefs and ideas from other Mesoamerican cultures, specifically the Maya and the Toltec. However, there are some defining characteristics of Aztec religion that help shed some light on what life might have been like in 15th century Mexico.

Creation, Life, Death, and the Four Suns

The Aztecs believed that the Earth upon which we are currently living is in fact the fifth Earth to have existed. These Earths, or "suns," were created by the gods and ceased to exist on the day that had been predetermined according to the date in which they were created. Humans existed on each of these suns, but they were completely wiped out by catastrophe. This notion would come to define Aztec religion and also Aztec way of life. Essentially, it created the idea that life on Earth was in constant danger. If the current sun on which people lived was not given all its nourishment, then the Aztecs believed it may cease to exist and that they would be wiped out of existence just like when the previous suns were destroyed.

The first sun was named Nahui-Ocelotl, which translates to Four-Jaguar. This name was chosen because it was believed that on the first sun human beings were destroyed by jaguars. The second sun came to an end because of Nahui-Ehecatl, or Four-Wind. The belief was that a magical hurricane turned all the people on Earth into monkeys. The third sun, Nahui-quiahuitl, Four-Rain, ended as Tlaloc, the god of rain and thunder, unleashed a rain of fire on the Earth. Lastly, the fourth sun, Nahui-Atl, Four-Water, ended in a flood that lasted 52 years. It is said that only one man and one woman survived this flood, and they were promptly turned into dogs by the god Tezcatlipoca because they disobeyed his orders.

The fifth sun, which represents present humanity, was created by Quetzalcóatl, the Feather Serpent god. Legends speaks of Quetzalcóatl sprinkling his blood on the dried bones of the dead which in turn helped bring the bones to life and create humanity as we know it. This present sun is called Nagui-Ollin, or Four-Earthquake because it is supposedly doomed to disappear in a giant earthquake in which skeleton-esque monsters from the west, the *tzitzimime*, will come to kill all the people.

Aztecs believed two primordial beings were responsible for the creation of life and all living things, including the gods. They were Ometecuhtl, the Lord of the Duality, and Omeciuatl, the Lady of the Duality. This Earth exists between 13 heavens, which are above the Earth, and 9 hells, which are found below the surface of our world. These supreme creators live in the 13th heaven, and although they have largely withdrawn themselves from the management of the world, they are still responsible for all creation and death.

The descendants of the Lord and Lady of the Duality were the gods responsible for the creation of this Earth. The story in Aztec religion is that the gods had gathered at Teotihuacán in twilight, and one god threw himself into the fire as a sacrifice. When he emerged from the fire, he had been transformed into a sun. Yet he could not move. He needed blood to break his idleness, which the other gods willingly provided by sacrificing themselves. Life was essentially created from death, an ideology that would be at the center of Aztec religion and thought throughout their period of dominance in the Valley of Mexico.

The Aztec beliefs on life after death are rather bleak as compared to other cultures and religions. According to Aztec tradition, anyone who died of leprosy, dropsy, gout, or lung diseases was sent to the old paradise of the rain god Tlaloc because it was believed that he had been the reason for their death. Because of this special selection by one of the gods, the souls of these individuals were sent to paradise.

After that, there were two main categories of people that went up to the heavens with the sun when they died. These two categories were: warriors who had died in battle or who were sacrificed and the merchants who had been killed in faraway lands, and women who had died giving birth to her first child.

The rest of the people were sent to Mictlan, the land of the 9 hells that exists underneath the Earth. It is said that it took them four years to travel through all 9 hells, and once they finally got there, they would disappear altogether. Back on Earth, ancestors would give offerings 80 days after someone's death, and then at every anniversary of their death for the next four years. After the fourth year, the connection between the living and the dead was broken.

This version of reality is no doubt shocking for modern-day readers, but it helps to better understand the Aztecs and their way of life. Two important themes emerge from this creation story. The first is that the Aztecs believed that the world was in constant peril. Four worlds had been created before this one, and there is no reason to believe this world will not suffer the same fate.

The other key takeaway from the Aztec creation story is the importance of blood in keeping this world alive. Since the first god who threw himself in the fire was turned into a sun but could not move until he was given the blood of the other gods, Aztecs felt it was their primary duty to provide blood to the Earth so that it would continue moving and fend off its impending doom. And the Aztec version of what happens after life served to reinforce this idea. Nothing was waiting for them after death, so the only motivation for living was to provide blood for the continued existence of this Earth. This is the primary reason why human sacrifice became such an essential aspect of Aztec religion and way of life, and also why war was such an integral part to the running and managing of the Aztec Empire.

Human Sacrifice

Perhaps some of the more influential images of the Aztecs that has come out of Hollywood and other pop culture outlets is that of an Aztec priest, standing at the tip of one of their pyramid temples, holding the beating heart of a person who had just been sacrificed. This image does not reflect the totality of the Aztec Empire. But it would be a mistake to downplay just how important this practice was to the Aztecs and also how much of a role it played in the day-to-day decisions of nearly everyone in the empire, from sovereign to slave.

Since the fate of the Earth depended on people feeding it blood every day, the Aztecs believed life itself also required blood. To deny the Earth the blood it needed to survive would be to kill all the life that lived on Earth and eventually the Earth itself. Because of this perspective, sacrifice became an essential duty for nearly every Aztec.

Sacrifices took place in a variety of different ways. The most common was at a temple. The victim was stretched out on their back over a circular stone. This would leave their torso exposed to the skies with their head and feet near the ground. Four priests would be responsible for holding the subject down, and when they were secure, a fifth would come in with a flint knife to slit their chest and tear out their bleeding heart.

Another form of sacrifice resembles the tradition of gladiators in Ancient Rome. First, the victim had a huge stone tied to his leg to slow him down and limit his movement. He would then be given wooden weapons and be sent to battle Aztecs armed with regular weapons. It was an unfair fight to say the least, and it usually ended with the subject to be sacrificed bloody and wounded. He'd then be taken to a stone where the priests would perform a similar ceremony as with other sacrificial victims. When sacrifice was carried out in this manner, though, there was a possibility the victim could escape. If they were successful in fighting off the Aztec warriors, then they would be spared from sacrifice. However, this rarely happened given the disadvantageous position of the captive.

There were other ways of sacrificing people besides cutting out their heart. Women were sacrificed in the name of the goddess of the Earth, and this was done by chopping off their heads unsuspectingly while they danced. To make offerings to Tlaloc, the rain god, children were drowned, and sacrifices to the fire god were made by tossing people into a fire. To honor the god Xipe Totec, captives were tied up, shot with arrows, and then flayed. It was common practice to dress up those to be sacrificed in the image of the gods. This way, when blood was spilled, it was the blood of a god that was being offered, which is reflective of the way the Aztecs understood the creation of the Earth and all the living things that occupy it.

This commitment to human sacrifice had a considerable impact on the overall course of the Aztec Empire in a variety of different ways. First, it created the need for near constant warfare. The initial expansion of Aztec city-states created a large area of pacified communities. It would not have been sustainable for priests and rulers to draw from their own people for sacrificial subjects. But the need to quench the thirst of the gods remained, which is why most Aztec city-states were constantly at war. It was a source of great pride for the warriors who took part in these conflicts to be able to bring home captives to be sacrificed to the gods. Because of this, battles with Aztecs often looked rather strange. Many of the warriors were trying to kill as few people as possible, hoping instead to take prisoners back with them, as this would bring them glory and respect.

The other way in which the practice of sacrifice affected Aztec civilization was in how it made them appear to the Spaniards when they eventually made contact with the "New World" civilization. While the Spaniards were no saints, the image of people having their hearts ripped out from their chests while bent over a stone was one that was rather difficult for the newcomers to swallow. It was because of this that Spanish settlers came to view the Aztec gods as demons and the Aztec religion as something of evil. This instilled a responsibility in them to rid Mexico and its people from these evil ways.

While the idea of human sacrifice seems cruel to those of us armed with hindsight, it would be unwise to judge the whole of Aztec society based on this one practice. It was indeed violent, but it was also in line with their view of the world and what was needed to preserve its existence. Civilizations throughout time, up to and including the present day, have come up with diverse reasons and methods for killing large amounts of people at one time. We may look back and question the practices of the Aztec, but in doing so, it's important to also look at what is currently being done that might be viewed with the same level of shock and awe by someone arriving from the outside.

The Gods

It's clear that Aztec life was very much centered around religion. The central tenet of nearly all their military and civil expansion was to make sure the gods were satisfied and that the Earth had the blood it needed to continue existing. Furthermore, one of the principle duties of any sovereign, dignitary, or noble was to protect the local temple so that the gods could receive the worship that was owed to them.

Formal religions practice had two forms: human sacrifice and ceremonies that took place at the temples, and home worship. Most cities and towns had a patron god to which they were dedicated, and commoners would set up altars in their homes with idols of these gods so that they could worship them as they saw fit. One of the responsibilities women undertook as homemakers was to light incense, keep the house clean for the gods, and make sure the altar was sufficiently maintained, as well as gather offerings for anyone who had died in the previous four years.

But who exactly were these gods? How did the Aztecs understand the supernatural? As is evident from the various creation stories and reasons for sacrifice, the Aztecs had many gods, almost too many to count. It was believed that all gods descended from the aforementioned Lord and Lady of the Duality. But these gods were far removed from the actual administration of the Aztec world. Instead, the Lord and Lady of the Duality sat in the 13th heaven, creating gods, humans, and Earths as they saw fit.

Many of the Aztec gods are manifestations of other Aztec gods but in different forms, but many others stand on their own as separate deities. So, while it's impossible to compile a list of all the gods the Aztecs worshiped, it is possible to narrow the list down to a few main gods who would form the basis of the Aztec religion.

Quetzalcóatl

The story of Quetzalcóatl, one of the most important gods in Aztec religion, is vital to both the origin and the eventual demise of the Aztecs. The Aztecs traced their roots back to the Toltec people of Northern Mexico. In this culture, Quetzalcóatl was the priest-king of Tula, the Toltec capital. As ruler, Quetzalcóatl never offered human victims for sacrifice, choosing instead to spill the blood of snakes, birds, and butterflies. However, he was expelled from Tula by another Toltec god, Tezcatlipoca. When this happened, Quetzalcóatl began wandering to the south. After walking along the "divine water" (the Atlantic Ocean), Quetzalcóatl killed himself and emerged as the planet Venus (yet another connection between destruction and creation).

There is reason to believe that some version of these events actually happened. Early Toltec civilizations practiced theology and were focused on peaceful, non-violent living. However, the rulers responsible for disseminating this worldview were overthrown by a military aristocracy with a decidedly more militaristic perspective. Quetzalcóatl's travels to the southeast could refer to the invasion of Yucatan by the Itza, a tribe that was closely associated to the Toltecs.

One of the most significant connections between Quetzalcóatl and history, though, actually refers to the eventual downfall and destruction of the Aztec Empire. Legend said that Quetzalcóatl would return from his journey in a 1 Reed year (see the description of the calendar below). The year 1519 when Hernán Cortés and his team of conquistadors arrived on the coast of the Mexican Gulf was in fact a 1 Reed year. This led the ruler of the Aztecs at the time, Montezuma, to consider the arrival of the Spanish as something divine. He thought that the newcomers could be the incarnation of Quetzalcóatl, and this caused him to welcome them with open arms. This obviously proved to be a fatal mistake, as the Aztec Empire would crumble within just a few years after their first contact with the Spanish.

Quetzalcóatl represented many things to many different people. He was first conceived to be the god of vegetation, or of earth and water. In this sense, he was closely related to Tlaloc, the rain god. After a while, Quetzalcóatl's cult began to revere him as a heavenly body, linking him with the morning and evening star. During the peak of the Aztecs, Quetzalcóatl was the patron of priests, the inventor of the calendar and books, and the protector of goldsmiths and other craftsmen. And he was also closely related to the planet Venus. Quetzalcóatl is also credited with bringing life to this Earth. He was the one who traveled down into Mictlan to gather the bones of the dead. and used his blood to bring them to life, further emphasizing the role of blood and sacrifice in creating life.

Huitzilopochtli

Huitzilopochtli, or Uitzilopochtli, as it's sometimes spelled, is, together with Tlaloc, is one of the two principle deities in Aztec religion. Considering Huitzilopochtli was the god of the sun and war, it should not be a surprise that he occupied such a prominent position in Aztec religion. Aztecs believed that warriors would come back to Earth as hummingbirds, and this is why Huitzilopochtli is often depicted in paintings and sculptures as such.

Part of the reason why Huitzilopochtli occupies such a prominent role in Aztec religion is that he is credited for guiding the journey the Aztecs took from Aztlan, their traditional home in Northern Mexico, to the Valley of Mexico. Priests who went on this expedition carried statues and idols in the form of a hummingbird. It's said that at night Huitzilopochtli would appear and give orders to the travelers as to where they could find a suitable place to settle. It was Huitzilopochtli who informed them of the prickly pear cactus and eagle that would mark the spot of the Tenochtitlán settlement. Because of this, one of the first construction projects to take place in the new city was a shrine to Huitzilopochtli. This shrine would later turn into a temple and was enlarged by each ruler until 1487 when the emperor Ahuitzotl built another larger temple dedicated to the god.

While human sacrifice was seen as necessary to appease all of the gods, it took a prominent role in the Aztec worship of Huitzilopochtli. Since he was the sun god, and since suns require blood to exist, it was important that Huitzilopochtli received an adequate amount of blood each day. If he didn't, then the Aztecs believed they would be putting their entire world at risk of total annihilation. Since Aztecs believed people to be children of the sun, they saw it as their responsibility to provide the blood for Huitzilopochtli and the sun to continue to exist.

Another way you can see the importance of Huitzilopochtli in Aztec religion was in how they organized the clergy. Huitzilopochtli's high priest, along with that of Tlaloc the rain god, were together the head of the entire Aztec clergy. A full month of the ritual year calendar was dedicated just to Huitzilopochtli. These ceremonies would involve warriors dancing in front of the god's temple day and night. War prisoners and some slaves were bathed in a sacred spring before being sacrificed. Additionally, a giant image of Huitzilopochtli was made of corn, which was then killed ceremoniously, with the corn being divided among the priests and novices. If one consumed the body of Huitzilopochtli, then they were expected to serve him for at least one year, although most evidence suggests priests would extend this service obligation voluntarily.

Huitzilopochtli was far and away one of the most important gods in Aztec religion. His connection to war, and the direct link between his appeasement and human sacrifice helped to shape the way the Aztec world would develop and expand throughout the Valley of Mexico.

Tlaloc

Next to Huitzilopochtli in the divine hierarchy is Tlaloc, the Aztec rain god. The word Tlaloc translates from Nahuatl to mean "He Who Makes Things Sprout." Tlaloc was usually represented as a man with a peculiar mask, large eyes, and long fangs. Similar representations were used for the Maya rain god, Chac, suggesting a close relationship between the gods worshiped during the Maya and Aztec period.

The adoption of Tlaloc as not only the rain god but as one of the main gods of the Aztec pantheon represents the syncretistic nature of Aztec religion. Evidence suggests agricultural tribes in Mesoamerica had been worshiping Tlaloc for centuries. Living in more fertile lands, war was less of a priority for these people, meaning they found it more prudent to dedicate their spirituality to maximizing the yields given to them by Mother Earth. As the Aztecs moved into the Valley of Mexico from the north, they brought with them their warlord gods, but they slowly adopted Tlaloc as an equal.

A full six months of the ritual calendar were dedicated to Tlaloc. During these months, people would engage in a wide array of ceremonies and rituals designed to honor Tlaloc and thank him for gifting them with rain and water to support life. Some of these rituals included bathing in the lake, dancing and singing using magic fog rattles (devices that made a loud rattling sound) to obtain rain, and making, killing, and eating idols made of amaranth paste.

Part of the reason Tlaloc was given so much attention was because he was both revered and feared. While he was responsible for bringing rains and for helping make the land bountiful, he could also be quite vengeful. Droughts, lightning, and hurricanes, among other natural disasters, were all attributed to Tlaloc. He could also send different types of rain depending on his mood, and he was also credited for certain diseases, such as dropsy and leprosy. Because Tlaloc could be both benevolent or ill-spirited, the Aztecs found it necessary to dedicate both time and energy to his worship, hoping that doing so would keep him happy and prevent him from unleashing his wrath on the Aztec people.

The high priest of Tlaloc joined the high priest of Huitzilopochtli to form the top of the Aztec clergy. Furthermore, the Teocalli (Great Temple) in Tenochtitlán had equal spaces dedicated to Huitzilopochtli and Tlaloc. This shared importance between Huitzilopochtli and Tlaloc helps us better understand how the Aztecs viewed the world. They understood their existence as something precious that was in constant danger. It was up to them to serve the gods enough to make sure they would allow them the time and space to continuing living on Earth.

Chalchihutlicue

> As the wife of Tlaloc, Chalchihutlicue is one of the most important goddesses from the Aztec pantheon. Her name translates from Nahuatl into "She Who Wears a Jade Skirt." Chalchihutlicue is the goddess of rivers, lakes, streams, and other freshwater bodies, and she was the ruler of the previous sun that existed before this one. It was during her reign that maize was first planted and cultivated; therefore, she is associated with this significant crop.

Coatlicue

Another important goddess is Coatlicue (Nahuatl: "Serpent Skirt"). She is the goddess of the Earth, and she is both the creator and destroyer. As the mother of both the gods and mortals, she occupies a position of prominence that is above most other deities. She is closer to the Lord and Lady of the Duality than most.

This dualism of creation and destruction defines the Aztec understanding and depiction of Coatlicue. Two fanged serpents are used to create her face, and her skirt is made up of woven serpents. Since she was responsible for nourishing both the gods and people, she had large, flabby breasts. She wears a necklace that is made up of hands, hearts, and a skull. These items were used because it was believed that Coatlicue fed off corpses—the Earth eats all that dies. Because of her position of power and dominance in Aztec religion, Coatlicue appears in many different forms, taking the form of both Cihuacóatl, the goddess of childbirth, and also Tlazoltéotl, the goddess of sexual impurity and wrong behavior.

Aztec gods are diverse and numerous. But they played a central role in shaping the way Aztecs lived their lives. Much of their day-to-day lives were spent trying to appease the gods, and one component of the empire's expansionist strategy was to acquire captives to be sacrificed. We may look back on it now and consider it crude, but this approach was in line with their worldview and belief system.

The Calendar

One important part of Aztec religion was their calendars. Yes, they had more than one. The calendars helped to organize agricultural practices and festivals, but they were also important in coordinating ceremonies and rituals throughout the year. The purpose of this calendar was to make sure that each god got their due worship.

The two calendars are quite different. The *xiuhpohualli*, or year count, is the agricultural calendar. It was based on the sun and the seasons, helping the Aztecs keep track of time and to make decisions about when to plant, water, harvest, etc. This calendar had been in use in Mesoamerica in some form or another since the time of the Maya.

This Aztec calendar is quite a bit different than the one we use today, although it has some similarities. For example, the Aztecs knew that one year lasted 365 days; they could figure this out by tracking the movement of the sun in the sky over the course of a year. However, the calendar is different in that it is divided into 18 months, with each month having 20 days. If you do the math, you'll realize that 18 multiplied by 20 is only 360. The other five days were left for the end of the year and were given no name. Aztecs considered these days to be very unlucky. They would spend the end of each year in temples making sacrifices to prevent anything bad from happening during these days of bad luck.

The *tonalpohualli*, or day count, is the ritual calendar of the Aztecs. There are only 260 days in this calendar, and each day has a corresponding number and sign. In total, there are 20 signs, with each one representing a different deity. These include:

- Crocodile
- Wind
- House
- Lizard
- Serpent/snake
- Death
- Deer

- Rabbit
- Water
- Dog
- Monkey
- Grass
- Reed
- Jaguar
- Eagle
- Vulture
- Earthquake
- Flint
- Rain
- Flower

The first day of the *tonalpohualli* is 1 Crocodile. The numbers increase, lining up with their appropriate sign, until 13. It's unclear why this number was chosen. But after 13, the numbers reset. But since there are twenty signs, the next month does not start on 1 Crocodile. So the first month ends on 13 Grass and begins on 1 Reed. The second month then continues 13 days and ends on 13 Death, and the third month begins on 1 Deer and ends on 13 Rain, with the fourth month starting on 1 Flower. This cycle continues, and after 260 days, it returns to 1 Crocodile, and a new ritual year begins.

The two calendars run side by side, with the ritual calendar used as a way of keeping track of which god should be worshiped at a particular part of the year. The two calendars line up every 52 years. This moment marks the beginning of a new Aztec century. But the day when the two calendars coincided was one of great distress. Fifty-two years were considered to be one life cycle of the Earth, and at the end of each life cycle, it was within the gods' rights to take all that they had created and destroy it. Yet again we can see how the Aztec worldview was one dominated by the belief that this world could be destroyed by the gods at virtually any moment.

Another way in which the two calendars were tied together was in the naming of the years. Each year in the 365-day *xiuhpohualli* was named for the day on the *tonalpohualli* in which it ended. So, for example, the first year in the Aztec calendar is named 1 Reed because the first 365-day calendar ended on 1 Reed in the *tonalpohualli*. Since each year ends on a different day, each year has its own name. A year could be 12 Crocodile, 4 Grass, 5 Death, and so on. This helps to organize the years and to specify when events happened, although the mixing of the two certainly make it a challenge for outsiders to understand how the Aztecs measured time.

Much work has been done to try and completely recreate the Aztec calendar and to link it to other Mesoamerican calendar systems. In doing this, historians and archaeologists have been able to verify the dates of some of the more important events in Aztec history, specifically the birth and death dates of prominent rulers, the dates of conquest and military campaigns, and also the dates of interactions with the Spanish.

Chapter 8 – Sports

While much of Aztec life was occupied with worshiping the gods, working the land, and supplying tribute to the nobility, it was not all work. There was time for recreation, and an Aztec ballgame was one of the most popular activities.

This particular game, which is similar in rules and nature to volleyball or racquetball, was played throughout Mesoamerica. It took on special significance in the Aztec Empire largely because it was used both as an arena for human sacrifice, but also because it was connected to military training.

The game is played on a stone court and with a rubber ball. Players pass the ball back and forth using pretty much any body part they can, except their hands. , They could use their forearms, legs, hips, or head. There were many different variations of the game, with each town, village, or city having their own rules of play.

The significance of the game also varied greatly across Mesoamerica. It was frequently played in informal settings, with groups of villagers gathering and playing for fun. However, as the Aztecs advanced, large arenas were built where the game would be played in front of large crowds of people. These formal games were highly ritualistic, and some cultures even tied them into human sacrifice. The winners, losers, or both would be sacrificed to the gods after the game. It's for this reason that the Aztec ballgame, which is often referred to as *ulama* or *pok-a-tok* although its original name is still unknown, has been brandished as a bloody, brutal, and violent game.

But the truth is not all those who played the game did it for the purpose of sacrifice. That being said, though, the game has been known to cause serious injuries and even death. The large, heavy ball can inflict quite a bit of damage on a person's body when it strikes. When the Spanish arrived in Mexico, they were in awe of the game, but quickly labeled it as the devil's work when they witnessed some people using it as a means for human sacrifice.

Patolli is another sport that was popular among the Aztecs, although people had been playing it in Mesoamerica for centuries before. It's a board game of chance and skill. The table is in the shape of a cross and players need to move their stones across the table. Betting was common and in some places even integral to the game. People would gamble stones, gems, food, and sometimes even their own lives. Patolli is one of the oldest games in the world, and it's still played in many parts of Central America today.

Conclusion

In just a few hundred years, the Aztecs were able to advance themselves from a group of unwelcome hunters and gatherers to one of the largest and most advanced civilizations of the ancient world. Over time, a dedicated military tradition was combined with cultural hegemony and effective political institutions to form a fully-functional and expanding empire.

However, the Aztec civilization was far from perfect. Its despotic state required constant war, and the extractive system of taxes and tribute, as well as a heavily stratified society, meant that the Aztecs had many enemies when the Spanish arrived thirsty for blood and gold in 1519. In just a few short years after Cortés landed on the coast of the Mexican Gulf, the mighty Aztec Empire would fall and disappear into history books. But this did not happen before the Aztec people made a significant contribution to the historical and cultural development of Mesoamerica.

There are still many people alive today who can trace their heritage back to the Aztecs and the great empire forms a part of modern-Mexican identity. There's no telling what the Aztecs could have accomplished had the Spanish not arrived or had they had immunity to the many diseases that the invaders carried with them. Yet despite a sudden and untimely defeat, the Aztecs are still considered to be one of the greatest human civilizations to ever have formed.

If you enjoyed this individual book on the Aztecs, can you please leave a review for it?

Thanks for your support!

Read more Captivating History Books about Ancient History

THE ROMAN EMPIRE
A CAPTIVATING GUIDE TO THE RISE AND FALL OF THE ROMAN EMPIRE INCLUDING STORIES OF ROMAN EMPERORS SUCH AS AUGUSTUS OCTAVIAN, TRAJAN, AND CLAUDIUS
CAPTIVATING HISTORY

ANCIENT EGYPT

A CAPTIVATING GUIDE TO EGYPTIAN HISTORY, ANCIENT PYRAMIDS, TEMPLES, EGYPTIAN MYTHOLOGY, AND PHARAOHS SUCH AS TUTANKHAMUN AND CLEOPATRA

CAPTIVATING HISTORY

ANCIENT GREECE

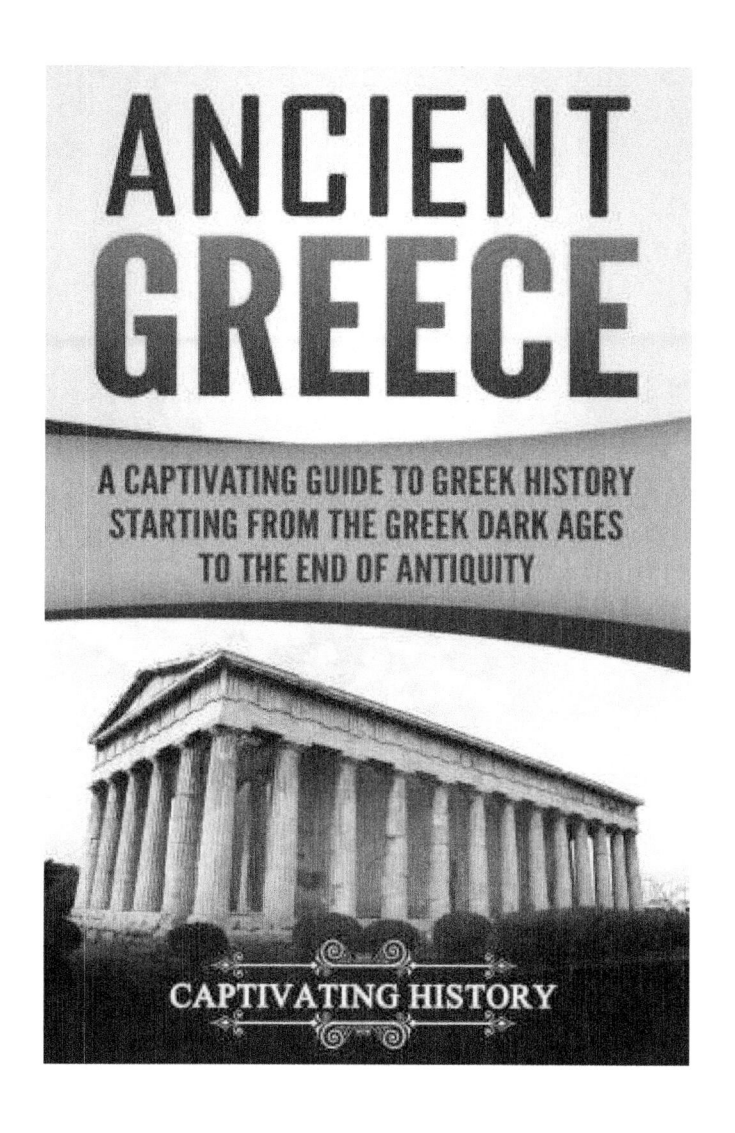

A CAPTIVATING GUIDE TO GREEK HISTORY STARTING FROM THE GREEK DARK AGES TO THE END OF ANTIQUITY

CAPTIVATING HISTORY

MAYA CIVILIZATION

A CAPTIVATING GUIDE TO MAYA HISTORY AND MAYA MYTHOLOGY

CAPTIVATING HISTORY

AZTEC

A Captivating Guide to Aztec History and the Triple Alliance of Tenochtitlan, Tetzcoco, and Tlacopan

CAPTIVATING HISTORY

INCAS

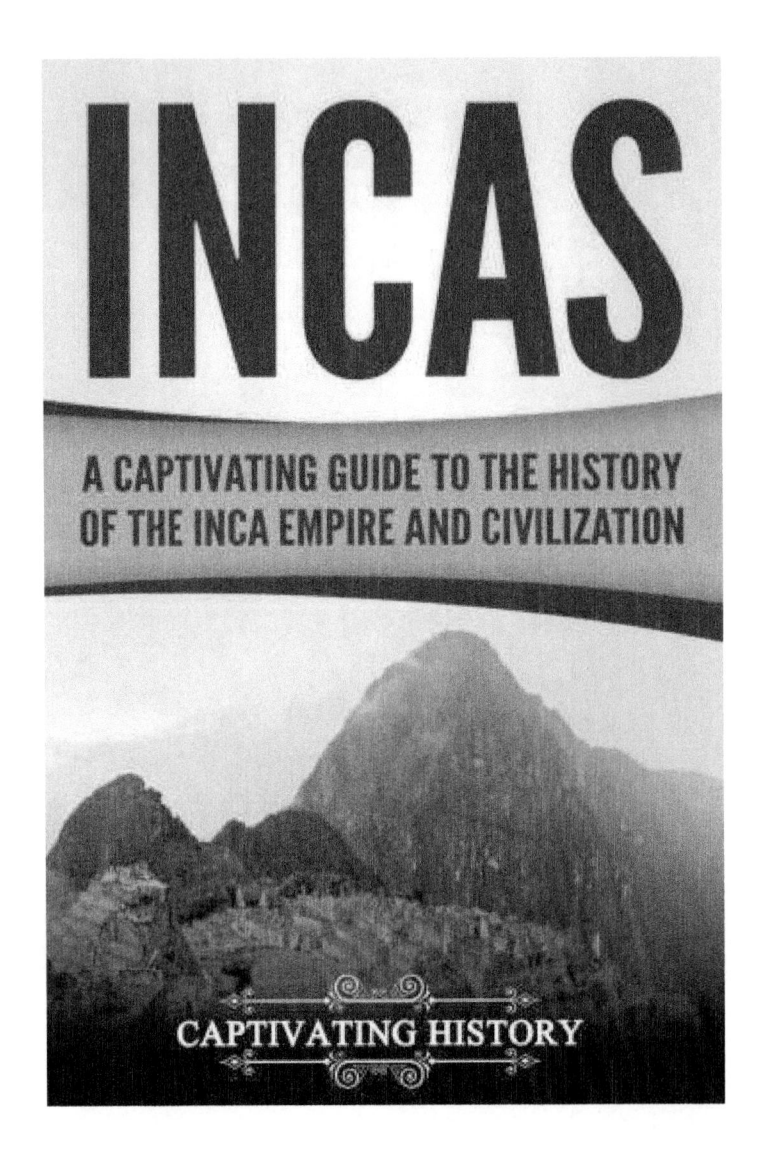

A CAPTIVATING GUIDE TO THE HISTORY OF THE INCA EMPIRE AND CIVILIZATION

CAPTIVATING HISTORY

Bibliography

Adams Richard E. W. and MacLeod Murdo J., *The Cambridge history of the native peoples of the Americas Volume II: Mesoamerica*, Cambridge, Cambridge University Press, 2008.

Carmack R.M., Gasco J. and Gossen G.H., *The Legacy of Mesoamerica: History and Culture of a Native American Civilization*, New York, Routledge, 2007.

Coe Michael D. and Koontz Rex, *Mexico – From the Olmecs to the Aztecs,* London, Thames and Hudson, 2013.

Bernal Ignacio, *The Olmec world* , Berkley, University of California Press, 1969.

Hassig Ross, *War and Society in Ancient Mesoamerica*, Berkley, University of California Press, 1992.

Koontz R., Reese-Taylor K. and Headrick A., *Landscape and power in ancient Mesoamerica*, Boulder , Westview Press, 2001.

Pool Christopher, *Olmec Archeology and Early Mesoamerica*, Cambridge, Cambridge University Press, 2007.

Staller John E. and Carrasco Michael, *Pre-Columbian Foodways: Interdisciplinary Approaches to Food, Culture, and Markets in Ancient Mesoamerica*, New York, Springer, 2010.

Rosenswig Robert M*.*, *The Beginnings of Mesoamerican Civilization: Inter-regional interactions and the Olmecs*, Cambridge, Cambridge University Press, 2010.

The Olmec and Toltec: The history of early Mesoamerica's most influential cultures, by Charles Rivers Editors, 2016.

Hernán Cortés Biography, Biography.com,

The Lost Zapotec: Vibrant Mesoamerican Civilization of the Cloud People, Ancient Origins, 2013-201.

These Zapotec Facts are Really Intriguing, Historyplex, 2018.

Zapotec Civilization, Ancient History Encyclopedia, Mark Cartwright, October 28, 2013.

Zapotec Civilization, Maya Inca Aztec, 2017.

Zapotec Civilization: A Civilization of the "Cloud People," Ancient Civilizations, June 18, 2016.

Zapotec Digs in Mexico Show Clues to Rise and Fall, National Graphic News, John Roach, March 9, 2009.

https://study.com/academy/lesson/why-is-monte-alban-historically-important.html - Image

Adams Richard E. W. and MacLeod Murdo J., *The Cambridge history of the native peoples of the Americas Volume II: Mesoamerica, part 1*, Cambridge, Cambridge University Press, 2008.

Adams Richard E. W. and MacLeod Murdo J., *The Cambridge history of the native peoples of the Americas Volume II: Mesoamerica, part 2*, Cambridge, Cambridge University Press, 2008.

Ardren Traci, *Ancient Maya women*, Lanham, Rowman & Littlefield Publishers, Inc., 2002.

Carmack R.M., Gasco J. and Gossen G.H., *The Legacy of Mesoamerica: History and Culture of a Native American Civilization*, New York, Routledge, 2007.

Coe Michael D., *Breaking the Maya code*, London, Thames and Hudson, 2012.

Coe Michael D. and Houston Stephen, *The Maya: 9th edition*, London, Thames and Hudson, 2015.

Foias Antonia E., *Ancient Maya Political Dynamics*, Tampa, University Press of Florida, 2013.

Foster Lynn V., *Handbook to life in the Ancient Maya world*, New York, Facts On File, Inc., 2002.

George Charles and Linda, *Maya civilization*, Farmington Hills, Lucent Books, 2010.

Goetz Delia, *Popol Vuh: The sacred book of Ancient Quiche Maya*, Norman, University of Oklahoma Press, 1950.

Hassig Ross, *War and Society in Ancient Mesoamerica*, Berkley, University of California press, 1992.

Koontz R., Reese-Taylor K. and Headrick A., *Landscape and power in ancient Mesoamerica*, Boulder, Westview Press, 2001.

Kurnick Sarah and Baron Joanne, *Political strategies in pre-Columbian Mesoamerica*, Boulder, University Press of Colorado, 2016.

Lohse Jon C. and Valdez Jr. Fred, *Ancient Maya commoners*, Austin, University of Texas Press, 2004.

Mazariegos Oswaldo C., *Art and Myth of the Ancient Maya*, London, Yale University Press, 2017.

McKillop Heather I., *The ancient Maya: new perspectives*, Santa Barbara, ABC-CLIO, Inc., 2004.

Sharer Robert J., *Daily life in Maya civilization*, London, Greenwood Press, 2009.

Thompson John S.E., *Maya history and religion*, Norman, University of Oklahoma Press, 1990.

Werness-Rude Maline D. and Spencer Kaylee R., *Maya imagery, architecture, and activity: space and spatial analysis in art history*, Albuquerque, University of New Mexico Press, 2015.

Alcock et al. *The Aztec Empire and the Mesoamerican World System* in *Empires: Perspectives from Archaeology and History*, ed. Susan E. Alcock pp. 128–154. Cambridge University Press: New York.

Del Castillo, B. D. (1910). *The True History of the Conquest of New Spain* (Vol. 2)

Getty Research Institute (2010). *The Aztec Calendar Stone*. Los Angeles.

Murphy, J. (2015). *Gods and Goddesses of the Maya, Aztec and Inca.* Britannica Educational Publishing: New York

Smith, M. E. (2013). *The Aztecs*. John Wiley & Sons.

Soustelle, J. (1968). *Daily Life of the Aztecs*. Courier Corporation.

Villela, Khristaan D., and Mary Ellen Miller (eds.)

Whittington, E. Michael, ed. (2001) T*he Sport of Life and Death: The Mesoamerican Ballgame.* Thames and Hudson: New York.

Printed in Great Britain
by Amazon